TH

HISTORY
OF
BRITAIN
IN
3,000 QUIZ
QUESTIONS

CONTENTS

QUESTIONS

IN THE BEGINNING...

1. According to current theories, how long ago is the Big Bang said to have occurred?

2. To the nearest 0.5 billion years, how long ago did the Earth form?

3. The earliest life, microscopic organisms, comes from when?

4. A prokaryote (a single-celled organism) that existed around 3.5 billion years ago is believed to hold which distinction?

5. What term is used to describe the major event, around 541 million years ago, during which most major animal groups began to appear in the fossil record?

6. What name is given to the creatures that evolved from fish and began to venture onto land around 380 million years ago?

7. Dinosaurs first appeared around 240 million years ago, during which period of Earth's history?

8. The oldest dinosaur fossil found in Britain, discovered in North Yorkshire in 2015, belonged to which species?

9. What name is given to the most recent supercontinent, which formed 335 million years ago and began to break apart around 175 million years ago?

10. The term homo erectus, referring to the first human ancestor to spread throughout Eurasia 2 million years ago, translates as what?

answers on page 317

GEOLOGY

1. The crust of the Earth beneath Britain is estimated to be how thick?

2. What is last believed to have occurred in Britain around 60 million years ago?

3. What's the name of the World Heritage Site that runs for 96 miles from East Devon to Dorset, and which spans approximately 185 million years of geological history?

4. In 2019, the largest meteorite crater in Britain – around 0.6 miles wide – was found where?

5. What's the oldest type of rock found in Britain?

6. The Whin Sill is a layer of igneous rock in the northeast of England, and forms part of the North Pennines. Igneous rock forms following the cooling of what?

7. What's the name given to the Paleozoic microcontinent that now underlies parts of the southwest of Britain?

8. Salisbury Plain is mainly comprised of which type of rock?

9. The Greensand Ridge is part of which area in South East England, which sits between the North and South Downs?

10. What part of Britain is said by various organisations to be between 7,500 and 19,000 miles long?

answers on page 317

PALAEOLITHIC BRITAIN (THE OLD STONE AGE)
c. 3m years ago to 15000 BC

1. The palaeolithic period is distinguished by the earliest example of what?

2. During this period, humans gradually evolved from the earliest members of which genus?

3. The earliest evidence of human occupation in Britain, from 900,000 years ago, was found in which present-day county?

4. Around 425,000 years ago, the Anglian Glaciation led to a megaflood that destroyed the Weald-Artois Anticline. What was created as a result?

5. Fossils of early Neanderthals, dating from around 400,000 years ago, were discovered in which Kent town?

6. What's the name of the Torquay cave system that provides evidence of human habitation around 40,000 years ago?

7. What name is given to a set of bones, discovered in Wales and dating from c.33,000 BC, featuring a distinctive colour?

8. What name is given to the culture that was centred around an area of Derbyshire 12,000 years ago?

9. Britain endured its final period of extreme cold, which was also the final period without human habitation, from c. 12,500 to 11,700 BC. What is this period called?

10. What name is given to Stone Age tools that were characterised by oval or pear-shaped hand axes?

answers on page 317

MESOLITHIC BRITAIN (THE MIDDLE STONE AGE)
c. 15000 – 4000 BC

1. From around 9,700 to 9,400 BC, Britain was partially occupied by Ahrensburgian hunter gatherers. Ahrensburg is located in which part of Europe?

2. What was their primary prey?

3. During this period, tools began to incorporate what extra feature, which made it harder for prey to escape?

4. What animal is believed to have first become domesticated during the mesolithic period in Britain?

5. A mesolithic house – dating from c. 7,800 BC – was discovered close to which Northumberland village?

6. Which location in North Yorkshire, near Scarborough, is one of the most important mesolithic sites in Britain?

7. The mesolithic period also marks the start of the current geological epoch. What is this epoch called?

8. What name is given to the plains of land, now submerged, that existed between Britain and continental Europe until around 6,500 BC?

9. A submerged mesolithic settlement near the Isle of Wight is known by what name?

10. Britain's oldest complete human skeleton – dating from around 7,000 BC – was discovered in 1903 in a cave in which part of the country?

answers on page 318

NEOLITHIC BRITAIN (THE NEW STONE AGE)
c. 4000 – 2500 BC

1. The introduction of agriculture led to the end of what lifestyle?

2. In order to create their new farms, the inhabitants of neolithic Britain had to engage in what process, permanently altering the country's landscape?

3. What name is given to the ancient causeway that ran through the valley of the River Brue, and which was later replaced by the Sweet Track?

4. Skara Brae, in the Orkney archipelago of Scotland, contains ten houses made of what?

5. Which neolithic site, in Wiltshire, is the largest megalithic stone circle in the world?

6. What name is given to the central monolith at Stonehenge?

7. Stonehenge Avenue is 3km long, and connects Stonehenge to which other location?

8. What name is given to the archaeological site in Orkney, Scotland that is believed to feature a large Neolithic temple?

9. To date, the earliest depiction of a human face ever found in Britain was discovered in Orkney in 2009. By what name is it known?

10. A late period of neolithic Britain, featuring the first metalworking, is known by which name?

answers on page 318

BRONZE AGE BRITAIN
c. 2500 – 800 BC

1. Bronze is made by mixing copper (which was widely used in Britain up until this point) with which other metal?

2. Earlier versions existed, but what weapon became more common during the Bronze Age, due to the use of copper?

3. What name, derived from a Dorset henge enclosure, is used to refer to the earliest period of the Bronze Age in Britain?

4. Which prehistoric monument, built around 2000 BC, features a timber circle surrounding an upturned tree root?

5. A 360ft long crushed chalk figure at Uffington, Oxfordshire takes the form of what creature?

6. What name is given to the mysterious group – of unknown origin – that is believed to have invaded much of Europe and Egypt during the 12th century BC, including Britain?

7. Bush Barrow, an early Bronze Age settlement from around 2,000 BC, is located less than a mile from which site?

8. What's the name of the Proto-Celtic population of central Europe that expanded during the Bronze Age, and which reached Britain in the 6th century BC?

9. What pottery style arrived in Britain around 2,000 BC, and is named after a distinctive type of drinking vessel?

10. Which culture was dominant in central and southern Britain during the Bronze Age?

answers on page 318

IRON AGE BRITAIN
c. 800 BC – 43 AD

1. Cassivellaunus, Mandubracius and Addedomarus were all leaders of which powerful pre-Roman British tribe?

2. Which Greek writer, who visited Britain in the 3rd century BC, reported that the country was named both Prettanike and Brettaniai, which led to the name Britannia?

3. The Ancient Greeks referred to Britain as part of the Cassiterides, referring to an abundance of which commodity?

4. Traders from which eastern Mediterranean civilization are believed to have traded with Britain during this period?

5. Lugus, Taranis and Teutatis are gods in which religion, which was widely practised by Britons during the Iron Age?

6. Which Iron Age hill fort near Dorchester is one of the largest in Europe?

7. What name is given to an Iron Age hillfort, located about 2 miles from Stonehenge?

8. Camulodunon, said to be the oldest town in Britain, is now better known by which name?

9. The earliest coins found in Britain, from the 2nd century BC, were the result of trade with which European power?

10. Large quantities of amphorae (jars) have been discovered at the Iron Age trading port of Hengistbury Head, in Dorset. Amphorae were used in the transport of what commodity?

answers on page 319

ROMAN BRITAIN
43 AD – 410 AD

1. Rome had an extensive trading arrangement with Britain, but this was disrupted by the territorial expansion of the Catuvellauni tribe. Who was their leader during this period?

2. As of 2021, recent research suggests that Julius Caesar first landed in Britain in 55 BC at which location in Kent?

3. Following Caesar's earlier landings, which Roman emperor ordered the full invasion of Britain in 43 AD?

4. Which battle, shortly after the invasion, took place in Kent between Roman forces and the native Cantiaci tribe?

5. Roman forces invaded which Welsh island in the 1st century CE, as part of their campaign against Celtic druids?

6. Which 1st century queen of the Brigantes led her people into a pact of peace with the Romans?

7. Which battle in north-east Scotland is said to have concluded the Roman subjugation of British tribes?

8. Aldgate, Bishopsgate, Ludgate and Newgate were the four main routes through which defensive structure?

9. Hadrian's Wall was built in the 2nd century AD to defend Roman Britain from which northern tribe?

10. Which 5th century Roman Emperor refused to send Roman forces to defend Britain, effectively abandoning Roman rule of the land?

answers on page 319

EARLY RELIGION
& THE ARRIVAL OF CHRISTIANITY

1. What name was given by the Romans to the priests of Britain, who left no written records of their beliefs?

2. Following the Roman invasion of Britain, which Welsh island – a religious centre for the the pre-Roman priests – was invaded between 60 and 77 AD?

3. Which goddess was worshipped at Bath's thermal spring?

4. Which 2nd century King of the Britons is traditionally credited with introducing Christianity to Britain?

5. Who is regarded as the first British Christian martyr?

6. What declaration, issued in 313 AD by the Roman emperors Constantine and Licinius, aimed to end the persecution of Christians through the empire?

7. Which figure, later canonised, was born in Britain in the 4th century and later helped establish Christianity in Ireland?

8. During the 5th century, which figure was sent to convert the Picts (in what is now Scotland) to Christianity?

9. Odin is a deity in Germanic and Norse mythology. What name was he given by Anglo-Saxon pagans?

10. Christianity faded following the withdrawal of the Romans, but returned when a mission was sent by the Pope to convert the Anglo-Saxons. Who headed this mission?

answers on page 320

BATH

1. What was the Roman name for the small town that once stood on the site of Bath?

2. In the Roman baths, the hot bath was called the caldarium and the warm bath was called the tepidarium. What name was given to the cold bath?

3. During the Anglo-Saxon period, Bath was known by the name Akemanchester. What does this name mean?

4. What's the name of the bun or teacake, similar to French brioche buns, that was first recorded in Bath in the 1680s?

5. Who designed the Circus, a ring of Bath townhouses built in the mid-18th century?

6. Which Bath-based entrepreneur, best known for reforming the British postal system, owned the mines that were used for much of the local Bath stone?

7. What's the name of the 18th century Bath bridge, designed by Robert Adam, that features a shopping arcade?

8. Which 18th century figure, known as a dandy and a fashion leader, was Bath's Master of Ceremonies from 1704 until his death in 1761?

9. In the late 1930s, which African emperor spent part of his exile at a house in Bath?

10. Which British food writer, born in Bath in 1935, was awarded the Freedom of the City in 2014?

answers on page 320

EARLY LITERATURE

1. Which late 7th century figure is the earliest English poet whose name is known?

2. In the Old English epic poem *Beowulf*, what's the name of the monster that attacks the mead hall of the Danish king?

3. Although it's regarded as one of the great English epics, *Beowulf* is actually set in which part of the world?

4. At the end of *Beowulf*, the titular hero is killed in a battle with a dragon. Only one of his compatriots remains behind to witness his death. What is this man's name?

5. What's the title of the Old English poem, by an unknown author, about a lonely exile who looks back on his old life?

6. The epic poem *Waldere*, or *Waldhere*, is a telling of the life of which legendary Visigoth king?

7. What name is given to the earliest British prose stories, compiled in the 12th and 13th centuries from oral traditions?

8. Which chivalric romance, which has existed since at least the 12th century, tells the story of the romance between a Cornish knight and an Irish princess?

9. What title is given to the 13th century author who composed the earliest extant scholarship on Old English literature?

10. Which late 14th / early 15th century anchoress wrote *Revelations of Divine Love*, which is the first book written in English by a known female author?

answers on page 320

BOUDICA
died c. 60 AD

1. Boudica was a queen of which Celtic tribe?

2. What part of modern Britain was Boudica's tribe based in?

3. Boudica's husband ruled before her. When he died, the kingdom was seized by the Romans, and Boudica and her daughters were flogged and raped. What was the husband's name?

4. What was the name of the Roman governor who fought against Boudica?

5. According to legend, Boudica invoked the name of the goddess Andraste. What animal – sacred to this god – is she said to have released from her gown at this moment?

6. Boudica's forces destroyed a settlement called Verulamium. What modern city is on the site of Verulamium?

7. During one of her attacks, Boudica's forces decapitated a bronze statue of which Roman emperor?

8. What name is generally given to the event that ended Boudica's rebellion against Roman forces in 60 or 61 AD?

9. Although the exact circumstances of Boudica's death are unknown, the Roman historian Tacitus suggests that she suffered what fate?

10. Thomas Thornycroft's statue *Boadicea and Her Daughters* now stands at which location in London?

answers on page 321

ROMAN LONDON

1. Although there is no evidence of his existence, some medieval sources claim that London is named after which pre-Roman king of Britain?

2. What name did the Romans use for London?

3. What name was given to the Roman road that linked Londinium to Silchester (modern-day Calleva)?

4. Which part of Roman London was known as Battle Bridge?

5. Which historic landmark, now on Cannon Street, is believed to have originally been part of the Roman governor's palace near Cannon Street Station?

6. Which river, now subterranean, was a major waterway in Roman times and ran along the western side of the city's wall?

7. What structure, discovered in 1988 and located beneath the Guildhall Art Gallery, was used in Roman times for events such as gladiator games and the execution of criminals?

8. A marble slab, dating from the Roman era, contains the earliest known reference to the people of London. What name does it give to them?

9. Which Roman naval commander led a brief revolt in the 3rd century, during which he declared himself emperor of Britain?

10. London declined rapidly after the Romans, and was in ruins by the 6th century. Which 9th century Anglo-Saxon king is credited with restarting the settlement?

answers on page 321

ROADS

1. As of 2021, the oldest British road dates from the 1st century BC and was found in a quarry near which Shropshire town?

2. One of the major ancient roads was Watling Street, established by the ancient Britons and paved by the Romans. The section between the English Channel and London is today known by what name?

3. Corpse roads were special roads designated for the transportation of dead bodies. What name was given to the corpse road that passed through Fryup in Yorkshire?

4. What medieval term was used for the payment paid to use certain roads?

5. Which riots in mid-19th century Wales saw farmers attack toll-gates in protest at tax levels?

6. On January 28th 1896, Walter Arnold of East Peckham became the first person to do what on an English road?

7. When driving licences were introduced in 1904, what was the minimum age for a driver?

8. What was first installed in Britain in November 1927, in Wolverhampton's Princes Square?

9. What was invented by Percy Shaw of Halifax, West Yorkshire in 1934?

10. First installed in the United Kingdom on the M40 in 1991, a Gatso is a common brand of what instrument?

answers on page 322

SAINT GEORGE
died in 303 AD

1. George is believed to have been born in Cappadocia, which is now better known as part of which modern-day country?

2. Both the Greek and Latin versions of George's story claim that he joined which army in his late teens?

3. The Greek version of the story claims that George was beheaded during the persecution of Christians in c. 303 AD. This persecution was ordered by which Roman emperor?

4. In this version of the story, the emperor's wife was also martyred after hearing of George's suffering and converting to Christianity. What was her name?

5. According to legend, George faced a dragon that was causing panic in which Libyan city?

6. The Muslim version of George's story claims that he was martyred after opposing a statue of which god?

7. In 494 AD, George was canonised by which pope?

8. George is sometimes referred to as George of Lydda. Lydda is better known as which modern Israeli city?

9. Which English king, in 1552, banned all saints' banners other than that of George?

10. When is St. George's day?

answers on page 322

THE END OF THE ROMAN ERA

1. By the late 4th century, the Roman Empire was under increasing threat from which group of people?

2. In 383, which Roman general withdrew forces from the north as part of his attempt to seize the imperial throne?

3. The withdrawal from the north led to increased raids by Picts from Scotland. Which Roman commander led a campaign against the Picts in 398?

4. Which Irish king is said to have raided Britain's southern coast during this period?

5. Which transgression in mainland Europe, which occurred at the end of the year 406, is widely seen as having marked a decisive turn against Rome?

6. Fearing an attack by Germanic tribes, the remaining Roman troops in Britain chose which new leader in 407 AD?

7. What name was given by the Romans to the social body of its citizens, united by common laws?

8. In 410 AD, which Roman emperor told the British that they would receive no more help and must defend themselves?

9. While this was happening, Rome was being sacked by which Germanic group?

10. What was the name of the Germanic group that began to launch an increasing number of raids on Britain, once the Romans were gone?

answers on page 322

ANGLO-SAXON BRITAIN
c. 500 - 1066

1. Which high king of the Britons is said to have been instrumental in securing Anglo-Saxon help in the fight against the Picts and the Scots?

2. Which two Germanic brothers are said to have led the Angle, Saxon and Jute invasion of Post-Roman Britain?

3. After the Anglo-Saxons began to rebel against the Britons, the latter won a brief victory in which late 5th century battle?

4. What term was used in Anglo-Saxon England to denote a prince who was in line for the throne?

5. What name was given to the assemblies of wise men that met regularly to advise the king?

6. Which Anglo-Saxon king, ruler of Kent from c. 589 to 616 AD, is said to have been an early convert to Christianity?

7. The English church gave its allegiance to the Pope following a 664 AD synod in which North Yorkshire location?

8. Which Wessex king led his forces to victory against the Britons at the Battle of Deorham (or Dyrham) in 577 AD?

9. Which 6th century British monk wrote *De Excidio et Conquestu Britanniae*, about the coming of the Saxons?

10. An Anglo-Saxon helmet, widely associated with King Rædwald of East Anglia, was discovered during an archaeological dig at which location in Suffolk?

answers on page 323

THE HEPTARCHY

1. The term 'heptarchy' refers to the seven kingdoms of Anglo-Saxon Britain, that existed for about 300 years from the 5th century. Which 11th century historian first used this term?

2. What term is sometimes used for the period in history immediately following the end of Roman occupation?

3. Which Staffordshire town was once a key location in Mercia?

4. Which 7th century Mercian, a pagan when most Anglo-Saxon rulers were Christians, defeated the king of Northumbria in 633 AD and became the most powerful king in the country?

5. Which Northumbrian king, who died in 641 or 642 AD, is now venerated as a saint?

6. Which king of Wessex conquered Kent in 686 AD, prompting the kingdom to fall into a state of chaos?

7. What was the name of the dynasty that ruled East Anglia between the end of Roman occupation and the 8th century?

8. Sigered, who reigned until 825 AD, was the last king of which region?

9. What term was used to describe a king who had gained overlordship of multiple kingdoms?

10. The heptarchy ended when most of the Anglo-Saxon kingdoms came under the rule of which Wessex king in 829?

answers on page 323

THE LEGEND OF KING ARTHUR

1. Which legendary king of sub-Roman Britain is said to be Arthur's father?

2. According to some versions of the legend, Arthur was conceived at which Cornish castle?

3. Arthur is said to have journeyed deep into which Welsh mythological Otherworld?

4. In chivalric romantic versions of Arthur's story, which figure is said to be the orphaned son of King Ban, and was subsequently raised by the Lady of the Lake?

5. What name was supposedly given to the empty seat at the Round Table, reserved for the knight who would one day find the Holy Grail?

6. In many versions of the legend, the Holy Grail is kept in the possession of which wounded figure?

7. Which figure, said to be Arthur's half-sister, becomes an apprentice of Merlin and harbours a deep hatred for Guinevere?

8. Which enchanted forest is said to be the last resting place of Merlin?

9. Who wrote *Le Morte d'Arthur*, an influential 15th century retelling of the Arthurian legend?

10. Arthur is said to have either died, or been mortally wounded, in which final battle against Mordred?

answers on page 323

OFFA OF MERCIA
died 796, Mercian king 757 - 796

1. Through his father Thingfrith, Offa was descended from which late 6th, early 7th century Mercian king?

2. Offa assumed the Mercian throne following a period of chaos and civil war, which had erupted following the assassination of which earlier king?

3. A coin minted by Offa provides the earliest evidence of what influence in England?

4. What name is given to the period between c. 626 and 825 AD, during which Mercia was the dominant Anglo-Saxon kingdom?

5. Within a few years of taking the Mercian throne, Offa was also the ruler of which other part of the country?

6. Offa's wife was the only Anglo-Saxon queen who ever appeared on a coin. What was her name?

7. Offa was briefly allied with the Holy Roman Emperor. What was this emperor's name?

8. Which large earthwork, once believed to have been built during Offa's reign, approximately marks the border between England and Wales?

9. What was the dominant power in Wales at this time?

10. What was the name of Offa's son, who succeeded him as king in 796 AD but lasted only a few months on the throne?

answers on page 324

THE VIKING AGE
from c. 793

1. The first recorded Viking raid in Anglo-Saxon England occurred in 789 AD on which island?

2. In 793 AD, an attack on which monastery is said to have marked the start of the Viking age?

3. What name is usually given to the Scandinavian forces that invaded England in 865 AD?

4. Established in 865 AD and lasting for approximately a century, what name was given to the area of England in which Danish laws held sway?

5. Many Viking leaders of this period flew a flag containing a symbol of which bird?

6. What name was given to an Anglo-Saxon tax that was raised for the purpose of bribing Vikings to stop their attacks?

7. What name, derived from the Old Norse word for a type of animal, was given to Norse warriors who fought in a kind of furious trance?

8. Which Old Norse god is often portrayed as having one eye and a long beard?

9. What name did Vikings give to the huge hall that they believed was home to the dead?

10. Which Viking warrior became the first ruler of Normandy, once his people had begun to settle northern France?

answers on page 324

KENNETH MACALPIN, KENNETH I OF SCOTLAND
810 – 858, King of Alba 843 - 858

1. Kenneth MacAlpin is believed to have been born in 810 AD in which part of modern-day Scotland?

2. In 841, MacAlpin inherited which throne from his father Alpin mac Echdach?

3. Around 850 AD, MacAlpin conquered the Picts. The legend of MacAlpin's treason, which is disputed by some scholars, states that he did what to the Pictish king and his nobles?

4. Which village in Strathearn is believed to have been the initial capital of MacAlpin's kingdom?

5. Following his campaign to seize all of Scotland, MacAlpin was given what nickname?

6. Which oblong block, moved by MacAlpin to his new kingdom, was used for centuries during the coronation of Scottish monarchs and was most recently used in the 1953 coronation of Britain's Queen Elizabeth II?

7. After MacAlpin's death in 858, who succeeded him as king?

8. One of MacAlpin's daughters, Máel Muire ingen Cináeda, is said to have married two separate holders of which title?

9. Which historical c. 5th century poem is said to prophesy the life of more than 20 Scottish kings, including MacAlpin?

10. Almost 200 years after MacAlpin's death, which king was the last member of the House of Alpin?

answers on page 325

ORKNEY & SHETLAND

1. What name refers to the hollow-walled drystone structures that were common in Scotland during the Ice Age, many examples of which can still be found on Orkney and Shetland?

2. What name is given to the chambered tomb, dating from the megalithic era, that stands in a valley on the island of Hoy?

3. What name did the Ancient Greeks and Romans give to the farthest north location on their maps, with some experts believing that this location was Orkney and Shetland?

4. Norsemen colonised the islands in the 9th century. What's the name of the resulting West Nordic language that developed, and which survived for ten centuries?

5. In 1379, which Scottish earl took control of Orkney on behalf of the Norwegian king Håkon VI Magnusson?

6. Which 16th century Lord of Shetland was known for his despotic rule?

7. What name was given to the Norwegian naval unit that used Shetland as its base during the Second World War?

8. What's the name of the natural causeway that links the islands of Hoy and South Walls?

9. Which Royal Navy battleship was torpedoed at Scapa Flow, Orkney in October 1939, with the loss of more than 800 crew?

10. Which 1980 musical piece by Peter Maxwell Davies was a response to fears of a planned uranium mine in Orkney?

answers on page 325

ALFRED THE GREAT
c. 848 – 899, Anglo-Saxon king c. 886 - 899

1. What was the name of Alfred's father, who ruled as King of Wessex between 839 and 858 AD?

2. In 876, Alfred escaped after a sudden Danish attack while he was staying in which town?

3. By early 878, what was the only part of England that hadn't been conquered by the Danes?

4. Which Danish leader commanded the forces that chased Arthur into seeming defeat?

5. In what part of the country was Alfred said to have burnt some wheaten cakes?

6. Alfred's forces defeated the Danish army at which battle in 878 AD?

7. What was the name of Alfred's wife, the daughter of a powerful Mercian nobleman?

8. What name is given to the document that lists Alfred's various fortified locations, as well as the taxes involved?

9. What name is given to the book of laws compiled by Alfred?

10. Alfred died in 899. Modern doctors believe that he suffered from which painful condition?

answers on page 325

WINCHESTER

1. What name did the Romans give to Winchester, in recognition of the local Belgae tribe?

2. Which 26-mile Roman road starts in Salisbury and ends in Winchester?

3. Which 9th century Bishop of Winchester gained a reputation as a miracle-worker, and has a feast day that is said to be a reliable predictor of weather?

4. Who founded the Hospital of St. Cross in Winchester, England's oldest almshouse, in 1136?

5. Winchester is said to have once been the capital of England, and remained important until the Norman Conquest in the 11th century. In the 13th century, which nobleman led a ransacking of the city's influential Jewish quarter?

6. What has hung in the Great Hall of Winchester Castle since the 15th century, and is linked to the legend of King Arthur?

7. In 1554, Wolvesey Castle was the location of the wedding breakfast for which royal couple?

8. In 1770, politician Thomas Dummer attempted – but failed – to move which structure from the city's centre?

9. *Night-Thoughts* is an 18th century poem by which author, who was born in Winchester in 1683?

10. Which 19th century author, who died in July 1817, is buried in Winchester Cathedral?

answers on page 326

ÆTHELSTAN
c. 894 – 939, reigned 924 - 927

1. What was the name of Æthelstan's father, Alfred's grandson, who ruled before him from 899 to 924 AD?

2. Upon his father's death, Æthelstan was immediately declared king of which part of the country?

3. Æthelstan secured a temporary truce with a Viking named Sitric Cáech, ruler of which territory in northern England?

4. As the first king of all the Anglo-Saxon peoples, Æthelstan launched an invasion of which territory in 934 AD?

5. Æthelstan subsequently won a major victory against the Norse and the Scots in which battle?

6. What name was given to those with the highest lay status under the king?

7. During Æthelstan's reign, where was the Anglo-Saxon capital city?

8. Æthelstan's reign saw the introduction of which system, whereby groups of ten or more men were responsible for peace-keeping in their local area?

9. Æthelstan was the first king whose coins declared him as holder of which office?

10. Although kings were traditionally buried at Winchester, the city had been opposed to his rule. Following his death in 939 AD, therefore, Æthelstan was buried at which location?

answers on page 326

ÆTHELRED THE UNREADY
c. 966 – 1016, reigned 978 – 1013 & 1014 - 1016

1. What was the name of Æthelred's brother, who ruled for just over two years before being murdered in 978 AD?

2. Which Archbishop of Canterbury – later canonised as a saint – officiated at Æthelred's coronation?

3. Æthelred's army failed to repel Viking forces in Essex during which battle in 991 AD?

4. The poem *The Homecoming of Beorhtnoth Beorthelm's Son* (1953), which commemorates the battle mentioned in the previous question, was written by which English author?

5. The mass killing of Danes in England occurred on which saint's day in 1002 AD?

6. Which Danish king briefly threw Æthelred off the throne and ruled for 41 days in 1013/14?

7. Where did Æthelred seek sanctuary during his time away from England?

8. Æthelred returned to England and briefly retook London, thanks in part to assistance to from which Norwegian king?

9. What was the name of Æthelred's son, who briefly succeeded him as king following his death before being toppled by Cnut the Great?

10. In its original form, 'the Unready' comes from the Old English word 'unræd'. What did this word mean at the time?

answers on page 327

OXFORD

1. What's the name of the woman, sister of Sweyn Forkbeard and wife of a Danish soldier, who is said to have been one of those killed in the St. Brice's Day Massacre in Oxford in 1002?

2. Who is the first foreign scholar known to have studied at Oxford university?

3. In 1517, an estimated 50% of the population of Oxford died from which mysterious, as-yet-unexplained illness?

4. Protestants Thomas Cranmer, Archbishop of Canterbury, and the bishops Hugh Latimer and Nicholas Ridley, suffered what fate in 1555?

5. What bridge, built in the late 18th century, spans the River Cherwell and is the site of the annual May Morning celebrations?

6. Which academic book retailer was founded in Broad Street, Oxford in 1879?

7. Which Scarborough-born architect designed Oxford Town Hall, which was completed in 1897?

8. In the early 20th century, which manufacturer and philanthropist established a car company near Oxford?

9. For what reason was Oxford largely spared by German bombers during the Second World War?

10. In 1954, at Oxford's Iffley Road track, who became the first athlete to run a mile in under four minutes?

answers on page 327

CNUT THE GREAT
c. 990 – 1035, reigned 1016 - 1035

1. What was the name of Cnut's grandfather, a legendary Scandinavian king?

2. Cnut was ruler of the North Sea Empire, which was made up of which three nations?

3. Cnut's father had briefly held the throne of England. Cnut fled following his father's death, but he swiftly returned with an army and landed in which Kent town?

4. Once he was king, Cnut provided protection against Viking attacks. However, he had to reassert his dominance in Scandinavia at which battle in 1026?

5. The story of Cnut (aka Canute) commanding the tide to stop rising first features in the *Historia Anglorum* by which 12th century historian?

6. What was the name of Cnut's wife, who had also been married to his predecessor Æthelred?

7. Which figure, at times both Archbishop of York and Bishop of Worcester, drafted many of the laws during Cnut's reign?

8. As a sign of his Christian faith, in 1027 Cnut went to Rome for the accession of which Holy Roman Emperor?

9. Cnut died at Shaftesbury in Dorset, and was buried at the Old Minster in which city?

10. Which of Cnut's sons subsequently ruled as Cnut III?

answers on page 327

MACBETH OF SCOTLAND
c. 1005 – 1057, Scottish king 1040 - 1057

1. Born around the year 1005, Macbeth is said to have been a grandson of which Scots king?

2. In 1031, Macbeth was one of those who offered their submission to which King of England?

3. A year later, Macbeth gained what title, most likely by killing its previous holder?

4. What name is used to describe the Gaelic system for passing on titles and lands, which explained how Macbeth's (probable) cousin became Duncan I around the year 1034?

5. In 1040, Duncan attacked Macbeth's lands, but Macbeth killed him and became king. He is believed to have made a pilgrimage to which location ten years later?

6. Which ruler of Orkney is said to have driven out a Scots king – possibly Macbeth – around this time?

7. In 1054, which English king sent an invasion force to Scotland, with the aim of overthrowing Macbeth?

8. Three years later, Macbeth was killed by the forces of the future Malcolm III, in which battle?

9. Macbeth was buried at which location, which was the traditional resting place for Scottish kings?

10. In Shakespeare's *Macbeth*, the king kills Duncan following a prophecy given to him by which characters?

answers on page 328

EDWARD THE CONFESSOR
c. 1003 – 1066, reigned 1042 - 1066

1. Edward is generally considered to have been the last king from which house?

2. After his father Æthelred's death, Edward is believed to have spent twenty-five years in exile in which country?

3. Following the death of Cnut in 1035, Edward and his brother Alfred travelled to England. Edward was swiftly captured by Cnut's son, Harold Harefoot. What was done to Alfred, to make him unsuitable for the throne?

4. In 1040, Edward sent an army to Scotland, resulting in the death of which king?

5. One year later, Edward was invited back to England by the king, Harthacnut. He was received as the next king, but he had to swear to do what?

6. St. Peter's Abbey, which was rebuilt on Edward's order as a royal burial church, is now known by what name?

7. In 1045, Edward married Edith of Wessex. Who was her brother?

8. In 1053, the head of which Welsh prince – who'd launched a raid against the English – was delivered to Edward?

9. Although there is some dispute about the facts, in 1051 Edward is said to have promised the throne to who?

10. Edward was canonised in 1161 by which pope?

answers on page 328

WESTMINSTER ABBEY

1. What's the name of the fisherman who is said to have once seen a vision of Saint Peter near the site of the present church?

2. Which Anglo-Saxon king is said to have installed a group of Benedictine monks on the site in the 970s?

3. When Edward the Confessor began to rebuild St. Peter's Abbey, it was the first church in England built in which architectural style?

4. The first documented coronation in the abbey was that of which king?

5. Construction of the present church began in 1245, under the direction of which king?

6. Is Westminster Abbey technically an abbey or a cathedral?

7. Which architect was responsible for the two western towers, which were constructed between 1722 and 1745?

8. Who was the first Pope to ever enter Westminster Abbey?

9. What's the name of the seat used by monarchs during their coronation at the abbey?

10. Who was the first poet interred in Poets' Corner?

answers on page 329

WILLIAM I & THE BATTLE OF HASTINGS
c. 1028 – 1087, reigned 1066 - 1087

1. William was often referred to as William the Bastard. This referred to the fact that he was the illegitimate son of which Norman duke?

2. What was the name of William's wife, who served as regent of Normandy during his absences?

3. What was the name of William's half-brother, who became Earl of Kent?

4. Prior to the Norman invasion, King Harold defeated a Norwegian force in which battle?

5. Where did William land when he arrived in England in 1066?

6. The Battle of Hastings took place roughly 7 miles from Hastings, close to which modern-day East Sussex town?

7. Who was briefly proclaimed king, but never crowned, following the death of Harold?

8. What name is used to describe William's 1069-1070 campaign to subdue rebels, which resulted in massacres in locations such as York?

9. What name is given to a 1075 conspiracy that aimed to overthrow William?

10. Construction began around 1078 on the White Tower, which is now part of which fortress?

answers on page 329

EXETER

1. What name did the Romans use for Exeter?

2. Two years after the Norman conquest, Exeter rebelled against William I. Which noblewoman was living in the city at the time?

3. Which diplomat and scholar, who founded the main research library at the University of Oxford, was born in Exeter in March 1545?

4. Which gardens, which opened Exeter in 1612, are the oldest public open space in England?

5. Temperance Lloyd, Mary Trembles and Susannah Edwards died in 1682 after which event?

6. In 1887, the worst theatre fire in British history saw 186 people die at the Theatre Royal in Exeter. What play, by Wilson Barrett, was being performed on that night?

7. Which Exeter-born sportswriter, who later moved to America, is often referred to as the Father of Baseball?

8. Which Exeter-born sculptor is known for medieval screens in churches such as St. Alban's Cathedral in Hertfordshire and Christ Church Cathedral in St. Louis, Missouri?

9. In April and May 1942, Exeter's city centre was devastated during which Luftwaffe bombing campaign?

10. Which Exeter shopping centre, opened in the 1950s, was the first pedestrianised shopping street in the UK?

answers on page 329

A BRIEF HISTORY OF THE ENGLISH LANGUAGE

1. English developed from which branch of the Germanic family of languages?

2. How did this language reach Britain?

3. The Bath curse tablets, discovered in the late 20th century, contain text mostly written in British Latin. Some sections, however, are believed to be written in which other language?

4. What name is generally given to this pre-Roman language?

5. What name is given to the runic script that was originally used in the writing of Old English?

6. When Vikings began to colonise parts of England, they spoke which language?

7. For many years after the Norman invasion of 1066, most common people in England spoke English. What language was usually spoken by high-ranking nobles during this period?

8. In 1362, the Pleading in English Act was passed. This ensured that English courts should use the English language, since most locals didn't understand the language that had been used up to that point. What was this other language?

9. Which English king was the first to speak English as his first language?

10. The first English dictionary, *A Table Alphabeticall*, was published in London in which year?

answers on page 330

EARLY SCOTLAND

1. What was the original name of Scotland during the Latin and Roman ages?

2. In *Scotichronicon*, Walter Bower claims (without any proof) that the Scots were descended from a king of which country?

3. Vipoig, Drest I and Oengus mac Fergusa were all kings of which tribe?

4. The name Scotland comes from Scoti, which was the Latin name for which group?

5. Which tribal confederacy ruled much of Scotland during the Iron Age and Roman era?

6. Which legendary king is said to have been the founder of Scotland?

7. Which Irish missionary is generally credited with spreading Christianity throughout Scotland during the 6th century?

8. Which 7th century Anglo-Saxon kingdom straddled what is now southeastern Scotland and the north-east of England?

9. Who, in 1371, became the first Scottish king from the House of Stuart?

10. In 1249, Henry III of England and Alexander III of Scotland attempted to end Anglo-Scottish conflict by establishing a 'buffer zone' between the two kingdoms. What name was given to this zone?

answers on page 330

ABERDEEN

1. Which Scottish king granted the first charter to Aberdeen in 1179 AD?

2. What fund, created after Robert the Bruce granted a Great Charter in 1319, is still used in the 21st century to benefit the people of the city?

3. Since at least the 14th century, the city's motto has been which French phrase, which translates as 'good agreement'?

4. What name is given to the six 17th century divines who were initially led by Patrick Forbes, Bishop of Aberdeen?

5. Architects such as Archibald Simpson and John Smith helped inspire which nickname for Aberdeen?

6. Between 1845 and 1922, Aberdeen was the headquarters of which Scottish train company?

7. Which Aberdeen-born artist is known for paintings such as *Pegwell Bay, Kent – a Recollection of October 5th 1858*, and a series of murals at the Palace of Westminster?

8. The Guild Street drill hall was home, in the early 20th century, to a battalion of which army group?

9. In 1964, more than 400 cases were diagnosed when the city was hit by an outbreak of which disease?

10. Which singer, born in Aberdeen in 1954, was part of the pop duo Eurythmics?

answers on page 331

EARLY WALES

1. Which neolithic Welsh monument, which now consists of seven stones, stands roughly 11 miles from Cardigan?

2. Which late-neolithic passage tomb, located on Anglesey, is believed to have once been a henge with a stone circle?

3. What name is given to the warlike tribe that occupied south east Wales during the first few centuries AD?

4. Which 5th century figure, who gave her name to a Welsh town, was the daughter of a Welsh king named Brychan?

5. 6th century Welsh leader Dewi ap Sanctus is better known today by what name?

6. Which 7th century king was a key figure in the stories of Geoffrey of Monmouth, and is closely associated with the symbolic Welsh dragon?

7. Which 9th century leader came to rule much of Wales before his death at the Battle of Sunday in 873?

8. What was the name of the kingdom that emerged following the end of Roman rule, and which was based in north-east Wales until its fall at the end of the 13th century?

9. Which 11th century leader was the only Welsh king who ever truly united and ruled the entire country?

10. Welsh independence ended in 1283, when the country was finally conquered by which English king?

answers on page 331

THE DOMESDAY BOOK

1. The Domesday Book was written in which language?

2. The book is made up of two separate works. What title is given to the work that covers Norfolk, Suffolk and Essex?

3. The main aim of the book is generally agreed to have been to discover what taxes were owed during the reign of which previous king?

4. According to the book, approximately what percentage of England's 1086 population were slaves?

5. Land in the Domesday Book was divided into portions, each amounting to approximately 30 modern acres. What were these portions called?

6. What name is given to the part of the Domesday survey that covers south-west England?

7. During the 11th century, the book was generally known by what title?

8. Which 12th century churchman is believed to have coined the phrase 'Domesday Book', due to the fact that the book's findings were – like the Last Judgement – unalterable?

9. Following the Great Fire of London in 1666, the Domesday Book was temporarily moved to which location in Surrey?

10. As of 2021, the Domesday Book is held at which location in London?

answers on page 331

WILLIAM II
c. 1056 – 1100, reigned 1087 - 1100

1. William II was often referred to by which other title?

2. On his deathbed, William I declared that one son, Robert, would rule Normandy, while the other, William, would rule England. What name is given to Robert's subsequent attempt to overthrow his brother?

3. Lanfranc, Archbishop of Canterbury, died in 1089. Who did William II eventually nominate as his replacement?

4. William II's customary oath is said to have been a reference to which wooden carving in Northern Italy?

5. In 1091, William II repelled an invasion by which Scottish king?

6. William II began construction of which London site, which still exists today?

7. William II subsequently built which castle, with the aim of controlling Cumberland and Westmorland?

8. William II's death in 1100, by an arrow in the lung, is believed to have occurred near which New Forest village?

9. Who is said to have fired the arrow that killed the king?

10. What name is generally given to the stone that's said to mark the spot where William II fell?

answers on page 332

HENRY I
c. 1068 – 1135, reigned 1100 - 1135

1. Following the death of his brother William II in 1100, Henry rushed to which city in order to press his claim to the throne?

2. The same year, Henry married which Scottish princess?

3. Henry was initially challenged by his other brother, Robert. Which agreement, in either 1101 or 1102, settled the matter?

4. What name was given to the noblemen appointed by the king during this time to guard the border between England and Wales?

5. On 25th November 1120, Henry's heir and only legitimate son William Adelin was killed in the sinking of which vessel?

6. What caused the vessel to sink?

7. The death of the heir to the throne caused instability in the kingdom. Which Welsh king launched an ill-fated rebellion against Henry?

8. What was the name of the new wife taken by Henry during this period, likely in an attempt to produce a new heir?

9. While campaigning in France in 1135, Henry – who was already sick – took a turn for the worse. According to the chronicler Henry of Huntingdon, this came after he'd eaten too much of what food?

10. Henry attempted to arrange for which of his daughters to take the throne following his death?

answers on page 332

STEPHEN, MATILDA & THE ANARCHY
1135 - 1153

1. Stephen was born in which northern region of France?

2. Stephen persuaded which royal steward to swear that the dying king Henry I had chosen Stephen as his successor?

3. Between 1136 and 1137, Stephen tried (but failed) to stamp his authority on which part of his kingdom?

4. In 1139, Empress Matilda took a French army to England, aiming to overthrow Stephen. What was the basis for her claim to the throne?

5. Who was Matilda's husband during this period?

6. Stephen was captured at which battle in February 1141?

7. After being released, Stephen fought back. Following a siege, the Empress Matilda had to escape barefoot across an icy river from which castle?

8. After ten years, the conflict had reached a stalemate. In 1147, the Empress Matilda's son launched a small, failed attack. What was his name?

9. In 1153, Stephen finally decided to end the war by recognizing the Empress Matilda's son as his successor. What was the name of this agreement?

10. In late 1154, Stephen suddenly fell ill and died at which location in Kent?

answers on page 332

DAVID I OF SCOTLAND
c. 1084 – 1153, Scottish king 1124 – 1153

1. Born in 1084, David is believed to have been the son of which Scottish king?

2. David's mother was Margaret of Wessex, who was also known by which name?

3. David was a member of which Scottish royal house, which originated in the 11th century with Duncan I?

4. After his uncle Donald seized the Scottish throne, David was sent into exile in England. Who did his sister Matilda marry in 1100?

5. Around the year 1113, David gained which title?

6. David later opposed the reign of the English king Stephen. What battle in June 1138 saw David's force defeat the English in Lancashire?

7. David's advance into England was halted two months later at which battle in Yorkshire?

8. Which Cistercian abbey was founded by David in Moray, Scotland in 1150?

9. David's son Henry, Earl of Huntingdon and Northumbria died in 1152. Who did David arrange to have succeed him as king?

10. David died in 1153 at which location in the north of England?

answers on page 333

WINDSOR CASTLE

1. Windsor Castle was one of a number of castles established by which king?

2. The castle has a keep on a raised area of ground, with a walled courtyard surrounded by a protective ditch. What name is given to this type of fortification?

3. Who was the first king to use Windsor Castle as a residence?

4. Which chivalric order, established by Edward III in 1348, has its base at Windsor Castle?

5. Which French king was briefly held captive at Windsor Castle in 1356, following his capture during the Hundred Years' War?

6. Who – or what – occupied Windsor Castle during the Interregnum that followed the English Civil War?

7. Seventy-six heraldic statues on the roof of St. George's Chapel are generally known by what name?

8. What was first created by George Bickham in 1753, as the castle became an early tourist attraction?

9. Queen Victoria and her husband Albert are buried at the Royal Mausoleum, which is located on which estate near the castle?

10. The November 1992 fire that damaged much of the castle began in which room?

answers on page 333

HENRY II
1133 – 1189, reigned 1154 - 1189

1. Henry became king following Stephen's death, at which point he became the first monarch from which house?

2. In 1152, Henry married which former French queen?

3. What overall name is given to Henry's possessions, encompassing not only England but also his substantial lands in France?

4. In 1157, northern parts of England were returned to the English throne by which Scottish king?

5. What title is generally used to refer to Henry's oldest surviving son, who was crowned during his father's reign but predeceased him by six years?

6. Henry had a long-running and bitter rivalry with which French king?

7. In 1171, Henry took an army to Ireland in support of which recently deposed king?

8. What name is given to the rebellion against Henry that was launched in 1173 by a group that included his wife and three of his sons?

9. Written in the late 1180s, what name is given to the earliest treatise on English law, which allowed Henry to define for the first time the legal processes that existed in the country?

10. Henry was buried at which location in France?

answers on page 334

THE ASSASSINATION OF THOMAS BECKET
1170

1. In his twenties, Thomas Becket worked in the household of which Archbishop of Canterbury?

2. In 1155, at the age of approximately thirty-five, Thomas was given which powerful rank?

3. Becket became Archbishop of Canterbury in 1162, and Henry II thought he would be easy to control. Instead, within three years Henry tried to force Becket to sign which document confirming the crown's power over the church?

4. Becket fled to France, but he eventually returned. In December 1170, four knights arrived at Canterbury Cathedral and demanded that he follow them to which city?

5. In what part of the cathedral was Becket murdered?

6. The knights who killed Becket eventually travelled to Rome, where they were ordered to do what as penance?

7. Which Pope canonised Becket, two years after his death?

8. In 1174, Henry gave public penance at Becket's tomb, and at which Canterbury church?

9. In Scotland, King William the Lion – who had known Becket personally – ordered that which newly-constructed abbey should be dedicated to Becket?

10. What day is now celebrated as Saint Thomas Becket's feast day?

answers on page 334

CANTERBURY

1. What was the name of the Roman settlement that once existed on the site of Canterbury?

2. Which Archbishop of Canterbury, later canonised, refounded St. Augustine's Abbey in 978 AD?

3. What's the name of the Canterbury gatehouse, the largest surviving city gate in England, that has at various times served as the city's jail, a museum, and an escape room?

4. By the 17th century, around 40% of the city's population consisted of which religious group, members of which had fled the Spanish Netherlands?

5. The Canterbury and Whitstable Railway, opened in 1830 as one of the world's first passenger railways, was also known by what nickname?

6. Canterbury Cathedral's organ was originally built in 1886 by which master organ maker?

7. Mary Tourtel, who lived in Canterbury, created which fictional bear?

8. Which band, part of the 1960s and 1970s Canterbury Scene, included Robert Wyatt and Kevin Ayers as members?

9. The University of Kent at Canterbury opened in 1965. The following year, who was appointed as its first Chancellor?

10. Which company, based in Blean near Canterbury, produced TV shows such as *Noggin the Nog* and *The Clangers*?

answers on page 335

DOVER CASTLE

1. Which military and trading confederation – which includes Dover, Hastings and Hythe – was established during the Anglo-Saxon period?

2. Which Saxon church, built between c. 600 and 1000 AD, stands next to the castle's Roman lighthouse?

3. Between 1179 and 1188, Henry II is said to have spent £6,500 fortifying the castle. What was the king's annual revenue during this period?

4. What name is given to the eastern gate on the castle's outer curtain wall?

5. What stood on the castle's 22nd tower between the 13th and 19th centuries?

6. The castle's royal chapel is dedicated to which figure?

7. A Dover merchant named Richard Dawkes achieved what feat in 1642?

8. In Rudolf Erich Raspe's 1785 novel *The Surprising Adventures of Baron Munchausen*, the protagonist says that he donated what item to the governor of Dover Castle?

9. What item from Dover Castle, which dates from around the year 1600, can now be found on display at the Science Museum in London?

10. The Lord Warden of the Cinque Ports also holds the title Constable of Dover Castle. As of 2021, who holds this office?

answers on page 335

RICHARD I
1157 – 1199, reigned 1189 - 1199

1. Richard was born in 1157 at which palace in Oxford?

2. Prior to the deaths of his older brothers, Richard was not expected to take the throne. Instead, his father Henry II granted him the duchy of which French region?

3. Richard's second great seal was the first English royal emblem to feature which symbol?

4. What happened to the Jewish leaders who arrived at Richard's coronation with gifts for the new king?

5. In 1191, during the Third Crusade, Richard's army secured a key victory by conquering which Mediterranean island?

6. Which victory in 1192 forced Richard's opponents to negotiate an end to the Third Crusade?

7. During his return to England in 1192, Richard was captured and held prisoner for a year by which Holy Roman Emperor?

8. While Richard was imprisoned, much of the English throne's land in France was squandered in battle by his brother. What was this brother's name?

9. In March 1199, while organising a siege in France, Richard was killed by a young boy who wanted revenge for the deaths of his father and brothers. What weapon did the boy use?

10. By the time of his death, Richard had ruled for 10 years. How much of this time had he actually spent in England?

answers on page 335

THE CRUSADES

1. What was the name of the Turkish warlord whose capture of much of the Middle East, including Jerusalem in 1073, directly led to the Crusades?

2. The First Crusade resulted from a call to arms issued by Pope Urban II in 1095. What name is given to this gathering in France?

3. Which preacher led the People's Crusade, which saw thousands of peasants travel to the Holy Land?

4. What was the name of the Seljuq sultan who ruled the Sultanate during the period of the First Crusade?

5. The First Crusade ended in 1099 with the foundation of the Christian Kingdom of Jerusalem. Which Frankish nobleman established this Crusader State?

6. Which Catholic military order, founded in 1119, was based on the Temple Mount in Jerusalem and fought during the Second and Third Crusades?

7. The Third Crusade, launched in 1189, came after Jerusalem was taken by which Muslim leader?

8. During the Third Crusade, the Crusaders won an important victory in 1191 following the two-year siege of which city?

9. In 1204, Crusaders sacked which city?

10. How many Crusades took place before the final one ended in 1272?

answers on page 336

JOHN
1166 – 1216, reigned 1199 - 1216

1. Aged 11, John was given which title by his father Henry II?

2. What nickname was given to John, due to the fact that he was expected to inherit very little in the way of territory?

3. While Richard was in the Holy Land, John was left in charge. As he began to lose his brother's land in France, John tried (but failed) to strike an alliance with which French king?

4. Once he was king, John enraged the French by abandoning his first wife in favour of which countess?

5. Between 1202 and 1204, John lost most of what remained of his French territories, including which large region?

6. Under pressure from the barons, in 1215 John signed a document, later known as Magna Carta, that laid out the rights of free men. Where was this document signed?

7. What name is given to the civil war that subsequently raged from 1215 to 1217, led by landowner Robert Fitzwalter?

8. Which figure, the son of the French king, sailed to England during this period and was briefly hailed as the new king?

9. As John tried to fight back against the rebels, what did he supposedly lose in the Wash (an estuary in East Anglia)?

10. John's death (probably from dysentry) in 1216 saw a change in the royal fortunes during the civil war. Which treaty saw the French pretender give up his claim on the throne?

answers on page 336

MAGNA CARTA

1. Defeat in which 1214 battle saw King John face increased resistance to his taxes?

2. The full title of Magna Carta is Magna Carta Libertatum. What does this mean in Medieval Latin?

3. Which Archbishop of Canterbury created the initial draft of Magna Carta in 1215?

4. One particular clause, clause 61, caused particular controversy. What does this clause state?

5. Magna Carta failed to bring peace under King John, but it was revived under his son Henry III. Which other important charter from this period, issued by Henry III in 1217, concerned the rights of free men to access royal land?

6. What was created in 1508 by Londoner Richard Pynson?

7. What principle, espoused by monarchs such as Charles I, was later seen to be in direct opposition to Magna Carta?

8. Magna Carta exerted influence on the formation of the Thirteen American Colonies. As of 2021, a replica of Magna Carta can be found in the crypt of which US building?

9. Who designed the Magna Carta Memorial at Runnymede which was erected by the American Bar Association in 1957?

10. As of 2021, three clauses of Magna Carta remain on statute. These relate to the freedom of the English Church, the liberties of the City of London, and which legal matter?

answers on page 337

THE LEGEND OF ROBIN HOOD

1. The first definite reference to Robin Hood is found in which late 14th century poem by William Langland?

2. Most early ballads claim that Robin had which status in society?

3. According to legend, what's the name of the villain hired by the Sheriff of Nottingham to kill Robin Hood?

4. Maid Marian is believed by many scholars to have originally been a personification of the Virgin Mary. Before becoming part of the Robin Hood legend, she was supposedly part of which annual celebration?

5. Robin Hood is traditionally associated with which colour, which originates from the East Midlands?

6. William de Wendenal occupied which position while Richard I was away on the Third Crusade?

7. Who wrote *The Merry Adventures of Robin Hood* (1883), which influenced many subsequent depictions of the Robin Hood legend?

8. A statue of Robin Hood, unveiled outside Nottingham Castle in 1952, was created by which English sculptor?

9. In Disney's 1973 animated version of the legend, what type of animal is Robin?

10. According to the 1991 film *Robin Hood: Prince of Thieves*, Robin Hood's family come from which castle?

answers on page 337

NOTTINGHAM

1. Prior to the Anglo-Saxon era, Nottingham was known by which title?

2. Nottingham's name is believed to have been derived from the name of which Saxon chieftain, who once ruled the area?

3. Which pub, which claims to have been established in 1189, rests against Castle Rock in the shadow of Nottingham Castle?

4. Which annual event, which occurs in the first week of October, was first referenced in borough records in 1541?

5. Which chemist was born in Radcliffe-on-Trent, near Nottingham, in 1815?

6. Which Nottingham cricket ground, opened in 1841, hosted its first Test March in 1899 when England played Australia?

7. Who owned a large tobacco factory in Nottingham in the late 19th century?

8. What was the name of Nottingham's first railway station, which opened in May 1839?

9. The Adams Building, which opened in 1855, was originally a showroom and warehouse dedicated to which hugely successful Nottingham industry?

10. Which bicycle manufacturer was founded in Nottingham in 1885?

answers on page 337

HENRY III
1207 – 1272, reigned 1216 - 1272

1. How old was Henry when his father John died, and he assumed the throne?

2. Which knight was Henry's guardian while he was young?

3. Which battle, in 1217, saw English forces repel French forces and capture their flagship?

4. Henry upheld Magna Carta, which his father had reluctantly signed. What term was first used during Henry's reign to refer to gatherings of the royal court under this new system?

5. What 1253 law aimed to stop the construction of synagogues and force the wearing of Jewish badges?

6. In 1258, facing revolt from the English barons, Henry accepted which set of measures, which transferred further power from the king to the various councils?

7. The Second Barons' War erupted in 1264. Which nobleman led the barons in their campaign against Henry III?

8. Henry was captured by his opponents during which 1264 battle in Sussex?

9. The Barons' War ended when royalist forces won which battle, and freed the captured king, in August 1265?

10. Henry died in 1272. Twenty years later, his body was exhumed and what part was removed?

answers on page 338

EDWARD I
1239 – 1307, reigned 1272 - 1307

1. Edward was named after which figure?

2. As a boy, Edward was also known by which name?

3. Where was Edward in 1272 when he learned of his father's death?

4. One of Edward's earliest challenges came from which Welsh leader, who refused to do homage and instead sought to take advantage of the chaos following the Second Barons' War?

5. Edward's wife Eleanor of Castile died in 1290. What monuments were erected by Edward to mark the stops where her body rested during its journey to Westminster Abbey?

6. In 1290, Edward signed the Edict of Expulsion, which was aimed at which part of the English population?

7. What name is given to the succession crisis in Scotland, which erupted in 1290 following the death of the seven-year-old heir to the throne Margaret (the Maid of Norway)?

8. Which figure was chosen as the new Scottish ruler following a hearing in 1292?

9. Following conflict with Scotland, Edward imprisoned the new king in the Tower of London and confiscated which item which had traditionally been used in Scottish coronations?

10. Edward died of dysentery in July 1307, while preparing to confront which Scottish rebel?

answers on page 338

WILLIAM WALLACE
c. 1270 - 1305

1. William Wallace was born around 1270. Which Scottish king, who brought relative peace to the country, was on the throne at this time?

2. One of Wallace's first known acts came in 1297, when he killed which English Sheriff?

3. Many Scottish nobles submitted to the English, but Wallace and his followers continued their rebellion. During this time, Wallace was based in which location?

4. Which battle in September 1297 saw Wallace and the Scottish force inflict a major defeat on the English?

5. Six months later, Wallace's forces were defeated in which battle?

6. In 1305, Wallace was turned over to the forces of Edward I by which Scottish knight?

7. During his trial in London, Wallace was crowned with which item, which signified his status as king of the outlaws?

8. Following his conviction, what fate befell Wallace on 23rd August 1305?

9. Who wrote *The Wallace*, an epic poem recounting the life of William Wallace, written two centuries after his death?

10. The Wallace Monument, a tower commemorating his life, stands on which hilltop?

answers on page 339

ROBERT THE BRUCE
1274 – 1329, Scottish king 1306 - 1329

1. Early Scottish forces supported a claim on the throne by which individual, who claimed to be a close relative of King David I?

2. When Robert succeeded William Wallace as Guardian of Scotland in 1298, he did so alongside which Scottish baron?

3. Robert is believed to have spent some time in the Hebrides, in the company of which Scottish noblewoman?

4. In 1309, Robert held his first parliament in which location?

5. For almost a decade, Robert operated as a guerilla warrior, continually attacking the English but avoiding a full confrontation. This changed in 1314, when Robert's forces secured a famous victory against the English in which battle?

6. Which treaty, signed in 1328, saw Edward III of England finally recognize Scotland as an independent kingdom?

7. Robert the Bruce died in 1329. Although the cause of his death has been debated, many English chroniclers at the time claimed that he had suffered from which condition?

8. Where was Robert buried?

9. What was the name of Robert's son, who succeeded him as king and ruled for four decades until his death in 1371?

10. In the early 1800s one of Robert's descendants, Thomas Bruce, secured which controversial sculptures for Britain?

answers on page 339

EDWARD II
1284 – 1327, reigned 1307 - 1327

1. Edward was born in which Welsh castle in 1284, less than a year after his father had conquered the region?

2. What was the name of the household knight to whom Edward II was particularly close, resulting in rumours of a homosexual relationship?

3. What name is given to the regulations, imposed upon Edward II by the peerage, designed to restrict his power?

4. While Edward tried to deal with political tensions at home, he suffered a humiliating defeat against Robert the Bruce, who in 1314 laid siege to which castle?

5. What devastating event struck Britain, and most of Europe, between 1315 and 1317?

6. By the early 1320s, Edward had a new favourite. What was his name?

7. Which leader, long an opponent of Edward II, formed a coalition against the king once civil war broke out in 1321?

8. What nickname was given to the king's enemies during the subsequent trials?

9. Edward was captured by his enemies, and in 1237 the king died (probably murdered) at which castle in Gloucestershire?

10. Ten years later, the Fieschi Letter – sent to Edward's son Edward III – made what claim about the king's death?

answers on page 339

CHESTER

1. Chester was originally founded by the Romans around AD 70, and was given what name?

2. Which 2nd century shrine, now in the Handbridge area of Chester, is dedicated to the Roman goddess of wisdom, justice and strategic warfare?

3. Which 7th century Anglo-Saxon king scored an important victory over the native Britons in the Battle of Chester?

4. In the year 973, which English king is said to have held his court at Chester?

5. What name is given to the covered walkways, dating back to the 13th century, that feature in several of the city's streets?

6. From the 14th to the 18th centuries, the city was also known by what name?

7. In 1645, which composer and musician was one of the casualties in the English Civil War Battle of Rowton Heath, which occurred close to Chester?

8. Which 18th century folk song, originally part of the play *Love in a Village* by Isaac Bickerstaffe, tells the story of a man who works next to the River Dee?

9. What name is given to the accident in 1847, in which five people died after a Chester passenger train fell into the river?

10. Who designed the Eastgate Clock, which was installed in 1899?

answers on page 340

EDWARD III
1312 – 1377, reigned 1327 - 1377

1. Before becoming king, Edward was known by which name?

2. Aged 12, Edward was given which earldom by his father?

3. Edward was only 14 when he was crowned. The real power behind the throne was his mother's lover. What was his name?

4. Three years later, Edward seized the English throne in his own name. He captured his mother's lover at which castle?

5. Edward also claimed the French throne, marking the start of the Hundred Years' War. Which early battle on 26th August 1346, saw Edward's army defeat a much larger French force?

6. In 1344, Edward is said to have briefly planned to revive which symbolic item of furniture?

7. A statute from Edward's reign, still in force today (in a modified form), defines acts that constitute which crime?

8. Edward often relied upon the assistance of which Chancellor, who became unpopular during the 1360s?

9. What name is given to the 1376 parliament that, though called to grant taxation, ended up checking the power of many of the king's most senior servants?

10. Edward died of a stroke in 1377. By this point, he was increasingly reliant upon the help of which of his sons?

answers on page 340

THE HUNDRED YEARS' WAR
PART I: THE EDWARDIAN WAR
1337 - 1360

1. The Hundred Years' War was initially fought between the English House of Plantagenet and which French royal house?

2. The war began when Edward III of England claimed the French throne. What was his basis for this claim?

3. Who became French king instead?

4. English coastal defences mostly held, but which unwalled town was burned to the ground by a French attack in 1339?

5. Which battle in June 1340 resulted in a victory that allowed the English to gain naval supremacy in the English Channel?

6. English forces also had to worry about Scotland during this period. Which Scottish king was eventually defeated at the Battle of Neville's Cross in 1346?

7. In 1356, King John II of France was captured. His ransom was set at 2 million ecus, but how did John react to this?

8. What name is given to a 1358 revolt by French peasants, who objected to their suffering during the war?

9. At Easter 1360, the English army was badly damaged by a freak hailstorm. What name was given to this event?

10. Edward agreed to negotiate a truce, thereby ending the first phase of the war. He renounced his claim to the French throne in exchange for full rights over which part of France?

answers on page 341

THE BLACK DEATH

1. The Black Death was an outbreak of the bacterium Yersinia pestis, which is commonly known by which name?

2. The first known case in the late 14th century English epidemic was a seaman who arrived in which town on the south coast?

3. What was the first major British city that was struck by an outbreak?

4. What creature is believed to have been the primary vector of the plague's spread?

5. Who was the only member of the British royal family who is known to have died from the plague?

6. Which well-known nursery rhyme has lyrics that are said by some to refer to symptoms of the Black Death?

7. What name is usually given to individuals who wore a mask that took the form of a bird's beak?

8. Who wrote *A Journal of the Plague Year* (1722), an account of the disease's outbreak in 1665?

9. Who was Lord Mayor of London during the worst of the plague outbreak in the mid-17th century?

10. What was the name of the large municipal burial ground that was used for the burial of many plague victims, and which was extensively excavated during construction of the Crossrail line?

answers on page 341

BRISTOL

1. What was the name of the market town that was founded on the site of Bristol some time before the 11th century?

2. Which 15th century merchant was Mayor of Bristol five times, and spent much of his fortune rebuilding the church of St Mary Redcliffe?

3. Which 18th century building, commissioned by John Wesley, was the first ever Methodist chapel and is still in use in 2021?

4. During the 18th century, Bristol was a key player in the slave trade. A statue of which merchant, who made money from the trade, was toppled in 2020 and pushed into the harbour?

5. Which 18th century philosopher, who wrote *A Vindication of Natural Society* (1756) and *Reflections on the Revolution in France* (1790), was MP for Bristol between 1774 and 1780?

6. The company W.D. & H.O. Wills, formed in Bristol in 1786, was the first British company to mass-produce what item?

7. The deadly Bristol Riots of 1831 were caused by the refusal of the House of Lords to pass which piece of legislation?

8. What name is given to the feature of Bristol dialect that sees an extra letter added to the end of some words?

9. In 1963, the Bristol Bus Boycott was organised in response to what policy by a local bus company?

10. In November 2003, what happened for the last time at Bristol Filton Airport?

answers on page 341

EDWARD THE BLACK PRINCE
1330 - 1376

1. Edward was born in 1330 at which Oxfordshire royal residence?

2. He was the first holder of which dukedom, which still exists in the 21st century?

3. In 1335, with fears growing of an imminent French invasion, Edward's household was moved to which location?

4. Aged sixteen, Edward was already known as a highly capable military leader. In July 1346, he was involved in his father's capture of which French-held town in Normandy?

5. Two years later, following a successful campaign in France, Edward was invested by his father with which new honour?

6. Which battle, which took place in August 1350, saw an English fleet defeat a larger group of Castilian vessels?

7. In 1355, Edward sacked – but failed to take the citadel of – which southern French town?

8. In 1361, aged 31, Edward finally married. What was the name of his wife, who also happened to be his cousin?

9. Edward used a shield decorated with an image of three feathers, which is believed to have influenced the shield of later Princes of Wales. The feathers were from which animal?

10. Edward died in 1376, most likely of dysentery. His tomb can still be seen today in which location in England?

answers on page 342

CORNWALL

1. During the Bronze Age, Cornwall was first mined for which metal?

2. What language, spoken by the Celtic occupants of Cornwall during the Iron Age, developed to become modern Cornish?

3. From the Iron Age until the early Saxon period, Cornwall and Devon were both occupied by which tribe?

4. What creature – which also exists in the folklore of Devon and Wales – is said to be a small, Leprechaun-like figure that wears miner's garb and causes mischief?

5. Which tribe, established in Cornwall by the 5th century, is believed to have been the origin of the name Cornwall?

6. The last recorded king of Cornwall died in 875 AD. What was his name?

7. The Cornish rebellion of 1497, against Henry VII's taxation levels, ended with defeat at which battle?

8. Which 1755 event caused damage to the Cornish coast, with the sea rising by 6ft at St. Michael's Mount?

9. What name is given to the organisation that collected tin coinage, which was a duty that ended up in the hands of the Duchy of Cornwall?

10. Which pub, which still exists on Bodmin Moor, was the setting for a Daphne du Maurier novel and is said to have a long association with Cornish smuggling?

answers on page 342

THE HUNDRED YEARS' WAR
PART 2: THE CAROLINIAN WAR
1369 - 1389

1. Peace reigned for a decade after the first phase of the war. Conflict returned in 1369 when England and France supported different sides in a civil war of succession in which country?

2. This conflict had been stoked earlier, when the Black Prince restored which figure to the throne in that region?

3. The Carolinian War is named after which figure?

4. In 1378, the Western Schism caused a split in the Catholic Church. Rival bishops claimed to be the true Pope, one in Rome and one in which French city?

5. The Breton knight Bertrand du Guesclin, who fought for the French, was known by which two nicknames?

6. England had generally commanded the sea, but this came to an end with defeat in which 1372 battle?

7. What name is given to the 1373 military campaign, led by the English king's son John of Gaunt, that ended in defeat?

8. What was the name of the agreement signed by France and England in 1375, which led to a brief truce?

9. French soldier Olivier de Clisson was better known by what nickname?

10. By 1389, both sides were struggling to raise taxes. Which agreement, signed in July, ended this phase of the war?

answers on page 343

RICHARD II
1367 – 1400, reigned 1377 - 1399

1. Richard was born in 1367 in which French city?

2. How old was Richard when his grandfather Edward III died, and he became king of England?

3. What was the name of Richard's cousin, who was denied his inheritance and fled to France, only to return later as the king's sworn enemy?

4. What was the name of the group of nobles who attempted to impeach several of the king's favourites in 1388?

5. Several of Richard's closest advisors were sentenced to death in 1388 by which parliament?

6. Which poet served Richard as a diplomat?

7. What animal was considered to be a symbol of Richard?

8. Richard surrendered to the rebels at which Welsh castle?

9. At first, the new king Henry IV planned to let Richard live. However, this changed following the discovery of a plot to restore Richard to the throne. What name is given to this plot?

10. Richard died, supposedly of starvation, in February 1400 in which West Yorkshire castle?

answers on page 343

THE PEASANTS' REVOLT
1381

1. Following an outbreak of the Black Death, labourers were in short supply. How did the Ordinance of Labourers (1349) and the Statute of Labourers (1351) attempt to rectify this?

2. As the Hundred Years' War drained the treasury, a new poll tax was introduced. The Peasants' Revolt began in 1381 when villagers failed to pay the tax in which county?

3. The rebellion quickly spread to Kent. What was the name of the man who became the leader of the Kentish rebels?

4. On their way to London, the rebels encountered – and mocked – the king's mother. What was her name?

5. In London, the rebels made a camp at which location?

6. Which radical preacher gave a speech to the Kentish rebels, encouraging them to continue with their cause?

7. Richard agreed to meet the rebels at which location in London, on the south side of the Thames?

8. As they entered London, the rebels destroyed which grand building that was owned by the king's uncle??

9. The rebel leader was killed during a meeting with Richard, but the rebellion had spread throughout the country. Who commanded a rebel force that marched from Essex to Suffolk?

10. The rebels sought, and by the end of the revolt gained, the abolition of which feudal status?

answers on page 343

HENRY IV
1367 – 1413, reigned 1399 - 1413

1. Henry was born at which location in Lincolnshire?

2. Henry was the son of which powerful and influential figure?

3. Having participated in an early rebellion against Richard II, in 1390 Henry supported a siege of Vilnius led by which religious order?

4. Richard II stopped Henry inheriting his father's land. Henry immediately teamed up with which former Archbishop of Canterbury in order to mount a campaign against the king?

5. When Henry's forces arrived in England, where was Richard II?

6. In 1402, the Welsh joined with another group of rebels. This group was led by which figure, who had been Richard II's heir presumptive prior to the reign of Henry?

7. In 1403, Henry defeated a challenge from 'Harry Hotspur' Percy in the Battle of Shrewsbury. This battle was the first to prove the effectiveness of which medieval weapon?

8. A long-standing prophecy, which the king himself believed, stated that he would die in which city?

9. In reality, Henry died in 1413, in which location in London?

10. Henry was buried at Canterbury Cathedral, close to a shrine dedicated to which figure?

answers on page 344

OWAIN GLYNDŴR AND THE WELSH REVOLT
c. 1359 – c. 1415

1. Owain Glyndŵr was born in the mid-14th century and is believed to have studied at which London institution?

2. Upon his return to Wales, Glyndŵr married Margaret, daughter of which local justice?

3. Glyndŵr initially served in the English army. In 1389, he gave evidence in which early case of heraldic law?

4. Which medieval Welsh bard wrote poems addressed to several key figures during this period, including Glyndŵr?

5. Glyndŵr led a revolt following a dispute with a neighbour. In June 1401 his forces defeated the English in which battle?

6. In 1404, Glyndŵr called his first full Welsh parliament at which town in Powys?

7. What name is given to the 1405 agreement between Glyndŵr, Henry Percy and Edmund Mortimer, which aimed to divide England and Wales between the three of them?

8. Glyndŵr was the last native Welshman to hold which title?

9. Glyndŵr's fortunes faded, and nothing is known of his fate after the year 1412. Various theories have arisen, including one that suggests he became which folklore character?

10. By 1415, the rebellion was over and many Welsh families were ruined. Gruffydd Young, one of Glyndŵr's supporters, eventually became the bishop of which African location?

answers on page 344

CARDIFF

1. Houndemammeby, a name rooted in a strong Viking presence, is now better known as which Cardiff street?

2. Which nobleman, who led a revolt in Wales in 1316 against Edward II, was executed two years later at Cardiff Castle?

3. Which 1648 battle in the English Civil War took place in Cardiff, and saw a Royalist army lose to a much smaller group of Parliamentarian soldiers

4. Which 19th century aristocrat and industrialist is credited with building Cardiff Docks?

5. Which composer and actor was born in Cardiff in 1893 and went on to have success with songs such as *Keep the Home Fires Burning* (1914)?

6. Cardiff City F.C. was founded in 1899 under what name?

7. What did Edward VII grant to Cardiff in 1905?

8. Which Cardiff inhabitant, who lived in Victoria Park from 1912, died in April 1939?

9. Which Welsh singer was born in Tiger Bay, Cardiff on 8th January 1938?

10. The Senedd building, which serves as the debating chamber of the Welsh Parliament, was designed by which architect?

answers on page 344

GEOFFREY CHAUCER & THE CANTERBURY TALES
c. 1340s - 1400

1. Geoffrey Chaucer was born in the early 1340s. His father and grandfather both worked in which trade?

2. Chaucer studied law at which London institution?

3. One of Chaucer's earliest poems is *The Book of the Duchess*, from the late 1360s or early 1370s. This was written to commemorate which figure?

4. In 1374, Edward III gave Chaucer which unusual grant?

5. At the start of *The Canterbury Tales*, the narrator is at which London pub?

6. The characters in *The Canterbury Tales* are about to set out on a pilgrimage to the shrine of Thomas Becket. What prize is offered to the pilgrim who can tell the best story?

7. *The Canterbury Tales* contains structural parallels to which Italian work by Giovanni Boccaccio, which also features narrators who tell stories while on a journey?

8. Another of Chaucer's works was a manual titled *A Treatise on the Astrolabe*. What is an astrolabe?

9. What's the title of Chaucer's mid-1380s poem about two lovers, set during the siege of Troy?

10. Chaucer died of unknown causes in 1400. One of his sons, Thomas, became a butler to four English kings and an envoy to France. He also held which parliamentary position?

answers on page 345

HENRY V
1386 – 1422, reigned 1413 - 1422

1. Henry had a nickname, derived from the location of his birth in Wales. What was this nickname?

2. Once his father was king, Henry became heir to the throne. What injury did he subsequently suffer during the Battle of Shrewsbury in 1403?

3. Henry was friends with Sir John Oldcastle, who is said to have been the basis for which Shakespearean character?

4. Henry became king in 1413. His coronation was marked by what type of unusual weather?

5. Henry's most famous victory came in 1415, at the Battle of Agincourt, which occurred on the feast day of which saint?

6. The French king, Charles VI, was sick. At one point, he is said to have believed he was made of what material?

7. In 1415, Henry was inducted into which European chivalric order?

8. Following Agincourt, Henry began to progress through France. In 1417, he left fleeing French women and children to die during a siege of which French city?

9. Sir John Oldcastle was executed in 1417 following his role in a rebellion by which Christian group?

10. Henry died in 1422, aged 35. At this time, according to the Treaty of Troyes, Henry expected to soon receive which title?

answers on page 345

SOUTHAMPTON

1. Southampton is on the site of which Saxon town?

2. What's the name of the 13th century gatehouse that once permitted access to the south of the city?

3. The Wool House was built in Southampton in the late 14th century, to store wool primarily for export to which country?

4. In 1415, the Southampton Plot aimed to depose which English king?

5. Upon his death in 1550, which English churchman left £100 for the establishment of a grammar school in the city?

6. Which minister and hymn writer, born in Southampton in 1674, wrote compositions such as *Joy to the World* and *When I Survey the Wondrous Cross*?

7. Which 18th century engineer, born in Southampton, was a key figure in the development of wooden rigging blocks for the Royal Navy?

8. On April 10th 1912, which boat left Southampton on her maiden voyage?

9. Which English actor, comedian and singer was born in Southampton in 1924, and had early jobs in the city at Woolworths and as a milkman?

10. During the Second World War, German bombs aimed to destroy a key factory in Woolston in Southampton. This factory was involved in the production of what wartime item?

answers on page 346

THE HUNDRED YEARS WAR
PART 3: THE LANCASTRIAN WAR
1415 - 1453

1. In 1415, the war erupted again when Henry V sailed to France and laid siege to which town?

2. Eventually Henry's army had to retreat. The Battle of Agincourt occurred as they tried to reach which town?

3. The English won at Agincourt. Between 6,000 and 8,000 English soldiers faced how many French soldiers?

4. Henry's reputation suffered following which order during Agincourt, which was unusual for the time?

5. Henry V insisted that the French must honour an agreement that his heir should become king of France. When this didn't happen, the English won a 'second Agincourt' at which battle?

6. Joan of Arc, who helped lift the 1428 Siege of Orléans, was given which nickname?

7. English fortunes suffered after Joan of Arc's execution. In 1435, which figure pulled his support of the English forces?

8. Which 1453 event is generally regarded as the final battle of the Hundred Years' War?

9. England and France remained technically at war for another 20 years, but this ended following which treaty in 1475?

10. English (and later British) monarchs continued to claim the French throne for years. Who was the last to make this claim?

answers on page 346

HENRY VI
1421 – 1471, reigned 1422 – 1461 & 1470 - 1471

1. Aged 9 months, Henry was the youngest person ever to take the English throne. What title did he gain a month later?

2. Henry's mother Catherine soon remarried, to which Welsh figure?

3. Henry assumed full royal powers when he turned 16, in 1437. This coincided with which event, which was caused by a shortage of precious metals?

4. In 1445, Henry married which French noblewoman?

5. What name is given to the economic disaster that saw some trades suffer collapses of up to 90%?

6. Who led a popular revolt in the south of the country in 1450, which resulted in violent scenes in London?

7. In 1451, Henry lost the Duchy of Aquitaine. By 1453, his only French territory was which town?

8. Henry's unpopular advisor William de la Pole, who was killed by a Dover mob in 1450, was known by what nickname?

9. After a breakdown in 1453, Henry spent a year in a catatonic state. What was the name of his cousin, who was put in charge as Protector of the Realm?

10. In 1458, Henry tried to stage a display of reconciliation between the warring factions. What name was given to this event, which took place at St. Paul's Cathedral on 25th March?

answers on page 347

THE WARS OF THE ROSES
1455 - 1487

1. The Wars of the Roses were fought by two rival branches of the House of Plantagenet. Which of these branches had a white rose as its symbol, and which had a red rose?

2. One of the first major battles occurred at Northampton in July 1460. What happened to Henry VI at this battle?

3. A few months later, the Duke of York died at which battle?

4. By this point, Henry had slipped once again into madness. He was recaptured and held at which location?

5. Edward of York took the throne as Edward IV in 1461. A rebellion in Yorkshire later broke out under which leader?

6. In 1463, supporters of Henry – led by Sir Ralph Percy – laid siege to which castle?

7. In 1470, Edward IV was forced to flee the country following a disagreement with which key supporter?

8. Although Henry VI was back on the throne, he was too weak to lead. After six months, Edward IV returned to England and defeated Henry's army in which 1471 battle?

9. Henry died in the Tower of London in May. What was the official cause of death given by Edward IV's supporters?

10. Henry was buried at Windsor Castle, and rumours of miracles soon spread. Pilgrims to his tomb would put on his hat, in the hope of receiving respite from what condition?

answers on page 347

EDWARD IV
1442 – 1483, reigned 1461 – 1470 & 1471 - 1483

1. Until the death of his father, Edward was known by what title?

2. What was the name of Edward's wife?

3. In 1461, Edward took which emblem?

4. Edward's first reign was from 1461 to 1470. He eventually fled into exile abroad, following the defection of which influential political figure?

5. Edward's second reign ran from 1471 until his death twelve years later. He was able to raise an army and return for the crown with backing from which group?

6. Edward was said to use emetics, which enabled him to do what during meals?

7. In the 1470s, Edward financed the building of the Great Hall at which at which palace in London?

8. In 1476, what was established by William Caxton at Westminster Abbey?

9. Edward was one of the main creditors who owed a great deal of money to which banking institution, which collapsed ten years after his death?

10. Shortly before he died in 1483, who did Edward name as Protector of his young son?

answers on page 347

LANCASTER

1. The name Lancaster refers to which river?

2. Which king created the House of Lancaster when he created the Earldom of Lancaster in 1267 for one of his sons?

3. Which 14th century military leader and statesman was the first to use the red rose as a heraldic badge for the House of Lancaster?

4. In 1612, which group of women were charged with using witchcraft to murder ten people, with all but one of the women being found guilty and executed by hanging?

5. During the 17th century, Edmund Arrowsmith, John Finch and Robert Nutter were among the Catholics who became known by what name?

6. Which Lancaster slave trader had a ship called the Barlborough?

7. Thomas Edmondson, born in Lancaster in 1792, devised a new form of what travel item?

8. Biologist Richard Owen, who was born in Lancaster in 1804, is best known for having coined which word?

9. The organ at Lancaster Priory, installed in the early 19th century, was the work of which prominent organ builder?

10. Musician John Waite, born in Lancaster in 1952, reached number one on the US Billboard Hot 100 in 1984 with which song?

answers on page 348

YORK

1. Which 7th century Roman missionary founded a wooden church and became the first Bishop of York?

2. During the 9th century, York was occupied by Vikings. What name is given to the land that they ruled from the city?

3. In 944 AD, which English king expelled the Vikings from York?

4. In 1154, what collapsed as a crowd gathered to greet St. William of York upon his return from exile?

5. Which figure, the leader of the city's Jewish community, was among those who died in the York pogrom of 1190?

6. The White Rose of York was first used as a heraldic badge by which 14th century prince?

7. What name is given to a series of 48 Middle English plays that supposedly cover history from the moment of creation to the Last Judgment?

8. In 1676, which highwayman is said to have ridden from Kent to York in a day, in order to establish an alibi for a robbery he'd just committed?

9. The name of the Shambles, one of York's oldest streets, comes from an old term for what type of activity?

10. Which 19th century Yorkshire politician at one point controlled so much of the railway network that he became known as 'The Railway King'?

answers on page 348

EDWARD V
1470 – c. 1483, reigned 1483

1. Edward and his brother Richard, Duke of York are today best known by what title?

2. Aged just 3, Edward was given which newly-created title?

3. Edward spent his childhood at which Shropshire location?

4. Who did Edward IV name as the princes' Protector?

5. Edward and his brother took up residence in the Tower of London. Their parents' marriage was declared invalid, making the new king illegitimate. What was the title of the act of parliament that declared Edward's uncle to be the new king?

6. Once their uncle was king, the fate of Edward and his brother is unclear. Thomas More, writing close to the time, claimed that they had been murdered in what manner?

7. A set of bones that might have belonged to the princes was interred in a marble sarcophagus in the 17th century. Who designed the sarcophagus?

8. Seven years later, a man claiming to be the other prince in the tower attempted to claim the English throne. What was this man's actual name?

9. What was this man's fate?

10. What was the name of the princes' sister, who later married Henry VII, thereby uniting the houses of York and Lancaster?

answers on page 349

RICHARD III
1452 – 1485, reigned 1483 - 1485

1. Richard suffered from what is believed to have been a mild form of which condition?

2. Shortly after becoming king, Richard established which administrative body, with the aim of improving justice in some of the more remote parts of the country?

3. Which tribunal, established by Richard in 1483, allowed poor people to seek restitution for their grievances?

4. Richard's personal device took the form of which animal?

5. Who led a 1483 rebellion that aimed to depose Richard and put Henry Tudor on the throne?

6. The rebellion culminated in which event, which was the last significant battle of the Wars of the Roses?

7. Richard's death marked the end of which house, which had ruled England for three centuries since the reign of Henry II?

8. Although there were various claims about the location of Richard's body, he was ultimately shown to have been buried at which friary, the location of which was subsequently forgotten?

9. In 2012, Richard's remains were finally discovered beneath which location in Leicester?

10. On 26th March 2015, more than five hundred years after his death, Richard was buried in which location?

answers on page 349

LEICESTER

1. What's the name of the 2nd-century wall, part of which still exists, that once formed part of a public building in Corieltauvorum (the Roman name for Leicester)

2. Which play by William Shakespeare tells a modified version of the life of the founder of Leicester?

3. In 1628, riots occurred in the city after King Charles I arranged to sell which site?

4. Which Leicester gaol keeper, notorious for his huge size, was born in 1770 and supposedly fought a bear in the street?

5. Which 19th century engineer designed the Leicester lifting bridge, so that a new railway could cross the Grand Union Canal?

6. Due to the influence of 19th century poet Thomas Cooper, Leicester became a stronghold for supporters of which political movement?

7. The Arch of Remembrance, a First World War memorial in Victoria Park, was designed by which British architect?

8. In 1927, Dr. Cyril Bardsley became the first person appointed to which position?

9. Born in Madras, India in 1936, which singer moved with his family to Leicester when he was 10 years old?

10. Which sculptor is responsible for The Leicester Seamstress, which since 1990 has stood in Hotel Street?

answers on page 350

BRITISH SCHOOLS & EDUCATION

1. Which Kent school was founded in AD 597 and is said to be the oldest continuously operating school in the world?

2. Which school near Windsor was founded by Henry VI in 1440, with the aim of providing a free education to poor boys who might then go on to study in Cambridge?

3. Which 16th century jurist founded a school in his own name in 1563, located in Sandwich, Kent?

4. 18th century philanthropist Robert Raikes was an early pioneer of which education system?

5. What term is generally used to describe the new public universities founded toward the end of the 19th century?

6. Which school, founded in London in 1849, was the first higher education college for women in the United Kingdom?

7. Which schools, mostly established in the 18th century by John Pounds, were set up for poor and homeless children?

8. As part of the 1870 Education Act, the Cowper-Temple Clause specified what change to religious teaching in schools?

9. What act, established in 1876, imposed a legal duty on parents to make sure that their children received an education?

10. The modern distinction between primary and secondary education was defined by the Education Act of 1944, which is also known by what title?

answers on page 350

DEAL

1. The town of Deal, in Kent, is referred to by what name in the Domesday Book of 1086?

2. The Battle of Deal, in July 1495, saw an attempted landing by which pretender to the throne?

3. Deal's shoreline is close to which treacherous sandbank?

4. Which explorer arrived in Deal when he returned from his first voyage to Australia in 1771?

5. Deal's first pier, built in 1838, was designed by which engineer?

6. The town's second pier, built in 1864 after the first was wrecked in a storm, was itself destroyed when it was hit by which ship in 1920?

7. A tower in Deal, established in 1855, features what old-fashioned time-signalling device?

8. From 1930 to 1996, Deal's barracks were the home of which musical institution?

9. Which folk custom, involving a wooden hobby horse carried by an individual under a sackcloth, was once common in Deal and other parts of Kent?

10. Deal Town F.C. won which football competition at Wembley in 2000?

answers on page 350

HENRY VII
1457 – 1509, reigned 1485 - 1509

1. Henry was the first Tudor king of England. What was the main basis for his claim to the throne?

2. For fourteen years prior to becoming king, Henry had been exiled in which location?

3. Since the Battle of Bosworth Field, Henry has the distinction of being the last English monarch (to date) to do what?

4. Which pretender to the throne claimed, in 1487, to be Edward Plantagenet, a key rival to Henry VII?

5. Henry's chancellor collected taxes based on a simple catch-22 principle: those nobles who spent little must therefore have saved a lot of money, while those who spent a lot clearly could afford to pay. What was the title of this principle?

6. A conflict in France, between 1485 and 1488, saw Henry support a group of rebels against the French monarchy. What name is given to this conflict?

7. Henry sought to end the traditional alliance between Scotland and France. By what title was this alliance known?

8. Henry relied heavily on the support of which legal body?

9. Henry is generally regarded as having been the last English king to use the Tower of London in what manner?

10. In 1509, Henry VII died of tuberculosis at which location in London?

answers on page 351

HENRY VIII
1491 – 1547, reigned 1509 - 1547

1. Until he was ten years old, Henry was not expected to be king. What was the name of his older brother, whose death in 1502 left Henry at the front of the line of succession?

2. How old was Henry when he became king?

3. What was the name of the anti-French group, formed in 1511, that Henry subsequently joined in the hope of eventually ruling France himself?

4. Which pope refused to annul Henry's first marriage in 1527?

5. What name is given to the process whereby Henry broke the Church of England away from the authority of the Roman Catholic Church?

6. What name was given French owned monasteries in England, many of which had existed since the time of the Norman Conquest?

7. In 1536, Henry suffered a leg wound that festered for the rest of his life. How did he get this wound?

8. What was the name of Henry's chief minister from 1534 to 1540, who was ultimately beheaded?

9. What name was given to the black trumpeter who was a regular figure at the king's court?

10. How many of Henry's six wives were still alive when he died in 1547?

answers on page 351

HENRY'S 1ST WIFE:
CATHERINE OF ARAGON
1485 - 1536

1. Henry VIII was distantly related to all six of his wives, through which common ancestor?

2. Henry's first wife, Catherine of Aragon, was the daughter of the king and queen of which country?

3. Catherine was born into which European dynasty?

4. Aged 15, Catherine married Arthur, son of Henry VII and heir to the English throne. Within a few months, they were both ill, most likely with which mysterious condition?

5. To avoid returning Catherine's dowry after Arthur's death, Henry VII decided to have her marry his son Henry (later VIII). Where was Catherine kept until Henry was old enough?

6. While waiting for her second marriage, Catherine became the first woman to hold what type of post in England?

7. Only one of Catherine and Henry's children, born in 1516, survived childhood. What was the name of this child?

8. By 1525, Henry wanted to annul his marriage to Catherine. Catherine refused to quietly retire to what type of location?

9. What was the name of the Catholic cardinal, ordered by Henry VIII to secure an annulment, who was later banished from court after communicating secretly with the Pope?

10. Catherine died in 1536, at which Cambridgeshire castle?

answers on page 352

HENRY'S 2ND WIFE:
ANNE BOLEYN
c. 1501 - 1536

1. Anne and her siblings grew up at which Kent castle?

2. Before becoming Henry's second wife, Anne served as a lady in waiting for which monarch?

3. What was the name of Anne's sister, who had previously been one of Henry's mistresses?

4. Anne was crowned queen consort in 1533. What item was used for her crowning, which otherwise had only been used to crown monarchs?

5. What was the name of the nun who was executed for making public pronouncements condemning the marriage?

6. Which lawyer and judge, executed following Anne's marriage to Henry, was convicted of treason after refusing to recognize the king's supremacy in matters of the church?

7. Like Catherine of Aragon, Anne only had one surviving child. Who was this?

8. Anne was accused of having multiple lovers, including her own brother George. Where was she taken after her arrest?

9. Which poem, about death as an end of suffering, is said to have been written by Anne while she awaited her execution?

10. Anne was beheaded with an axe on 19th May. What special arrangement was made for her benefit?

answers on page 352

HENRY'S 3RD WIFE:
JANE SEYMOUR
1508 - 1537

1. In her early years, Jane Seymour was regarded as particularly skilled at what?

2. Jane served in what role in the household of Henry VIII's first wife, Catherine of Aragon?

3. Jane is said to have been given which nickname, due to her ability to calm the royal court?

4. The day after Anne Boleyn's execution, Henry VIII arranged to marry Jane. She soon fell pregnant, and is said to have developed a craving for what delicacy?

5. What was Jane's motto as queen?

6. As queen, Jane formed a close bond with which figure, who ultimately became closer to Henry as a result?

7. Jane is said to have rarely meddled in royal affairs. One exception came in 1536, when she unsuccessfully asked Henry to pardon the participants in which Yorkshire revolt?

8. In October 1537, Jane finally produced something that Henry had been craving. What was this?

9. A week after giving birth, Jane died of complications at which London location?

10. Jane Seymour was the only one of Henry's wives to receive what honour upon her death?

answers on page 352

HENRY'S 4TH WIFE:
ANNE OF CLEVES
1515 - 1557

1. Anne of Cleves was a princess from which country?

2. Henry married Anne partly because he wanted to forge an alliance with her family. Who was her brother?

3. Henry was considering marrying Anne's sister Amalia instead. Which well-known painter was sent to produce portraits of the two women, to help Henry make his decision?

4. In January 1540, Henry met Anne for the first time at which location in Kent?

5. Henry is said to have been disappointed when he met Anne, feeling that the portrait had exaggerated her beauty. What other disappointment occurred on their wedding night?

6. Henry and Anne married shortly after, in a ceremony that was presided over by which Archbishop of Canterbury?

7. Henry had the marriage annulled six months later. He and Anne became good friends, however, and she was referred to at the court by what title?

8. Following the execution of the king's next wife, Anne is said to have briefly suggested what course of action?

9. Anne died in 1557 at which location in London?

10. Anne held which distinction, compared to Henry's other wives?

answers on page 353

HENRY'S 5TH WIFE:
CATHERINE HOWARD
c. 1523 - 1542

1. Through her paternal aunt, Catherine Howard was the first cousin of which figure?

2. Following the death of her mother, five-year-old Catherine was sent to be raised by which relative, who is said to have offered little in the way of discipline?

3. As a girl, Catherine had a controversial – and possibly abusive – relationship with which music teacher?

4. Catherine was also said to have been involved in a relationship with which secretary?

5. Catherine caught the king's eye at the royal court and was in her teens when they married. What motto did she adopt?

6. What painful medical condition is believed to have caused Henry to become particularly irritable during this period?

7. Controversy soon arose over Catherine's supposed relationship with which courtier?

8. Following various other allegations, Catherine was stripped of her title in November 1541 and imprisoned at which location in Middlesex?

9. Catherine supposedly spent her last night practising what?

10. Several years later, Catherine's cousin Henry Howard – a well-known poet – suffered which distinction?

answers on page 353

HENRY'S 6TH WIFE:
CATHERINE PARR
c. 1512 - 1548

1. When she met Henry, Catherine had which other suitor, who was sent to Brussels so that he would be out of the way?

2. Catherine was the first woman to publish a book under her own name in the English language. What was its title?

3. In 1543, partly due to Catherine's influence, Henry passed which act?

4. When Henry went to fight in France in 1544, Catherine stayed behind as regent. Subsequent rumours suggested that the king was attracted to which other woman?

5. What was issued against Catherine in 1546?

6. Catherine is also the English queen with the most marriages. Including Henry, how many times did she marry?

7. Published in 1547, following the death of Henry VIII, what was the title of Catherine's third book?

8. Catherine died in 1548 after giving birth to a daughter. Where was she buried?

9. The funeral of Catherine Parr has the distinction of being the first in England to be carried out under what faith?

10. Catherine's grave was disturbed during the English Civil War. Who designed her new tomb in the 19th century?

answers on page 354

EDWARD VI
1537 – 1553, reigned 1547 - 1553

1. Who was Edward's mother?

2. What was the name of the governess who looked after Edward in his early years, along with his siblings?

3. By his twelfth birthday, Edward had already written a treatise comparing the Pope to which figure?

4. What name is given to the 1543 – 1551 conflict between England and Scotland, during which Henry attempted to force a marriage alliance between his son Edward and Mary, Queen of Scots?

5. In 1547, Edward was in which town when he learned of his father's death?

6. Who was appointed as Edward's first Protector, due to the new king's young age?

7. Which battle, in 1547, was the last major combat between Scotland and England prior to the Union of the Crowns?

8. What name is given to the rebellion that broke out in Devon and Cornwall in 1549?

9. In the same year, who became Edward's second Protector?

10. As his death approached, Edward (just fifteen years old) issued a plan for his succession, overlooking his half-sisters in favour of which cousin?

answers on page 354

LADY JANE GREY

c. 1536 – 1554, claimed the throne in 1553 but never crowned

1. Who was Jane's great grandfather on her mother's side?

2. As a girl, Jane was an attendant to which former wife of Henry VIII, who had since remarried?

3. Jane was a follower of which religion?

4. Although there are some disagreements, Jane is generally said to have been queen for how many days?

5. Which body of advisers effectively turned against Jane on 19th July, instead pledging their support to Mary?

6. Jane was subsequently convicted of treason. At the time, what was the traditional punishment for women who had been convicted of this crime?

7. At first, there was a chance that Jane would be spared death. What name is given to the 1554 rebellion that is widely regarded as having sealed her fate?

8. What was the name of Jane's husband, who was executed on the morning of her own death?

9. How was Jane eventually executed, aged 16 or 17, on February 12th, 1554?

10. Jane is the only English monarch of the past 500 years who lacks what?

answers on page 354

MARY I
1516 – 1558, reigned 1553 - 1558

1. Who was Mary's mother?

2. At the age of 9, Mary – a practising Catholic – was sent to live with her own court at which Shropshire castle?

3. Although she was never invested with the role, Mary was widely known during this period by what title?

4. Excluding earlier disputed claimants, upon her accession to the throne in 1553 Mary became the first person in England to hold which title?

5. Who did Mary marry in 1554, defying significant opposition?

6. What name is given to the Protestants who fled to Continental Europe during Mary's reign?

7. Which papal legate was appointed Archbishop of Canterbury in March 1556?

8. Mary encouraged English colonists to settle in Ireland. Which county town was originally established during her reign as Maryborough?

9. Mary died on November 17th 1558 at which London location?

10. By what name did Mary come to be known by her Protestant opponents?

answers on page 355

ELIZABETH I
1533 – 1603, reigned 1558 - 1603

1. Who was Elizabeth's mother?

2. Where did Elizabeth spend two months imprisoned, between March and May 1554, on the orders of her half-sister Mary?

3. Elizabeth was said to have been in love with which childhood friend, who was married to another woman?

4. Who was Elizabeth's chief adviser for most of her reign, up until his death in 1598?

5. What name is given to a plot, launched in 1586, that aimed to assassinate Elizabeth and put Mary, Queen of Scots on the English throne?

6. What was the name of Elizabeth's principal secretary from 1573 to 1590, who was generally regarded as her 'spymaster'?

7. When the Spanish Armada was launched in 1588, English ships set sail from which city?

8. While the threat of the Armada loomed, Elizabeth gave a rallying speech to her troops at which location in Essex?

9. What name is generally given to Elizabeth's 1601 speech in the Palace Council Chamber, in which she declared that she was in her final Parliament?

10. Elizabeth died in 1603. With which other figure does she share her tomb in Westminster Abbey?

answers on page 355

THE EARLY AMERICAN COLONIES

1. Following the first voyage of Columbus to America in 1492, which Italian navigator was sent by Henry VII of England to explore the coast of the new continent?

2. Many explorers followed. Martin Frobisher and Henry Hudson were looking, in particular, for which sea route?

3. In 1607, the London Company established a permanent colony in which location on Chesapeake Bay?

4. Colonists in Virginia soon began to make money growing what plant?

5. The Somers Isles, an early English colony, is now better known by what name?

6. Which Puritan group was one of the first to lead an English colonisation of the Bahamas?

7. Between 1636 and 1638, Puritan settlers fought (and won) a war with which Native American group?

8. Following a series of conflicts between the two nations, England signed a treaty with which country in 1674, thereby forcing that country off the continent?

9. What name is given to the disastrous scheme that saw the Scottish government lose huge amounts of money during their attempt to establish colonies of their own?

10. By the time of the Declaration of Independence in 1776, how many English colonies existed in the new world?

answers on page 356

SIR FRANCIS DRAKE
c. 1540 - 1596

1. Francis Drake was born in Devon in c. 1540. As a young man, he worked on boats as an apprentice to which figure?

2. At some point during the 'Troublesome Third Voyage' of 1567, Drake gained the captaincy of which ship?

3. For his first major attack on the Spanish, Drake formed an alliance with which group of African former slaves?

4. Drake was involved in which 1575 incident in Ireland, in which more than 600 defenders and civilians died?

5. Following an expedition between 1577 and 1580, Drake became the first person to achieve what feat?

6. What was the name of Drake's galleon during this voyage?

7. Following his return to England, Drake purchased which manor house in Devon?

8. What name is given to the series of attacks that Drake led against the Spanish in 1587?

9. Although the account is likely to be apocryphal, what is Drake said to have been doing on Plymouth Hoe when he was informed of the Spanish Armada's approach?

10. Drake died in 1596 during an attack on a Spanish town in Puerto Rico. What happened to his body?

answers on page 356

PLYMOUTH

1. Which location in Plymouth is believed to have been one of the key trading ports in Bronze and Iron Age Britain?

2. Which naval commander, an early figure in the Atlantic slave trade, was born in Plymouth in 1532?

3. In June 1616, which Native American woman arrived at Plymouth with her husband, and was subsequently presented to English society?

4. The Mayflower Steps in Plymouth commemorate the departure of which group of settlers, who departed from the city on their journey to North American in 1620?

5. In the late 17th century, which English painter and engineer was responsible for the building of the first Eddystone lighthouse near Plymouth?

6. In 1768, who founded a factory in Plymouth for the production of porcelain?

7. What drink was first produced in the city in 1793?

8. In 1815, who spent two weeks on HMS Bellerophon off the coast of Plymouth, following his capture by British forces?

9. Which preacher, a former vicar of Plymouth's Charles Church, was nicknamed the 'star of the west'?

10. Which sailor arrived at Plymouth in May 1967, having completed the first single-handed Clipper Route circumnavigation of the world?

answers on page 356

SIR FRANCIS BACON
1561 - 1626

1. Bacon was born in 1561 to Sir Nicholas Bacon and his wife Anne. What title did Nicholas hold from 1558 to around 1571?

2. Bacon's maternal grandfather was which Renaissance humanist?

3. Which figure did Bacon first meet while studying at Cambridge?

4. Bacon worked for a period as a barrister, before becoming an MP. In 1597 he was given what role by the queen?

5. What title, created for Bacon, was bestowed upon him in 1618?

6. He became Solicitor General and later Attorney General under Elizabeth's successor James I, before falling from favour following charges of corruption instigated by which figure?

7. Bacon is perhaps best known for developing what empirical method of study?

8. What was the name of Bacon's wife, who remarried just two weeks after his death?

9. Bacon died of pneumonia in 1626. One popular legend states that he fell ill while studying what?

10. Which 19th century US president referred to Bacon as one of the greatest men who ever lived, due to his role in the establishment of early American colonies?

answers on page 357

CAMBRIDGE

1. What was the name of the Roman fort that once existed on Castle Hill, to the northwest of modern Cambridge?

2. What's the name of the chalk hills, named after a folkloric giant, to the southeast of Cambridge?

3. Which Anglo-Saxon church is dedicated to the founder of a number of Italian monasteries?

4. The design of which 12th century building was inspired by the rotunda in the church of the Holy Sepulchre in Jerusalem?

5. Founded in 1284 by Hugh de Balsham, Bishop of Ely, what's the oldest constituent college of the University of Cambridge?

6. What's the name of the watercourse that was built in the early 17th century in order to bring fresh water to the city?

7. In 1829, which side won the first Boat Race between the universities of Oxford and Cambridge?

8. Which author, born in Cambridge in 1952, is perhaps best known for writing *The Hitchhiker's Guide to the Galaxy* (1978)?

9. Which British art collector established the Kettle's Yard house, and gave the house and its collection to the University of Cambridge in 1966?

10. What name is generally given to a civil disturbance in Cambridge in 1970, in which students protested against the Greek military junta?

answers on page 357

SIR WALTER RALEIGH
c. 1552 - 1618

1. Little is known of Raleigh's early years. In his teens, he fought in France as a soldier for which Protestant group?

2. He later travelled to Ireland and helped suppress which revolt, which ran from 1579 to 1583?

3. Elizabeth I sent him to explore the New World. What colony was established in 1585 in what is now North Carolina?

4. What was the name of Raleigh's ship, which was Lord High Admiral Howard's flagship during the battle with the Spanish Armada?

5. What was the name of Raleigh's wife, a lady-in-waiting for the queen, who he married in secret in 1591?

6. After a period in the Tower of London, Raleigh was involved with the capture of which merchant ship off the coast of Flores?

7. Toward the end of the 16th century, Raleigh heard about a lost Spanish city in South America. What was this city called?

8. Some claims (subsequently questioned) suggest that Raleigh discovered which natural site during his time in Venezuela?

9. In 1603, Raleigh was again imprisoned, this time accused of participating in which conspiracy against James I?

10. In 1617, Raleigh was pardoned. What fate did he meet in South America, following an attack on a Spanish outpost?

answers on page 358

ELIZABETHAN LITERATURE

1. The word euphemism comes from the 1578 romance *Euphues: The Anatomy of Wit*, by which English dramatist?

2. Published in 1590, which play by Christopher Marlowe is based on the life of the Central Asian emperor Timur?

3. What's the name of the protagonist in Thomas Nashe's 1594 novel *The Unfortunate Traveller*?

4. *On Monsieur's Departure* and *The Doubt of Future Foes* are poems attributed to which figure?

5. *The Countess of Pembroke's Arcadia* (1593) and *An Apology for Poetry* (1595) were both works by which Elizabethan poet?

6. A gentleman named Kno'well and a servant named Brainworm feature in which 1598 play by Ben Jonson?

7. Which author, one of the first English women to become known for writing poetry, wrote work such as the play *Antonius* and a translation of Petrarch's *The Triumph of Death*?

8. *Poemata, a Collection of Latin Panegyrics, Elegies and Epigrams* (1595) was written by which English composer and poet?

9. Which poem by Edmund Spenser, published between 1590 and 1596, begins with the tale of the Redcrosse Knight and his battle with a monster called Errour?

10. A controversy involving Ben Jonson, John Marston and Thomas Dekker between 1599 and 1602 came to be known by what name?

answers on page 358

CHRISTOPHER MARLOWE
1564 - 1593

1. Marlowe was born in Canterbury in 1568. Rumours suggest that by his 20s, Marlowe was operating in what capacity on the orders of Elizabeth I?

2. One of Marlowe's first plays was, *Dido, Queen of Carthage* (1594), was based on parts of which Latin poem?

3. Which Marlowe play tells the story of a shepherd who rises to the rank of Emperor of Central Asia?

4. Marlowe was a member of which group of playwrights, who met while studying?

5. What's the name of the protagonist of Marlowe's play *The Jew of Malta*?

6. In Marlowe's *Doctor Faustus*, what's the name of the demon who visits the title character and strikes a deal?

7. Some scholars claim that Marlowe collaborated with William Shakespeare on which 1591 play?

8. One of Marlowe's final plays was a historical account of the relationship between Piers Gaveston and which English king?

9. Marlowe was accused of being part of which atheist group, along with Sir Walter Raleigh and George Chapman?

10. In 1593, Marlowe was accused of treason and a warrant was issued for his arrest. A few days later, he was killed in a fight while staying in which part of London?

answers on page 358

WILLIAM SHAKESPEARE
1564 - 1616

1. What was the trade of Shakespeare's father John?

2. Who did Shakespeare marry in 1582, when he was 18 and she was 26?

3. What was the name of the playing company (a group of actors) for which Shakespeare wrote during most of his career?

4. What name was given to the theatre that was built by members of the company in 1599?

5. At 29,551 words, what's Shakespeare's longest play?

6. *The Comedy of Errors* and *The Tempest* are the only two Shakespeare plays that observe which Aristotelian principle?

7. Mistress Quickly delivers a eulogy for Sir John Falstaff in which play?

8. Which actor, the star of Shakespeare's theatre company, played the title role in the first performances of many of the author's plays?

9. Following his death in 1616, where was Shakespeare buried?

10. What name is given to the collection of thirty-six Shakespeare plays, published seven years after he died?

answers on page 359

MARY, QUEEN OF SCOTS
1542 – 1587, Scottish queen 1542 - 1567

1. What was Mary's relationship to Henry VIII, who was the English king at the time of her birth?

2. Mary was born into which Scottish house?

3. Who was Mary's father?

4. When Mary was 10 years old, the Treaty of Greenwich proposed that she should marry which English figure?

5. Instead, Mary's first marriage was to which French king?

6. What was the name of Mary's second husband, her half-cousin, who she married in 1565?

7. What name is given to the rebellion of 1569 that attempted to depose Elizabeth and put Mary on the English throne?

8. In 1567, Mary's second husband was killed in an explosion at Kirk o'Field, a former abbey in which city?

9. What name is given to the documents that were used as evidence to suggest Mary's involvement in the murder of her second husband?

10. In 1587, Mary was executed at which Northamptonshire location?

answers on page 359

JAMES I OF ENGLAND / VI OF SCOTLAND
1566 – 1625, Scottish king from 1567 & English king from 1603

1. How old was James, the son of Mary, Queen of Scots, when he became the king of Scotland?

2. James spent much of his childhood at which location in Central Scotland?

3. Which peace agreement, between James and Elizabeth I in 1586, came a short time before the English queen had James's mother Mary executed?

4. Which 'philosophical dissertation', written by James, covers the dangers of creatures such as witches, werewolves and vampires?

5. In 1598, James sent the Gentleman Adventurers of Fife to colonise which remote location?

6. Which 1604 gathering, between James and leaders of the church, led to the commissioning of the King James Bible?

7. Under the terms of the Spanish Match, James's son Charles was at one time supposed to marry which European figure?

8. A policy, launched in 1609, saw British settlers colonise which part of Ireland?

9. Which political figure proposed the Great Contract of 1610, which attempted to increase the Crown's income?

10. What name is given to the two-month 1614 Parliament that marked a low point in the king's relations with his ministers?

answers on page 359

GUY FAWKES & THE GUNPOWDER PLOT
1605

1. What was the name of the first plot against James, in 1603, which aimed to capture the king and force him to be more tolerant to Catholics?

2. Two years later, which Catholic was the leader of the group that planned the Gunpowder Plot?

3. The plotters aimed to blow up the House of Lords during which ceremony?

4. The plot was originally scheduled for February 1605, but was delayed by eight months. This followed a decision to keep Parliament shut during which crisis?

5. Who did the plotters plan to install on the English throne?

6. The plot was revealed on 26th October 1605 in an anonymous letter written to which figure?

7. When Guy Fawkes was discovered beneath the House of Lords, he was guarding how many barrels of gunpowder?

8. What pseudonym did Fawkes use during the plot, including in the aftermath of his arrest?

9. Several of the plotters fled London, and made their last stand in November 1605 at which Staffordshire location?

10. Guy Fawkes night is held on 5th November every year. What name was given in the 17th century to a similar anti-Catholic night held in the colonial United States?

answers on page 360

CHARLES I
1600 – 1649, reigned 1625 - 1649

1. Who was Charles's mother?

2. Charles ruled for 24 years, from 1625 to 1649. What name is generally given to this period?

3. In 1625, Charles married – by proxy – which Catholic French princess?

4. What name is given to the war that was raging in Europe at this time, largely within the Holy Roman Empire?

5. Who led a disastrous naval expedition against Spain in 1625?

6. Charles's attempts to raise money to fight France led to which 1627 legal case, in which his authority to demand forced loans was challenged?

7. What name is given to the 1639 to 1640 conflict that saw Charles launch a disastrous campaign in Scotland?

8. Having attempted Personal Rule between 1629 and 1640, Charles finally summoned Parliament again in April 1640. How long did this so-called 'Short Parliament' last?

9. What was the name of the petition, presented to the Long Parliament in late 1640, that sought to abolish bishops?

10. Charles's conflict with the English Parliament finally came to a head in January 1642. On what grounds did he enter the House of Commons and attempt to arrest five members?

answers on page 360

THE ENGLISH CIVIL WAR
1642 - 1651

1. What was the name of the standing army formed by the Parliamentarians at the start of the war in 1645?

2. Which parliamentary leader, who had been one of those almost arrested by the king, headed the Committee of Safety and worked to keep the anti-monarchy coalition together?

3. What name was given to the bands of vigilantes that tried to protect their homes from both sides during the war?

4. The first pitched battle of the war was Edgehill in 1642. What is the definition of a 'pitched battle'?

5. What name is given to the events of December 6th 1648, when soldiers arrested 45 MPs who they viewed as sympathetic to the imprisoned Charles?

6. Oliver Cromwell led Parliamentary forces to an important victory on 2nd July 1644, in which battle?

7. Which series of discussions, about a new British constitution, ran from October to November 1647?

8. Which 1647 agreement saw an imprisoned Charles attempted to secure Scottish support for his cause?

9. Which Parliamentary leader, who was responsible for many victories, stepped aside to let Cromwell take control?

10. Charles was executed on 30th January 1649 outside which building in Whitehall?

answers on page 361

OLIVER CROMWELL
1599 – 1658, Lord Protector 1653 - 1658

1. Cromwell was a member of which religious group?

2. When he became an MP in 1628, Cromwell represented Huntingdon. Which constituency did he represent when the Long Parliament was convened in 1640?

3. What nickname did Cromwell gain following his role in the English Civil War?

4. Cromwell was a prominent member of the parliament that dealt with Charles's execution, and which sat from 1648 to 1653. What was this parliament called?

5. Which political group, publishers of a newspaper called *The Moderate*, was marginalised by Cromwell in the late 1640s?

6. In 1649, seeking to deal with a Catholic and Royalist threat, Cromwell led an invasion of which country?

7. Around 3,500 people, many of them civilians, were killed by Cromwell's troops in October 1649. This event took place in which town?

8. In 1653, Cromwell became the first holder of which office?

9. Which leather-seller and preacher gave his name to a parliament that briefly sat in 1653?

10. Which common phrase is said to have originated in a comment made by Cromwell while he was having his portrait painted?

answers on page 361

PURITANISM

1. The history of the Puritans is generally traced back to which mid-16th century disagreement concerning clerical dress in England?

2. Puritans were members of which branch of Christianity?

3. One aim of the Puritans was to ban bishops and instead have the church run by elders. This doctrine is otherwise known by what name?

4. Which leading Puritan figure wrote the Book of Martyrs?

5. In 1584, Puritans sought to replaced the Book of Common Prayer with which book?

6. Between 1588 and 1589, a series of pamphlets were released in England, credited to which pseudonymous puritan writer?

7. In July 1620, a group of Puritans travelled from England to the American colonies aboard which boat?

8. What was the name of the extreme Puritan sect that attempted in 1661 to seize London in the name of 'King Jesus'?

9. What name is given to the event in 1662 that saw thousands of Puritans forced out of their positions in the Church of England?

10. From this point on, Puritans generally became part of the group known as the Dissenters. In turn, the Dissenters eventually came to be known by which name?

answers on page 361

RICHARD CROMWELL & THE RESTORATION
1658 - 1660

1. How long did Oliver Cromwell's son Richard last as Lord Protector following his father's death in 1658?

2. What nickname, given to Richard Cromwell following his rapid fall from power, has since been used as a pub name and as the title of a 1736 play by Henry Fielding?

3. In the chaos that followed Cromwell's resignation, which military leader marched south from Scotland with an army?

4. What name is given to the parliament that met for the first time in April 1660, and which declared that Charles I's son Charles had in fact been the lawful monarch since 1649?

5. What name was given, retrospectively, by Parliamentarian soldiers to their reasons for their opposing Charles I?

6. Prior to his return to England, Charles II had been living in which country?

7. What name is given to the general pardon, issued by Charles II in 1660, that set out his promises in relation to the reclamation of the English throne?

8. A public holiday on 29th May, declared as a celebration of Charles's arrival to London, was known by what name?

9. Thomas Harrison was the first man to be convicted of which crime following Charles's return?

10. What fate befell Cromwell's corpse in early 1661?

answers on page 362

CHARLES II
1630 – 1685, reigned 1660 - 1685

1. When he returned to England to assume the throne, Charles II landed at which spot on the south coast?

2. In 1660, Charles granted a charter to which organisation, which still exists today and aims to promote scientific beliefs?

3. What did Charles sell to King Louis XIV of France in 1662, for £375,000?

4. Charles's interest in science continued when, in 1675, he commissioned which facility in Greenwich?

5. The king granted several charters – including the right to rule foreign territory and the right to mint money – to which organisation?

6. Under Charles II, several important penal laws were passed. By what name are these laws collectively known?

7. Between 1665 and 1666, 100,000 people – 25% of London's population – died in an outbreak of which disease?

8. In September 1666, the Great Fire of London began in a bakery in which London street?

9. Why were so many in England keen to remove Charles's brother James from the line of succession?

10. Charles collapsed and died in February 1685. One theory suggests that this sickness was caused by his experiments with which element?

answers on page 362

ART & LITERATURE DURING
THE RESTORATION

1. Beginning in 1660, which Member of Parliament began to write a diary that went on to become famous?

2. *The Comical Revenge* (1664), *She Would If She Could* (1668) and *The Man of Mode* (1676) were all Restoration comedies by which English dramatist?

3. Following the destruction of Old St. Paul's in the Great Fire of London, who designed its replacement?

4. Who wrote the epic poem *Paradise Lost*, which was first published in 1667?

5. Who was appointed as the first Poet Laureate of the United Kingdom in 1668?

6. Which actress, a mistress of Charles II, gained fame during the late 1600s for her stage performances?

7. What's the title of William Wycherley's 1675 comedy that features characters such as Mr. and Mrs. Pinchwife?

8. Which author, who for a time was sent by Charles II to work as a spy in Belgium, wrote novels such as *Agnes de Castro* (1688) and *Oroonoko* (1688)?

9. *Two Treatises of Government* (1689) is a work of political philosophy by which English writer?

10. Who wrote the 1989 novel *Restoration*, about a medical student who finds favour in the court of Charles II?

answers on page 363

JAMES II
1633 – 1701, reigned 1685 - 1688

1. In 1644, at the age of 11, James was given which title?

2. What was the name of James's first wife, a commoner, who he married in 1660 despite official advice to ignore her?

3. James was a Catholic, and many in England feared the idea of him becoming king. Which 1673 penal laws were designed to stop any Catholics holding high office in the country?

4. Following the death of his brother Charles II in 1685, James became king. What was the name of the nephew who led a military campaign in an attempt to dethrone James?

5. This rebellion was defeated at which battle?

6. What name is given to the 1688 plot that led to the removal of James as king, and his replacement by his daughter Mary and her husband William III of Orange?

7. What happened to seven bishops who refused to read James's Declaration of Indulgence in church?

8. In June 1688, what event led to fears that England would be ruled by a Catholic dynasty?

9. What did James throw into the Thames as he attempted to flee England?

10. James ended his days in France. What name is given to those who subsequently fought for the restoration of his line to the English throne?

answers on page 363

SIR ISAAC NEWTON
1642 – 1726/27

1. Isaac Newton was born on which day in 1642?

2. Early in his career, Newton became involved in a dispute over calculus with which German mathematician?

3. What did Newton invent in the 1660s, involving a primary concave mirror and a secondary flat mirror?

4. A story, possibly apocryphal, claims that Newton was inspired to formulate his theory of gravitation after being hit on the head by what item?

5. What title is commonly given to Newton's 1687 work that covers, among other things, his laws of motion and law of universal gravitation?

6. Newton was also interested in alchemy. What name is given to the mythical alchemical substance that is said to turn base metals into gold or silver?

7. Between 1689 and 1701, Newton served as an MP, representing which constituency?

8. In 1699, Newton took up which post in London, which he held for the next thirty years?

9. After his death in 1727, Newton's hair was discovered to contain traces of which element?

10. The Newton, named after Sir Isaac Newton, is an internationally recognised unit of what?

answers on page 363

WILLIAM & MARY

1650 – 1702 & 1689 – 1694, reigned 1689 – 1702 & 1689 - 1694

1. William was the Prince of Orange. Where was the Principality of Orange located?

2. Mary was named after her great-grand-mother. Who was she?

3. Following their marriage, where did William and Mary live?

4. William and Mary took the English throne in 1689. Which act, passed that year and still in force today, clarifies the line of succession?

5. William's forces defeated the army of his predecessor (and father-in-law) James II in which battle in 1690?

6. Five years into their reign, Mary died from which sickness?

7. Until 1697, William was largely absent from England as he fought in which conflict between France and a coalition that included the Dutch army?

8. The 1698 Treaty of the Hague, signed by William, sought to resolve the question of the monarchy in which country?

9. Neither William or his sister-in-law Anne also children. In 1701, the Act of Settlement determined that after Anne, the Crown would then pass to which European noble?

10. William died of pneumonia in 1702. According to legend, what had caused his horse to stumble?

answers on page 364

ANNE
1665 – 1714, reigned 1702 - 1714

1. As a child, Anne lived for a time in France with her paternal grandmother. What was the grandmother's name?

2. Anne married in 1683. What was her husband's name?

3. What was the name of Anne's close confidant, whose dramatic friendship caused a great deal of controversy?

4. John Churchill, a powerful military commander during Anne's reign, was most widely known by which title?

5. From at least 1698 until her death sixteen years later, Anne suffered from which painful condition of the joints?

6. Only one of Anne's children (from seventeen pregnancies and five live births) survived infancy. He died in 1700, at the age of 11. What was his name?

7. Britain fought alongside the Dutch and the Holy Roman Empire in which 1701 to 1714 conflict?

8. What natural disaster struck England in 1703, causing huge damage across the land?

9. Which acts, passed in 1707, officially combined the Kingdom of England and the Kingdom of Scotland, resulting in the formation of one country called Great Britain?

10. Following the death of Sophia, Electress of Hanover two months earlier, who – under the Act of Settlement – was next in line to the throne when Anne died in August 1714?

answers on page 364

GEORGE I
1660 – 1727, reigned 1714 - 1727

1. Who was George I's father?

2. George's mother, Sophia, was next in line to the English throne. How many Catholics with superior claims were bypassed by this decision?

3. In his 20s, George fought at the Battle of Vienna, part of a war between the Holy Roman Empire and which other force?

4. 83-year-old Sophia died in 1714, supposedly after doing what in her garden in Hanover?

5. Following George's accession to the throne, some members of the Tory party sought to replace him with which figure?

6. George helped form the Triple Alliance of Britain, France and the Dutch Republic against which country?

7. George's wife was accused of having an affair. What was her fate for the rest of her life, until she died in 1726?

8. The Bubble Act of 1720 aimed to control the flotation of joint-stock companies. This followed Britain's first major stock market collapse, caused by shares in which company?

9. Which figure, who assumed office in 1721 and dealt with the South Sea Crisis, is seen as the first British prime minister?

10. What chivalric order, which had its roots in early practices, was formally revived by George in 1725 as a means by which the prime minister might reward political supporters?

answers on page 365

EDWARD TEACH, AKA BLACKBEARD
c. 1680 - 1718

1. Little is known about Teach's early life, and Teach might not even have been his real name. Around 1715, already in his 20s, he arrived on which pirate-filled Bahamian island?

2. The island had been established as a pirate based by which former privateer?

3. Teach quickly joined the crew of which pirate captain?

4. In 1717, Teach (by now in command of his own ship) and his crew seized a French merchant vessel named La Concorde. What new name did they give to this boat?

5. Who was Teach's lieutenant during this period?

6. Teach grew in strength and enlarged his fleet. In May 1718, he and his crew blockaded which town in South Carolina?

7. In June 1718, Teach accepted a pardon from which figure, who was Royal Governor at the time?

8. What was the name of Teach's wife?

9. What was the name of the Governor of Virginia, who worried that Teach had returned to piracy and set out to track him down?

10. Teach was eventually killed by the governor's forces in a battle near which North Carolina island?

answers on page 365

SIR ROBERT WALPOLE
1676 – 1745, PM 1721 - 1742

1. Walpole was a member of which political party?

2. Although he entered parliament as a representative of Castle Rising in Norfolk, for most of his career Walpole was the member for which nearby borough?

3. In 1712, in relation to a political scandal involving contracts, Walpole was imprisoned for six months in which building?

4. Following the South Sea Bubble, Walpole helped protect a number of political figures who were accused of corruption. What nickname did he gain as a result?

5. Walpole was never formally referred to as 'prime minister' and rejected the title. Instead, his tenure in the role is generally dated from his assumption of which office in 1721?

6. What name was given to the Whig group that formed around 1725 in opposition to Walpole's policies?

7. What nickname did Walpole acquire in 1726, after he was made a Knight of the Garter?

8. Walpole commissioned which Norfolk country house, which today is a Grade I listed building?

9. Walpole resigned in 1742. George II, who wept at the news, elevated him to the House of Lords with which title?

10. In his later years, Walpole owned a large collection of what?

answers on page 365

10 DOWNING STREET

1. What is said to have stood on the site of Downing Street during the 15th century?

2. 10 Downing Street was built between 1682 and 1684, on the orders of which English statesman?

3. Who designed the house?

4. As First Lord of the Treasury (and effectively Prime Minister), Robert Walpole accepted the house in Downing Street in 1735 as a gift from which king?

5. Who was Mr. Chicken?

6. The numbering of the Downing Street houses has changed over the years. Until 1779, number 10 actually had which number?

7. What was installed at 10 Downing Street for the first time in 1884, during the premiership of William Gladstone?

8. Who, in 1902, revived the tradition of 10 Downing Street being the official residence of the prime minister?

9. What's the postcode of 10 Downing Street?

10. When the house was renovated in the 1950s, workers discovered that the black appearance was actually due to pollution. What colour was the front of the house really?

answers on page 366

THE WHIG PARTY

1. What were the core beliefs of the Whig party concerning the monarchy?

2. The name 'Whig' was short for the Scottish term whiggamor. What was a whiggamor?

3. What was the Whig view during the Exclusion crisis?

4. The Whig-supported Prohibition of 1678 banned what?

5. The Reform Act 1832, championed by the Whigs, saw an end to what type of political constituency?

6. The same year, the Whigs also abolished what in the British Empire?

7. Which London club – still running today – was founded in 1836 by Edward Ellice, a Member of Parliament and a Whig whip?

8. Whig politician Sir Robert Walpole is regarded as having been the first British prime minister. Who, between 1855 and 1858, was the last Whig prime minster?

9. The Whigs were eventually folded into which new political party, which lasted from 1859 to 1988?

10. Who wrote *The Whig Interpretation of History* (1931), which coined the idea of Whig history focusing on the journey from a dark part to a glorious present?

answers on page 366

GEORGE II
1683 – 1760, reigned 1727 - 1760

1. George II is the most recent British monarch to have which distinction concerning his birth?

2. When George first met his future bride, Caroline of Ansbach, he did so under which fake name?

3. In 1716, a would-be assassin attempted to kill the future king. Where did this event take place?

4. George's popularity led to a rift with his father. What was the name of his London residence, which became a base for the king's political's opponents?

5. George chose not to travel to Germany for his father's funeral. At his own coronation, four new anthems were performed, which had been written by which composer?

6. Shortly after becoming king, George donated what collection to the British Museum?

7. What 1739 – 1748 conflict with Spain takes its name from the unfortunate fate suffered by a British sea captain?

8. In 1743, George became the last British monarch (to date) to lead troops into battle, at which conflict?

9. The Seven Years' War, which erupted in 1756, followed a French invasion of which British-held island in the Balearics?

10. George died in 1760. What unusual request did he make regarding not only his own coffin, but that of his late wife?

answers on page 367

DICK TURPIN
c. 1705 - 1739

1. Richard 'Dick' Turpin was born around 1705 at which pub in Hempstead, Essex?

2. Documents suggest that Turpin might have initially followed his father into which profession?

3. What was the name of his wife?

4. Deer poaching was a major problem in the Royal Forest of Waltham. The Black Act of 1723 got its name from the fact that it outlawed what poaching tactic?

5. Turpin is believed to have become involved with which poaching gang?

6. The gang was broken up and Turpin turned to highway robbery. Turpin is believed to have spent time in which country?

7. Back in England, Turpin eventually adopted which alias?

8. Turpin was eventually captured and put on trial for stealing horses. On 7th April 1739, he was executed by hanging at which location in York?

9. A fictionalised account of Turpin's exploits, including a supposed 200-miles overnight ride from London to York, was popularised in the 1834 novel *Rookwood* by which author?

10. According to legend, what was the name of Turpin's horse?

answers on page 367

HENRY PELHAM
1694 – 1754, PM 1743 - 1754

1. Pelham became an MP at the age of 23, representing which constituency?

2. What was Pelham's first ministerial position?

3. He soon found favour with Robert Walpole. His meetings with Walpole and his own younger brother Thomas were usually known by what title?

4. Following the death of Spencer Compton in 1743, Pelham became Britain's third prime minister and worked closely with his brother. What name is given to this coalition?

5. At the time of Pelham's accession to the role, Britain was engaged in which conflict?

6. For two days in 1746, Pelham resigned while which other figure attempted (and failed) to form a government?

7. What act, introduced in 1751, was designed to curb problems cause by excessive drinking?

8. What happened to the calendar in 1752?

9. One of the final acts passed during Pelham's premiership, in 1753, allowed which group of people to become naturalised in the country?

10. Pelham died in office. Who succeeded him as prime minister?

answers on page 367

BONNIE PRINCE CHARLIE
& THE JACOBITE UPRISING OF 1745

1. Charles Edward Stuart, aka Bonnie Prince Charlie, was the grandson of which figure?

2. Charles was born and raised in which European city?

3. The Jacobite cause aimed to return the Stuart family to the British throne. In 1744, Charles attempted to gain the support of which country?

4. Charles travelled to Scotland, where the Jacobites still enjoyed support. Which folk song tells the story of his victory over a British government force at the Battle of Prestonpans?

5. What battle took place on 16th April, 1746, and saw Charles and his forces suffer a final defeat?

6. Who commanded the king's army during the battle with Charles?

7. Which song by Sir Harold Edwin Boulton commemorates the end of the battle, and Bonnie Prince Charlie's escape?

8. What name is given to the spot in the Highlands from which Charles made his final departure from Scottish soil?

9. Charles subsequently retreated to France. In a last attempt to gather support, he abandoned Roman Catholicism and switched to which religion?

10. Charles died in 1788. Where were his remains (minus his heart) buried?

answers on page 368

THE HEBRIDES

1. What name is given to the standing stones, erected in the Neolithic era, on the west coast of the Isle of Lewis?

2. During the 6th and 7th centuries, the Hebrides were part of which Gaelic kingdom?

3. In 1098, following a period of Viking raids, King Edgar of Scotland gave the Hebrides to which Scandinavian ruler?

4. Which Norse-Gaelic warrior led a rebellion in 1156, in which the Inner Hebrides were taken from the Vikings?

5. In 1266, which agreement formally gave control of the Hebrides to King Alexander III of Scotland?

6. Which 16th century Scottish clergyman, who wrote an early book about the history of the Hebrides, is sometimes referred to as the 'Dean of the Isles'?

7. Which islands in the Outer Hebrides are sometimes known as the Seven Hunters?

8. Which 17th century poet lived on North Uist and served as official poet to the chief of the Clan MacDonald of Sleat?

9. Which 1882 event saw local crofting tenants rebel against their landlords, by witholding rent and releasing sheep into forbidden parts of the island of Skye?

10. In 1918, which English industrialist bought the Isle of Lewis for £167,000, with the aim of establishing a new, more modern fishing industry?

answers on page 368

ROBERT CLIVE, AKA CLIVE OF INDIA
1725 - 1774

1. Robert Clive was born in Shropshire in 1725. When he was 19, Clive joined the East India Company. On his way to India, however, his ship ran aground off the coast of which country?

2. Clive eventually reached India. What name is given to the three wars, between 1746 and 1763, that saw the company vie for power with the French East India Company?

3. Clive is regarded as being one of two men who laid the foundations for British rule in India. Who was the other?

4. In 1751, Clive proved his military worth during which siege in eastern India?

5. Several years later, Clive led a military force that recaptured which city?

6. Clive secured a decisive victory over the Nawab of Bengal and his French allies in which 1757 battle?

7. While back in Britain for a few years, Clive was elected to which local office for 1762 – 1763?

8. In 1765, Clive secured what hugely important document from King Shah Aalum?

9. Clive died in London in 1774. The circumstances of his death have been debated, but he is believed to have cut his own throat with what object?

10. Which of Clive's associates died in March 2006 in Kolkata?

answers on page 369

GEORGE III
1738 – 1820, reigned 1760 - 1820

1. George III was born in 1738. He was a grandson of George II. Who was his father?

2. George and his family often spent their holidays in Britain. Which location in Dorset became one of the country's first seaside resorts, following several visits by the king?

3. What did George surrender to Parliament, in exchange for the creation of the civil list?

4. The American Revolution began in 1765. Who was George's prime minister at the time?

5. During the 1780s, George's mental health became a concern. One contemporary story claimed that he had shaken hands with what object, after mistaking it for the Prussian king?

6. Which would-be assassin attempted to kill the king during a performance at the Theatre Royal?

7. What title is George said to have turned down following the 1801 Act of Union?

8. In 1810, George suffered a further deterioration in his mental state. This was widely attributed to whose death?

9. Once his son George (later George IV) became Regent, George III retired to spend his final years at which location?

10. A 2005 study of a sample of the king's hair found that it contained high levels of which element?

answers on page 369

THE INDUSTRIAL REVOLUTION
from around 1760

1. Daily life was transformed by the Industrial Revolution. Who wrote the 1844 book *The Conditions of the Working Class in England*, which described many of these changes?

2. Derwent Valley Mills, one of the first modern factories in the world, was owned by which 18th century entrepreneur?

3. What was the name of the revolutionary weaving device patented by John Kay in 1733?

4. Which canal, which opened in 1761, allowed coal and other goods to be transported between Worsley and Manchester?

5. In 1784, Henry Cort patented a new version of which technique, which enabled the transformation of molten (crude) pig iron into wrought iron?

6. What term, credited to James Watt, is used to compare the output of steam engines with the power of a type of animal?

7. Who is credited with developing the first commercially-used steam engine?

8. What device, used in textile manufacturing, was invented by Samuel Crompton in the late 18th century?

9. Which 1799 act aimed to stop trade unions and collective bargaining among members of the British workforce?

10. Which secret organisation emerged in the 19th century and aimed to destroy machines that took away human jobs?

answers on page 369

SHEFFIELD

1. What name is given to the Central Europeans who migrated to the Sheffield area during the Bronze Age?

2. Northumbrian king Eanred submitted to King Egbert of Wessex in 829 AD at which village near Sheffield?

3. The Domesday Book of 1086 is the oldest surviving example of the area around Sheffield being referred to by what name?

4. Which Sheffield church was founded in the 12th century by Robert FitzRanulph, with some sources claiming that he'd been involved in the murder of Thomas Becket?

5. What organisation, still in existence today, was formed in 1624 in an attempt to oversee a certain trade in Sheffield?

6. Who was imprisoned at Sheffield Castle for 14 years, starting in the year 1570?

7. The Industrial Revolution transformed Sheffield. What was invented in the city in 1912, by Harry Brearley?

8. What nickname was given to Sheffield due to the rise of criminal gangs in the city in the 19th century?

9. Which 1984 film, written by Barry Hines and directed by Mick Jackson, is set in a future version of Sheffield in the aftermath of a nuclear war?

10. Which Sheffield nightclub was home to the Gatecrasher brand during the late 1990s and early 2000s?

answers on page 370

CANALS

1. In 1515, the City of Canterbury obtained permission to 'canalise' which river?

2. In 1605, which commission was appointed by James I to manage navigation on the Thames?

3. Which canal, which opened in 1757 and eventually connected St. Helens to the River Mersey, was the first modern canal and was built during the Industrial Revolution?

4. Canal operators didn't always cooperate with one another. What physical barrier was erected in the 18th century to block passage between two canals in the centre of Birmingham?

5. What name is given to the period between 1790 and 1810, in which the UK canal network became almost 4,000 miles long?

6. The longest aqueduct in Britain, the Pontcysyllte Aqueduct, is part of which canal?

7. What art style emerged in the mid-19th century as a way of decorating narrowboats, with some historians believing that Romani vardos were a major influence?

8. Which civil engineer designed the Manchester Ship Canal and the Anderson Boat Lift?

9. Which lock on the Rochdale Canal, built in 1996 and with a fall of 6m, is the deepest lock in the United Kingdom?

10. The Falkirk Wheel, which opened in 2002 in Scotland, connects the Forth and Clyde Canal to which other canal?

answers on page 370

TRAINS

1. In 1603, construction began on which overground wagon route, which was designed to carry coal in Newcastle?

2. Which 18th century narrow gauge line near Wakefield is generally recognised as the world's first public railway?

3. What was the name of the first commercially successful steam locomotive, which was built in 1812 by a Yorkshireman named Matthew Murray?

4. Opening in 1830 in Liverpool, what was the first intercity passenger station in the world?

5. Which British civil and mechanical engineer is generally regarded as the 'Father of Railways'?

6. Which London station, which opened in 1836, is (as of 2021) the oldest London terminus station still in operation?

7. Which Kent line, which opened in 1927, was originally conceived by racing drivers 'Jack' Howey and Count Louis Zborowski?

8. What were the 'big four' railway companies that were nationalised in 1948 to become British Railways?

9. In the 1960s, which physicist and engineer identified more than 2,000 stations and 5,000 miles of line for closure?

10. As of 2021, the world's oldest surviving steam locomotive is which train, constructed in the 19th century by William Hedley and first used to transport coal in Northumberland?

answers on page 371

THE AMERICAN REVOLUTION
1765 - 1791

1. Which 1765 act saw the British government impose direct taxation on the American colonies for the first time?

2. Many American colonists objected to this act not because of the cost, but because of which other factor?

3. What was the name of the group that formed to fight the act and protect the rights of American colonists?

4. Who wrote *Letters From a Farmer in Pennsylvania* (1767 – 1768), protesting against the regulation of American trade?

5. Which 1770 event saw British soldiers fire at an angry American crowd, killing five civilians?

6. What was the name of the British customs schooner that was burned by Americans in 1772?

7. Which 1773 event saw Americans board the ships of the East India Company and throw their cargo into the harbour?

8. The British government responded with the Massachusetts Government Act, the Administration of Justice Act, the Boston Port Act and the Quartering Act. By what collective name are these four acts better known?

9. Which 1774 declaration saw the so-called Provincial Congress reject the new British acts?

10. Which 1775 events are generally regarded as the first military engagements of the American War of Independence?

answers on page 371

THE AMERICAN WAR OF INDEPERNDENCE
1775 - 1783

1. Early American support for the war was bolstered by the pamphlet *Common Sense*, written by which political activist?

2. Which early battle in 1775, saw the British army lose more than 1,000 men despite scoring a somewhat pyrrhic victory?

3. The Americans made a last-ditch attempt to avoid war, through which July 1775 document?

4. The American Declaration of Independence was overseen by the Committee of Five. What were their names?

5. Who became American Commander-in-Chief in June 1775?

6. Who was the Commander-in-Chief of the British forces during the early stages of the war?

7. The Americans turned to France for assistance. What company, formed in 1775, was used by the theoretically neutral French and Spanish to help America fight the British?

8. In 1776, worried that the Iroquois might support the British, American forces entered French territory and were subsequently defeated at which battle?

9. The last major land battle of the American War of Independence, in October 1781, saw the Americans defeat the British at a siege of which Virginian location?

10. The war officially ended following the signing of which agreement in 1783?

answers on page 371

CAPTAIN JAMES COOK
1728 - 1779

1. James Cook was born in Yorkshire in 1728. His first merchant navy apprenticeship saw him work on which collier?

2. In 1768, Cook was sent on his first scientific voyage, the aim of which was to record what phenomenon?

3. For this voyage, Cook was given command of which vessel?

4. Cook subsequently discovered that he was also ordered to search for which continent?

5. During this search, Cook became the first European to communicate with which people?

6. Cook first set foot on Australian soil at a site he named Stingray Bay. He later gave this spot which other name?

7. In 1776, Cook was sent to locate the Northwest Passage. During this voyage, he became the first European to made full contact with islanders from which location?

8. Contemporary reports claimed that the islanders initially considered Cook to be an incarnation of which deity?

9. Cook was subsequently killed in a confrontation with the local population. Since they still considered him to be a deity, what did the islanders do to his body?

10. Cook's parents' last home in Yorkshire, known as Cooks' Cottage, was later moved to which location?

answers on page 372

ADAM SMITH
1723 - 1790

1. Adam Smith was born in 1723 in which Scottish town?

2. What was the title of Smith's 1759 book, which focused on the nature of human morality?

3. By this point, Smith was a friend of which Scottish philosopher, whose work included *A Treatise of Human Nature* (1739 – 1740)?

4. While visiting Paris, Smith spent time with which American writer and philosopher?

5. What shortened name is given to Smith's 1776 publication, which is regarded as the first modern work of economics?

6. What name did Smith give to the principle of specialisation, whereby workers were more productive if they focused on certain core tasks?

7. In a budget the following year, prime minister Lord North introduced what tax on employees, first suggested by Smith?

8. What principle, first described by Smith, refers to the ability of a party to produce more efficiently that its competitors?

9. He died in 1790. What was the title of the posthumous book that was released five years later, containing a number of his unpublished pieces?

10. What nickname is often used for Smith, reflecting his influence on modern political thinking?

answers on page 372

MARY PRINCE
1788 – c. 1833

1. Mary Prince was born into enslavement at Devonshire Parish, which is a parish of which country?

2. She was sold several times in her youth, eventually ending up in Antigua. During this period, she joined which church?

3. Who was her master in Antigua?

4. Around this time, Prince began to develop which medical condition, which limited her ability to work?

5. What was the name of her husband, a former slave who had bought his freedom?

6. A few years later, Prince's master took her along on a trip to London. Which 1772 legal case meant that slaves could not be transported out of England?

7. After leaving her master's service, Prince started working for which abolitionist writer?

8. Unable to go home, for fear of being enslaved again, Prince was encouraged to write a book about her life. This was transcribed for her by which Canadian author?

9. Following criticism of her book, Prince sued which Scottish writer and pro-slavery campaigner for libel?

10. Little is known of Prince's life after 1833. In 2007, a commemorative blue plaque was unveiled close to her former residence in which part of London?

answers on page 373

THE FRENCH REVOLUTIONARY WARS
1793 - 1802

1. The French Revolution began in 1789. Which French king was executed in January 1793?

2. Around this time, a young French artillery officer gained his first experience in combat. He would go on to become a major figure in the conflict. What was his name?

3. Revolutionary France swiftly declared war on many countries, including Britain. What name is given to the 1794 naval battle that saw both sides claim victory?

4. During this period, Britain also unsuccessfully tried to support French rebels in what region?

5. In 1796, France invaded which neighbouring country?

6. Britain was facing internal trouble at the time. In April 1797, a major mutiny broke out at which Portsmouth anchorage?

7. Austria made peace with France in late 1797, leaving Britain alone in facing the French. What was the name of the governing body in France at this time?

8. What name is used for the 1799 coup that saw this governing body overthrown?

9. In 1801, which battle saw the British destroy a smaller Danish-Norwegian fleet?

10. Which treaty, signed in 1802, saw hostilities between France and Britain end, at least for a short period?

answers on page 373

WILLIAM PITT THE YOUNGER
1759 – 1806, PM 1783 – 1801,1804 – 1806

1. William Pitt (the younger) was born in 1759 in which Kent village?

2. Pitt's uncle on his mother's side was which former prime minister?

3. Pitt's father, who was also prime minister, is sometimes referred to by which one-word nickname?

4. While prime minister, Pitt also occupied which other key government position?

5. After becoming prime minister in 1759, Pitt put forward an act that was designed to reorganise which company?

6. Following the American War of Independence, Britain could no longer send convicts to the New World. Under Pitt, which colony was founded in Australia for the same purpose?

7. In 1801, Pitt became the first holder of which office?

8. Pitt resigned from office and was replaced by his ally Henry Addington, but Addington resigned in 1804 and Pitt became prime minister again. Following the Battle of Trafalgar, he was toasted by some with which title?

9. He died in 1806, unmarried and with no children. Where was he buried?

10. What name was given to the national unity government that was formed by Pitt's successor, William Grenville?

answers on page 373

THE NAPOLEONIC WARS
1803 - 1815

1. Peace between Britain and France lasted less than a year, and ended in May 1803. What French policy aimed to stop neighbouring countries trading with Britain?

2. Britain paid some European countries, to help them raise armies against France. How were these payments known?

3. Which 1805 battle saw Napoleon defeat a large Russian and Austrian army, leading to the fall of the Holy Roman Empire?

4. Napoleon needed to assert naval superiority in order to invade Britain. This effort ended in failure in 1805's Battle of Trafalgar, which occurred off the coast of which country?

5. By 1808, which country had begun to trade with Britain again, leading to the Peninsular War?

6. In 1812, Napoleon suffered a disastrous failure when he tried to invade which country?

7. Which London-based German banker organised the financing of Britain's war effort during this period?

8. Following Napoleon's fall from power in 1814, he was exiled to which island?

9. Napoleon escaped and gathered a new force, only to be defeated at the Battle of Waterloo in 1815. Where is Waterloo?

10. After the war ended in November 1815, Napoleon was again sent into exile. He died six years later on which island?

answers on page 374

ADMIRAL HORATIO NELSON
1758 - 1805

1. Nelson was born in Norfolk in 1758, and was named after a distant relative who also happened to be the nephew of which former prime minister?

2. After school, Nelson began his naval career aboard which vessel?

3. In 1776, Nelson became sick and almost died from which illness?

4. Nelson was soon given command of his own vessel for the first time. What was the name of this vessel?

5. Nelson married in 1787. What was the name of his wife?

6. In 1794, Nelson's right eye was injured (though he was not permanently blinded) during which military offensive?

7. In 1797, shortly after the Battle of Cape St. Vincent, Nelson was promoted to what rank?

8. Which 1798 battle saw Nelson score an important victory after discovering Napoleon's fleet in Aboukir Bay, Egypt?

9. Who served as flag captain to Nelson at the Battle of Trafalgar, and was present at his death?

10. Nelson's Column in London was completed in 1843. Who designed the monument?

answers on page 374

THE WAR OF 1812

1. Which 1794 treaty was supposed to avert war between the US and Britain, by resolving issues that lingered following the American War of Independence?

2. Which 1811 skirmish between an American and a British vessel saw a number of British casualties?

3. In June 1812, which American president issued a list of grievances against the British?

4. In September 1813, the Americans secured an important victory in which battle?

5. Which Shawnee chief, who had sided with the British, was killed in the Battle of the Thames in October 1813?

6. Between 1813 and 1814, British forces tried (and failed) to support native American groups during which conflict?

7. Which battle in July 1814 saw the Americans try to defeat British forces to the north of the country?

8. Once Napoleon had been defeated in Europe, the British were able to send more troops to America. In August 1814, British forces invaded and set fire to much of which city?

9. Which American military leader, and future president, led his forces to an important victory over the British at the 1815 Battle of New Orleans?

10. The war finally ended in 1815, following which peace agreement?

answers on page 375

ARTHUR WELLESLEY, THE DUKE OF WELLINGTON
1769 – 1852

1. Arthur Wellesley was born in which city?

2. After joining the army, Wellesley saw action in India. In 1803, at the Battle of Assaye, he won an important victory over which enemy?

3. In 1806, having returned to England, Wellesley entered Parliament as a Tory MP for which constituency?

4. As the Marquess of Wellington, he won a key victory in Europe when he defeated the French at which 1813 battle?

5. After the war, Wellesley returned to domestic politics. In 1828 he became prime minister, and one year later he was appointed to which ceremonial position?

6. As a Tory prime minister, Wellesley oversaw the emancipation of which group within England?

7. How did Wellesley settle a dispute with the Earl of Winchilsea in 1829?

8. During this period, Wellesley's political stubbornness earned him which nickname?

9. Following his retirement, Wellesley briefly returned during the Europe-wide revolutions of 1848. What was his role during this short period?

10. Wellesley retained which rank in the army until his death in 1852?

answers on page 375

THE ROYAL NAVY

1. The Royal Navy was founded in 1546 by which king?

2. What name is generally given to the period between the mid-15th and mid-19th centuries, which saw a huge growth in the importance of seafaring trade and warfare?

3. What naval prefix was first used for vessels during the reign of Charles II?

4. What name is given to the period between 1815 and 1914, during which the Royal Navy effectively controlled most of the key maritime trade routes around the world?

5. The Naval Defence Act of 1889 stipulated that the Royal Navy should maintain a number of battleships at least equal to what number?

6. Launched in 1901, what was the name of the Royal Navy's first submarine?

7. Which hugely influential Royal Navy battleship, which entered service in 1906, eventually lent its name to an entire generation of vessels?

8. Formed in 1914, what name was given to the Royal Navy's main fleet during the First World War?

9. What's the name of the UK's nuclear deterrence system, which has been run by the Royal Navy since 1980?

10. As of 2021, the Royal Navy's basic training facility is which stone frigate at Torpoint in Cornwall??

answers on page 375

MEDWAY

1. What's the name of the Kent peninsula that separates the estuaries of the Thames and Medway rivers?

2. Which Medway town was known as Durobrivae – which can be translated to mean something related to a fort or bridge – by the Romans?

3. Gillingham is said to have been named after a local warlord who was known for which custom?

4. In 604 AD, St. Justus became the first holder of which title?

5. Which historical route crosses the River Medway near the village of Cuxton?

6. Matthew Baker, a master shipwright during the Tudor era, was known for a long-standing rivalry with which Chatham-based shipbuilding dynasty?

7. Which castle, constructed in the mid-16th century, was designed to protect Chatham Dockyard?

8. In 1667, the Raid on the Medway – in which numerous British vessels were burned or stolen – was a disastrous moment in which conflict?

9. Which influential botanical and ornithological illustrator was born in Strood in 1806?

10. Chatham Dockyard closed in 1984. What type of vessel were the last to be constructed there, with examples such as HMS Ocelot and HMCS Okanagan?

answers on page 376

GEORGE IV
1762 – 1830, reigned 1820 - 1830

1. George was known for his extravagant lifestyle. As Prince of Wales, he lived in which Westminster mansion?

2. In 1785, George married Maria Fitzherbert. Why did the marriage have to remain secret?

3. George became Regent in 1788, after his father's mental illness deteriorated further. Later, the recovered king forced George to marry which German-born figure?

4. When he became king in 1820, George is said to have been addicted to which opium-based substance?

5. The following year, George became the first monarch since Richard II to make a state visit which territory?

6. As a patron of new styles, George commissioned John Nash to design which building in Brighton?

7. George was a close friend of which fashionable Regency era figure, who is often used as an example of a dandy?

8. Due to his charm and sense of culture, George rapidly earned which nickname?

9. Which prime minister, in office for most of George's reign, had to deal with public anger at the king's spending?

10. George's health deteriorated rapidly, and he became obese due to his lifestyle. What was the name of the king's doctor during this period, who was criticised for his treatment?

answers on page 376

BRIGHTON

1. The name Brighton is believed to have developed from the name of an Anglo-Saxon farmstead on the site. According to this theory, who owned the farmstead?

2. What's the name of the Iron Age hillfort that still stands to the north of Brighton?

3. What name is given to the Neolithic earthwork, a kind of causewayed enclosure, just outside Brighton?

4. Brighton's annual Royal Escape yacht race commemorates the escape to France in 1651 of which royal figure?

5. What event caused considerable damage to Brighton in the early 18th century, and was subsequently described by the writer Daniel Defoe?

6. Which engineer, born in Brighton in 1851, is known for having built the world's oldest operating electric railway?

7. Which 19th century seaside architect was responsible for Brighton's West Pier?

8. Who pained the satirical artwork *HRH the Prince Regent Awakens the Spirit of Brighton*?

9. What's the name of the Brighton war memorial that commemorates the loss of Indian soldiers who fought for the British Empire in the First World War?

10. Which planning officer is widely credited with saving the North Laine area from redevelopment in the late 1970s?

answers on page 377

SPENCER PERCEVAL
1762 – 1812, PM 1809 - 1812

1. As of 2021, Spencer Perceval holds which unfortunate distinction?

2. Following the death of his father, Perceval went to which London school?

3. After studying law, wrote a series of anonymous pamphlets supporting the impeachment of which Bengal Governor-General?

4. In 1796, Perceval entered Parliament as MP for which East Midlands town?

5. Perceval was involved in defending the Prince Regent's wife Princess Caroline against the so-called 'delicate investigation', which was called following which accusation?

6. Shortly after becoming prime minister in 1809, Perceval had to contend with an investigation into which unsuccessful military expedition to the Netherlands?

7. Who shot and killed Perceval in the lobby of the House of Commons on 11th May 1812?

8. What was his killer's grievance against the government?

9. An inquest was held into Perceval's death at which public house near Downing Street?

10. What happened to the man who'd killed the prime minister?

answers on page 377

J.M.W. TURNER
1775 – 1851

1. Born in London in 1851, Turner was only fourteen years old when he enrolled at which institution?

2. Which 1796 painting by Turner showed a view of boats off the Isle of Wight at night?

3. Which Yorkshire landowner commissioned Turner to paint watercolours of the area surrounding his home near Otley?

4. Turner became more eccentric as he grew older. He never married, but he is believed to have fathered two daughters with which older widow?

5. Which 1839 oil painting by Turner depicts a Royal Navy ship being towed away so that it can be broken up for scrap?

6. Turner's friend Edward Thomas Daniell commissioned a portrait of the artist by which painter?

7. What was the title of Turner's early 19th century collection of prints, which includes over a hundred paintings?

8. In 1841, Turner famously rowed a boat out on the Thames, in order to avoid what?

9. Turner died in 1851 and left a small fortune. The main part of the Turner Bequest was housed in the National Gallery of British Art, which is now known by what name?

10. A portrait of Turner appears on which item, which came into circulation in Britain on February 20th 2020?

answers on page 377

JOHN CONSTABLE
1776 – 1837

1. Born in Essex in 1776, Constable initially joined his father working in which business?

2. In 1779, Constable entered the Royal Academy Schools. One of his early landscape paintings is a view of which green space near Colchester?

3. What was the name of Constable's childhood friend, who he eventually married (after conflict with her family) in 1816?

4. In 1819, Constable's first major sale, a view of a tow-horse being transported across a river, had which title?

5. What name is generally given to a series of large paintings that Constable produced during this period?

6. Originally titled *Landscape: Noon*, which 1821 painting depicts a rural scene on the River Stour?

7. One of Constable's most famous paintings, from 1823, shows a view of which English cathedral?

8. Constable was particularly popular in France during his lifetime, and is widely credited with inspiring which movement that embraced Realism?

9. Constable died in 1837, and was buried along with his wife in which part of London?

10. What name is generally given to the area around Dedham Vale that was made famous by many of the artist's paintings?

answers on page 378

JANE AUSTEN
1775 – 1817

1. Jane Austen was born in 1775 in which Hampshire village, where her father George served as rector of the parish?

2. When she was young, she nearly died when she caught which infectious disease?

3. What name is given to the collection of work, divided into three notebooks, that Austen produced during her childhood?

4. Which early Austen work, published after her death, is about a widow who causes trouble while visiting her brother?

5. Catherine Moreland is the protagonist of which Austen novel, completed in 1803 and published in 1807?

6. *Sense and Sensibility* was published anonymously in 1811. Instead of featuring Austen's name, the title page carries what three-word reference to its author?

7. In Austen's 1813 novel *Price and Prejudice*, what's Mr. Darcy's first name?

8, Which unfinished novel, originally titled *The Brothers*, tells the story of a small town that becomes a fashionable resort?

9. Which publisher purchased the rights to Austen's novels and re-released them in the 1830s, helping them gain greater popularity than before?

10. Who wrote *A Memoir of Jane Austen* (1869), which helped to popularise her work after her death?

answers on page 378

WILLIAM IV
1765 – 1837, reigned 1830 - 1837

1. George IV died without any legitimate heirs, so he was succeeded as king by his brother William. What was William's nickname, derived from his youth spent in the Royal Navy?

2. William was appointed to which naval position in 1827?

3. In his twenties, William moved in with which popular stage actress?

4. Which major London royal residence was built for William in the late 1820s?

5. William eventually married which German-born princess?

6. When he became king, William refused to have a lavish coronation ceremony. This led to the event being given what label by his critics?

7. The 1832 Reform Act saw the first legal ban on what happening at elections?

8. In 1833, the Slavery Abolition Act was passed, banning slavery in the British Empire with the exception of which three situations?

9. In 1834, William became the last monarch (to date) to do what, in relation to the appointment of a prime minister?

10. Shortly before his death in 1837, William had a very public disagreement with which figure?

answers on page 379

THE BRONTË SISTERS

1. What was the name of the imaginary North Pacific island created by Emily and Annie Brontë when they were young?

2. All four Brontë siblings were subsequently involved in the creation of another fictional world. What was this called?

3. What was the name of the Brontë sisters' brother, who translated numerous classics into English and also worked as a portrait-painter?

4. When they first published their work, the Brontë sisters shared which pseudonymous surname?

5. In Emily's book *Wuthering Heights*, what's the name of the new tenant who arrives at Thrushcross Grange?

6. At the start of Charlotte's novel Jane Eyre, 10-year-old Jane lives with her uncle's family at which house?

7. What's the name of the mysterious woman who rents the mansion in Anne's *The Tenant of Wildfell Hall*?

8. What was the name of Emily's dog?

9. Who wrote the 1857 biography *The Life of Charlotte Brontë*, which helped to popularise not only Charlotte herself but also her two sister?

10. The Brontë Parsonage Museum, housed in the family's former home, is located in which West Yorkshire village?

answers on page 379

SIR ROBERT PEEL
1788 – 1850, PM 1834 – 1835, 1841 – 1846

1. Robert Peel was born in Lancashire in 1788. His father was a wealthy manufacturer in which industry?

2. At Harrow School, Peel was a contemporary of which poet?

3. As Home Secretary in 1827, Peel opposed Catholic emancipation and subsequently earned which nickname?

4. What name is given to the 1939 crisis that occurred when Peel and others asked Queen Victoria to include more Tories in her household?

5. Peel's work modernising the police led to officers gaining two nicknames. What were they?

6. The Mines and Collieries Act of 1842 banned women from working in mines, and set what minimum age for boys?

7. What form of tax was reintroduced to Britain in 1842, at a rate of 2.9%?

8. In 1843, Peel was the target of a failed assassination attempt. The trial of the would-be assassin, Edward Drummond, gave rise to which type of criminal defence?

9. In 1846, Peel was forced to resign after he joined with opposition forces to repeal the Corn Laws. This was deemed necessary as a response to which event abroad?

10. Peel is generally regarded as one of the founders of which modern-day political party?

answers on page 380

THE METROPOLITAN POLICE

1. Prior to the establishment of the Metropolitan Police in 1829, what was the name of the detective force that is widely seen as London's first professional police force?

2. The Industrial Revolution saw an increase in London's population. Home Secretary (and future prime minister) Robert Peel set up the Metropolitan Police. What was the name of the first officer who was killed in the line of duty?

3. Although it was supposed to appear civilian, the force was allowed to purchase fifty examples of what weapon?

4. The Stratton Brothers case of 1905 saw the first conviction in the UK secured by the use of what type of evidence?

5. What award was introduced following the 1909 Tottenham Outrage?

6. Which 1911 event saw two Latvian revolutionaries seek refuge from the police in a house in Stepney?

7. Sofia Stanley holds what distinction?

8. What name is used for the force's headquarters, even though the building is now on Victoria Embankment?

9. What was the name of the investigation, conducted between 1978 and 1982, that sought to uncover evidence of corruption in London police forces?

10. In 2017, who became the first woman to serve as Commissioner of the Metropolitan Police Service?

answers on page 380

THE ISLE OF MAN

1. The Isle of Man became an island around 8,500 years ago. What name is given to the island's largest megalithic tomb, located in the village of Laxey?

2. What name is given to the Stone Age culture that existed on the Isle of Man from around the year 3,000 BC?

3. What's the name of the ancient sea god who, according to myth, once ruled the island?

4. Which 11th century Norse ruler was responsible for the construction of Peel Castle?

5. In the 13th century, which Scottish king finally secured the Isle of Man, which had previously been held by the Norse kings?

6. What's the name of the Isle of Mann's parliament?

7. Thomas Stanley, who died in 1504, was the last to use which title?

8. The 1765 Isle of Man Purchase Act saw the British Crown purchase the feudal rights of the island from which family?

9. Which town was the capital of the Isle of Mann until 1869, at which point that role was taken by the town of Douglas?

10. The three members of which pop group were born on the Isle of Man in the late 1940s?

answers on page 380

THE RNLI

1. Which soldier and philanthropist founded the RNLI as the National Institution for the Preservation of Life from Shipwreck in March 1824?

2. Who was appointed as the RNLI's first president?

3. In 1851, which naval commander and politician became the RNLI's new president and oversaw a major reorganisation?

4. In 1851, boat builder James Beeching came up with which important invention, which revolutionised the RNLI's fleet?

5. What's the name of the structure erected on St. Mary's Isle near the Isle of Man in 1832, following the rescue of the crew of RMS St. George a few years earlier?

6. The biggest rescue in the charity's history came in 1907, when all 456 passengers were rescued from which liner near Cornwall's Lizard Point?

7. In 1914, six lifeboats went to the aid of the hospital ship SS Rohilla, which had run aground off the coast of which town?

8. In February 1936, which lifeboat was involved in the rescue of the crew of a lighthouse ship named the Comet?

9. In 1940, lifeboats from Ramsgate and Margate were among the RNLI boats that were involved in which major operation?

10. In April 1947, eight lifeboat crew-members died in which incident off the coast of Wales?

answers on page 381

THE ISLE OF WIGHT

1. Who, in the 7th century, was the last Jutish King of the Isle of Wight and probably Anglo-Saxon England's last pagan king?

2. Which battle in July 1545 saw the English halt a French advance across the island?

3. Who was imprisoned in the island's Carisbrooke Castle from 1647 until shortly before his execution over a year later?

4. Which famous shipbuilding firm, based in East Cowes from the early 19th century, became one of the world's leading constructors of naval and merchant ships?

5. Which military installation was built in the 19th century to guard the Solent against possible French attacks?

6. In 1878, who demonstrated an early version of the telephone to Queen Victoria, by placing a call to Cowes?

7. The world's first paid telegram, sent from the Isle of Wight in 1898, was known by what name?

8. Which architect, who was born in London in 1856, subsequently moved to the Isle of Wight and is responsible for the Queen Victoria Memorial in Newport?

9. During the Second World War, which British plan aimed to construct submarine oil pipelines from the Isle of Wight to France in support of Operation Overlord?

10. Which American singer-songwriter opened the Woodstock Festival in 1969 and closed the Isle of Wight Festival in 1970?

answers on page 381

VICTORIA
1819 – 1901, reigned 1837 - 1901

1. What was Victoria's actual first name?

2. Early in her reign, Victoria's popularity suffered due to a scandal involving one of her ladies-in-waiting, who some said was pregnant out of wedlock. What was the woman's name?

3. Victoria and Albert had nine children, who married into royal houses across the continent. What sobriquet did she earn as a result?

4. Due to her closeness with the prime minister, Victoria was often jeered early in her reign and was given which nickname?

5. Victoria's popularity improved after she married Albert, but she was the target of a number of assassination attempts. Who was the first man who tried to shoot her, in 1840?

6. Victoria avoided public appearances following the death of her husband. What was her nickname during this period?

7. Later, she began to rely heavily on a Scottish manservant. What was his name?

8. What was the name of the Muslim 'munshi' who attended to Victoria in her later life?

9. Victoria died in 1901. She was the last British monarch of which house?

10. Who designed the Victoria Memorial, which stands outside Buckingham Palace at the end of The Mall in London?

answers on page 382

PRINCE ALBERT
1819 - 1861

1. Albert was born in August 1819, at which castle near Coburg in Germany?

2. Albert was a member of which ducal house?

3. After his marriage to Victoria, Albert was eventually given the title Prince Consort. What title was he almost given instead?

4. Albert is said to have taken a disliking to Baroness Lehzen, who ran the royal household. What nickname did he give her?

5. In 1844 Albert purchased Osborne House as a private residence for the royal family. Where is Osborne House located?

6. In 1847, Albert was elected to which position?

7. When Russia attacked an Ottoman fleet in 1853, false rumours in London claimed that Albert had suffered what fate?

8. In November 1861, Albert personally intervened to help defuse which crisis that briefly threatened war between Britain and the United States?

9. Albert died in December 1861. Contemporary doctors claimed that he had been suffering from which condition?

10. Who designed the Albert Memorial, which is located in Kensington Gardens in London?

answers on page 382

CHARLES DICKENS
1812 - 1870

1. Charles Dickens was born in February 1812 in which city?

2. At the age of 12, while his parents were in Marshalsea debtors' prison in Southwark, Dickens left school and worked where?

3. Dickens eventually began to work as a junior clerk for a law firm. After trying to become an actor, what was the title of the first short story he submitted for publication?

4. What nickname did Dickens adopt when he started writing newspaper sketches?

5. Dickens was invited to write a series of texts to accompany engraved illustrations. These eventually formed which novel?

6. In 1836, Dickens married Catherine Hogarth. However, he later began a long-term relationship with which actress?

7. Illustrator Habolt Knight Browne, who provided images for many Dickens novels, worked under which pen-name?

8. Dickens had a number of pets named Grip, which were all which type of animal?

9. In 1865, Dickens was returning from Paris when he was involved in a train crash close to which Kent village?

10. Following his death in 1870, Dickens was buried at Poets' Corner in Westminster Abbey. This was contrary to his wishes, as he had asked to be buried at which location?

answers on page 382

CHARLES BABBAGE & ADA LOVELACE
1791 – 1871 & 1815 - 1852

1. Born in 1791, Babbage is often referred to by what title?

2. Born in 1815, Ada Lovelace was the daughter of which English poet?

3. In 1812, Babbage helped to form which group, which aimed to promote the use of Leibnizian notation?

4. Ada's parents separated when she was very young. Which Scottish scientist and polymath became her tutor?

5. Babbage was one of the key figures in the formation of which organisation in 1820?

6. What name was given to Babbage's theory that workers should be assigned to tasks that match their skill level?

7. Created in the 1820s, what was the name of the automatic mechanical calculator that was able to carry out common mathematical functions?

8. First described in 1837, what was the name of Babbage's machine that came to form the logical structure of modern computer design?

9. Ada Lovelace is often regarded as the first computer programmer, and with creating the first example of what kind of computational instruction?

10. Which video game and electronics retailer started out in Dallas, Texas with the name Babbage's?

answers on page 383

ISAMBARD KINGDOM BRUNEL
1806 - 1859

1. Born in Portsmouth in 1806, Brunel studied in France and eventually worked under which master clockmaker?

2. One of Brunel's first projects was the Thames Tunnel. Contemporary sources claimed that the design of Brunel's tunnelling equipment was inspired by which creature?

3. Brunel was elected in 1830 as a fellow of which London organisation?

4. In 1831, construction began on which bridge, which spans the River Avon?

5. Two years later, Brunel was appointed chief designer of which railway network?

6. Which station, designed by Brunel, opened in 1854 as the London terminus of the new line referred to in the previous question?

7. What controversial decision did Brunel make when he began to work on the railway system?

8. Which bridge, designed by Brunel and opened in 1845, crossed the Thames close to the site of Charing Cross station?

9. What name was given to Brunel's pre-fabricated hospital that was designed to be shipped to Crimea during the war?

10. Brunel died in September 1859, and was buried at which location in London?

answers on page 383

THE GREAT EXHIBITION OF 1851

1. The Great Exhibition was primarily organised by Prince Albert and which British civil servant?

2. Where did the exhibition take place?

3. Who directed the exhibition's opening music?

4. The exhibition included the first modern example of what facility, which cost 1p to use?

5. One of the exhibits was the Koh-i-Noor (the Mountain of Light), which at the time was the world's largest example of what?

6. A man named William Chamberlin Jr. used the exhibition to present what type of machine?

7. Which firearms manufacturer showed off a number of weapons, including Walker and Dragoon revolvers?

8. Frederick Bakewell demonstrated an early example of what machine?

9. One stand helped to popularise pottery, leading to a craze for what material?

10. Once the exhibition was over, it was found to have made a large profit. This money was used to found the Victoria & Albert Museum and a number of other sites, in a part of London that subsequently gained which nickname?

answers on page 384

BLACKPOOL

1. What name is generally given to a 13,500-year-old animal skeleton that was discovered near Blackpool in 1970?

2. Which 19th century landowner is often referred to as the 'Father of Blackpool'?

3. In the mid-19th century, Blackpool became a popular seaside resort. Who designed the Central Pier, which opened in 1868?

4. Blackpool's success was aided by a tradition that saw factories close for a week so that they could be serviced and repaired. What name was generally given to this tradition?

5. Who was the first mayor of Blackpool, after the town was granted a Charter of Incorporation in 1876?

6. What was founded in 1896 by A.W.G. Bean and John Outhwaite?

7. In the late 1800s, Blackpool was a regular holiday destination for employees of which Staffordshire brewery?

8. Audrey Mosson, who turned on the Blackpool Illuminations in 1935 and again in 1985, was known as the 10th holder of which title?

9. In 1937, Blackpool was the home to the first high-street store opened by which company?

10. Which squadron, formed in Blackpool in 1940, claimed the largest number of aircraft shot down during the Battle of Britain?

answers on page 384

THE CRIMEAN WAR
1853 – 1856

1. What name is given to the 19ᵗʰ century plan that aimed to maintain the balance of power, and territorial integrity, of existing European nations?

2. The Crimean War followed a series of disagreements between France and Russia. France supported the rights of Roman Catholics in the Holy Land. Who did Russia support?

3. Who was the ruler of Russia during the Crimean War?

4. In July 1853, Russia occupied Moldavia and Wallachia, which were better known together under which name?

5. The Ottomans suffered a major defeat at a sea port on the Black Sea shore, in which battle?

6. British, French and Egyptian forces subsequently defeated a Russian force in September 1854 in which battle?

7. One month later, the Battle of Balaclava took place, with the Allies attempting to capture which Russian naval base?

8. During this stage of the war, who led the famous British Charge of the Light Brigade?

9. Who wrote a famous poem about the Charge of the Light Brigade, which was published a month later?

10. The Russians eventually sued for peace, which came after which the Treaty of Paris of 1856. This treaty made what declaration regarding the Black Sea?

answers on page 384

FLORENCE NIGHTINGALE
1820 – 1910

1. Florence Nightingale was born at Villa Colombaia, in which European city?

2. Following the outbreak of the Crimean War in 1853, Nightingale and her nurses travelled to which barracks?

3. Who did Nightingale appoint as her head nurse at the barracks?

4. Members of which Irish order arrived to assist with nursing duties?

5. What nickname did Nightingale gain during the Crimean War, following a report in The Times?

6. What was the title of her 1859 book about nursing procedures?

7. In 1860, Nightingale set up a training school at which London hospital?

8. Nightingale went on to train which woman, who is regarded as the first professionally trained American nurse?

9. In 1883, Nightingale was the first recipient of the Royal Red Cross. In 1907, she became the first women to receive the Order of Merit. In 1908, she was granted which honour?

10. Nightingale died in 1910. She was one of the historical figures feature in the book *Eminent Victorians*, by which author?

answers on page 385

MARY SEACOLE
1805 – 1881

1. Mary Jane Grant was born in Kingston, Jamaica in 1805. Her mother had which nickname, due to her work with local medicines?

2. Her father was a soldier from which country?

3. In 1836, Mary Grant married Edwin Seacole. Some claims suggest that Seacole was an illegitimate son of which British figure?

4. Following the outbreak of the Crimean War, Seacole established a hospital in the region. What name was given to this hospital?

5. After returning to London, Seacole was declared bankrupt. What was the title of her book, published in 1857, which was the first autobiography written by a black woman in Britain?

6. Around this time, her work in the Crimea was criticised in a letter written by which figure?

7. In 1871, a marble bust in her likeness was created by which sculptor, who was also a nephew of Queen Victoria?

8. By the following year, she was also working as a personal masseuse for which royal figure?

9. In 1991, Seacole was posthumously awarded which honour?

10. Thirteen years later, in 2004, Mary Seacole topped which poll organised by the BBC?

answers on page 385

THE GREAT STINK OF 1858

1. In the year 1831, London suffered its first major outbreak of which infection?

2. Which social reformer was instrumental in the 1848 establishment of the Metropolitan Commission of Sewers?

3. Which scientist, writing in 1855, warned that the entire River Thames was effectively a sewer?

4. Which theory, popular in the mid-19th century, suggested that contagious diseases were spread through bad air?

5. Which 1855 – 1857 serial (later a novel) by Charles Dickens mentions the terrible smells of the River Thames?

6. By mid-1858, the stench from the river was so bad that business in Parliament suffered. One extreme attempt to solve the problem involved soaking curtains in what substance?

7. Which civil engineer created a new sewer system for London, thereby starting to alleviate the problem?

8. Three embankments had to be built to allow the sewers to drain. What is the name of these embankments, which still exist today?

9. What was the name of the pumping station, built next to the Erith marshes, that was used to move sewage from the river?

10. What name was given to the first sludge boat, commissioned in 1887, that was designed to transport effluent to the North Sea for dumping?

answers on page 386

THE RIVER THAMES

1. The river's name is said to come from its old Brittonic name, Tamesas, which is believed to have had what meaning?

2. Part of the river running through Oxford is sometimes referred to by which other name?

3. The source of the Thames is often said to be at Thames Head in the Cotswolds. Some sources, however, claim that the source is at which location near Cheltenham?

4. During the Middle Ages, an island existed on the Thames called Thorney Island. What buildings are now on this spot?

5. What's the name of the largest island on the London stretch of the Thames?

6. A previous London Bridge was subsequently sold and now stands in which location?

7. What name is given to the festivities that were often held on the tideway of the river, up until the 19th century, during periods of severe bad weather?

8. St. John's Lock features a statue, by Raffaelle Monti, of which figure?

9. The Thames Tunnel, originally constructed in the mid-19th century for horse-drawn carriages, was the first tunnel built under a navigable river. What is it used for now?

10. What's the title of Jerome K. Jerome's 1889 book about a boating holiday on the Thames?

answers on page 386

THE BRITISH EMPIRE

1. At its greatest extent, in 1920, the British Empire covered 26.35% of the world. Which empire, with 17.81%, comes second on the list?

2. What name is generally given to the 15th and 16th century period during which European nations began to explore the globe and establish colonies?

3. What name is given to the period between 1815 and 1914, during which Britain was an unrivalled global power?

4. The 1888 Convention of Constantinople dealt with British and French rivalry by establishing a zone of neutrality around which important location?

5. What name is given to the centre or homeland of an empire?

6. Which island voted in 1956 for integration with the United Kingdom?

7. In 1960, Harold Macmillan gave a speech in South Africa. What name is given to this speech, in which he asserted that Britain was willing to accept decolonisation in Africa?

8. The 1979 Lancaster House Agreement formally recognised the independence of Rhodesia, under which new name?

9. The constitution of which country was finally patriated in 1982, ending British involvement in their governance?

10. Some historians consider the end of the British Empire to have come in 1997, with the handover of which colony?

answers on page 386

THE EAST INDIA COMPANY
1600 - 1874

1. The East India Company received a royal charter at the end of 1600 from which monarch?

2. Who was appointed as the company's first Governor?

3. In 1612, trying to gain influence abroad, the company achieved victory over the Portuguese at which battle in western India?

4. For most of its existence, the company was based at East India House, in which part of London?

5. In 1695, the company's position in India was imperilled when a Mughal convoy was attacked by which English pirate?

6. Which event in 1773 saw East India Company cargo thrown into an American harbour?

7. The company's Bengal opium was smuggled into China. The ensuing First Opium War (1839 – 1842) ended with China agreeing to cede which island to Britain?

8. Many of the company's ships had the prefix HCS in their titles. What did HCS stand for?

9. The East India Club, initially formed for officers of the company, still exists in which part of London?

10. The company lost India in 1857 and was dissolved in 1874. The company's fall led to the establishment of which new system of British rule in India?

answers on page 387

THE BRITISH RAJ
1858 - 1947

1. Following the Indian Rebellion of 1857, the British East India Company's rule was transferred to the Crown. Who became the first Viceroy of India under the new regime?

2. What name was generally given to the semi-sovereign principalities that existed in India at this time, which were not directly ruled by the British but still suffered interference?

3. Which political party, founded in 1885, was the first modern nationalist movement to emerge in the British Empire?

4. Which women's rights and education activist was a key figure in the emancipation of women in India?

5. What name was used for members of the lowest caste in India?

6. The 1905 Partition of Bengal was carried out by which figure, who served as Viceroy of India from 1899 to 1905?

7. Which activist and lawyer was known for undertaking long fasts, and led the 1930 Salt March?

8. In 1943, an estimated 3 million people died in a famine in which part of India?

9. What name is generally given to the day of nationwide riots on 16th August 1946, which left thousands dead?

10. The Partition of India, which occurred in 1947, divided British India into which two independent countries?

answers on page 387

CHARLES DARWIN
1809 - 1882

1. Charles Darwin was born in Shrewsbury in 1809. What was the name of the family home?

2. Darwin's grandfather Erasmus Darwin had already published a theory of common descent in which 1794 book?

3. After studying at Cambridge, Darwin was invited to join a voyage to South America aboard which vessel?

4. Who wrote the 1830s book *Principles of Geology*, which greatly influenced Darwin's work?

5. What was the name of Darwin's wife, who also happened to be his first cousin?

6. Darwin was also influenced by the work of Thomas Robert Malthus. What was the fundamental theory behind the idea of the Malthusian catastrophe?

7. Darwin made some of his most important observations concerning evolution on which archipelago of volcanic islands in the Pacific Ocean?

8. What was the title of Darwin's 1859 book, in which he laid out the foundations of evolutionary biology?

9. More than a decade later, Darwin published which book that applied evolutionary theory to human evolution?

10. Darwin died in April 1882, most likely of which illness?

answers on page 388

BIG BEN

1. Big Ben is the name of the largest bell, but the tower was referred to by what name during the reign of Queen Victoria?

2. The tower was part of the new Palace of Westminster, after the old palace was destroyed by fire in 1834. Charles Barry designed the palace, but who designed the tower?

3. How many steps are there, in the climb from ground level to the tower's belfry?

4. In 1880, atheist MP Charles Bradlaugh earned what distinction?

5. What name is given to the light, installed in 1873, that shines above the tower's belfry whenever the House of Commons sits at night?

6. The clock's speed can be increased or decreased by 0.4 seconds per day, by the manipulation of a stack of what item on the pendulum?

7. Erected in 1892, Little Ben is a much smaller clock tower located close to which train station?

8. What's the name of the twenty-note tune played by the quarter bells?

9. The origin of the name Big Ben is unclear, but it's thought to possibly refer to either Sir Benjamin Hall, how oversaw the bell's installation, or which heavyweight boxing champion?

10. Since 2012 the tower has been known by what name?

answers on page 388

BENJAMIN DISRAELI
1804 – 1881, PM 1868 & 1874 - 1880

1. Born in Bloomsbury in 1804, Disraeli is (as of 2021) the only British prime minister to have been born into which religion?

2. What was the title of his first novel, released in 1826, about a young man who attempts to enter the political world?

3. Disraeli became an MP while still in his 30s. In 1852, he served as Chancellor of the Exchequer in which short-lived government under Lord Derby?

4. Disraeli's first term as prime minister lasted less than a year, and was dominated by debate over which institution?

5. He became prime minister again in 1874. The following year, he arranged for a 100m franc purchase of a 44% share in which crucial transport operation?

6. In 1876, Disraeli pushed through the controversial Royal Titles Act, which gave Queen Victoria which new title?

7. The same year, Disraeli was elevated to which earldom?

8. Two years later, Disraeli was a central figure at which diplomatic meeting, which aimed to reorganise states in the Balkans following the Russo-Turkish War?

9. Disraeli is said to have coined which phrase, which describes a form of British politics?

10. Disraeli died in 1881. Queen Victoria wasn't allowed to attend his funeral. What did she send instead?

answers on page 389

WILLIAM EWART GLADSTONE
1809 – 1898, PM 1868 – 1874, 1880 – 1885, 1886 & 1892 - 1894

1. Born in 1809 in Liverpool, William Ewart Gladstone was the son of John Gladstone. Many years later, John received compensation following the abolition of which practice?

2. Gladstone was responsible for which 1844 act, which is seen as having marked the birth of the regulatory British state?

3. Around 1858, Gladstone took up which noisy outdoor hobby, for which he became somewhat notorious?

4. Gladstone became prime minister in 1868. He repealed duties on many basic food items, leading to the realisation of which common demand of the time?

5. Gladstone was popular with working-class voters, and accordingly was given which nickname?

6. What name is given to Gladstone's late 1870s speeches, which are regarded as having formed the first modern political campaign?

7. What was the title of Gladstone's 1876 pamphlet, which attacked Disraeli's handling of the Ottoman Empire?

8. In 1882, Gladstone ordered the bombardment of which city?

9. In 1886, Gladstone headed a short third government, during which he failed to push through what bill relating to Ireland?

10. Who succeeded Gladstone as prime minister after he retired in 1894?

answers on page 389

JACK THE RIPPER
active in 1888

1. Jack the Ripper's confirmed murders all took place in and around which area of London?

2. What was the name of the first confirmed victim, who died in August 1888?

3. What was the name of the chief inspector who was put in charge of the investigation?

4. Before the name Jack the Ripper was used, the killer was generally known by what title?

5. Following the murder of Catherine Eddowes, part of her apron was found nearby with graffiti on a wall. What name is given to this graffiti?

6. Which letter, claiming to be from the killer, was delivered along with half a preserved human kidney?

7. Who served as chairman of a special vigilance committee at the time of the murders?

8. An opinion written by police surgeon Thomas Bond, speculating on the murderer's abilities, is generally regarded as the first example of what crime-fighting device?

9. What happened to the majority of the original police files from the case?

10. In a 2002 book, crime novelist Patricia Cornwell claimed that Jack the Ripper was in fact which English painter?

answers on page 389

FOOD

1. Olive oil, gourds and cloves are first mentioned in which 14th century collection of recipes?

2. What name is generally given to the phenomenon, beginning in the late 15th century, that saw the transfer of food (among other things) between the New and the Old worlds?

3. Which king, who requested plum pudding as part of a Christmas feast, was referred to as The Pudding King?

4. Hannah Glasse's 1747 cookbook *The Art of Cookery Made Plain and Easy* is believed to contain the first published recipe for which item, previously referred to as 'dripping pudding'?

5. Authentic cullen skink, from Scotland, is supposed to use what type of haddock?

6. Opened by Sake Dean Mahomed in London in 1810, what was the name of England's first Indian restaurant?

7. Which Welsh meal, commonly a lamb or beef soup with vegetables, is often regarded as a national dish of Wales?

8. Who is said to have opened the first Chinese restaurant in Britain, Maxim's in Soho, in 1908?

9. Who opened his first fish and chips restaurant in Guiseley, West Yorkshire, in 1928?

10. Which British chef and restaurant critic, along with her husband Johnnie, began writing a Daily Telegraph column in 1950 under the pen name Bon Viveur?

answers on page 390

DRINK

1. Which 17ᵗʰ century English queen, wife of Charles II, is generally credited with having popularised tea in England?

2. Which brewer, established in Faversham in 1698, is the oldest in Britain?

3. *Gin Lane* (1751), designed to illustrate the perils of gin consumption, is an illustration by which English artist?

4. Robert and Mary White began making what drink in Camberwell, London in 1845?

5. In 1873, Cardinal Henry Manning launched which Roman Catholic total abstinence society?

6. Which drink was first produced by the Scottish firm A.G. Barr in 1901?

7. What was founded, in 1908, to provide support to the UK government's hospitality work?

8. In 1924, Yorkshiremen Fred and Tom Pickup launched a drink called Pickup's Appetizer. What is this drink called today?

9. S.M. Lennox of Bristol is credited with naming which drink in 1938?

10. What was the name of the character, created by Giles Andreae, that featured in a number of 1990s and 2000s adverts for Vimto?

answers on page 390

CECIL RHODES
1853 - 1902

1. Born in 1853, Rhodes suffered ill health as a child. He was eventually sent to live with his aunt on which island?

2. In the early 1880s he entered South African politics, and in 1894 he oversaw which law, which limited the amount of land that black South Africans were allowed to hold in the country?

3. Which railway line, which was never completed, did Rhodes hope would span the entire continent of Africa?

4. What was the name of the Polish princess who claimed at one time that she was engaged to Rhodes?

5. During the Boer War, Rhodes was involved in the defence of which besieged city?

6. What's the name of the diamond company, formed by Rhodes in 1888, that still exists in the 21st century?

7. The same year, Rhodes finally managed to get a mining concession from Lobengula, the king of which region?

8. Rhodes died in 1902, of heart failure, at his cottage in which South African seaside town?

9. Following his death, the postgraduate Rhodes Scholarship was established at which university?

10. What name was given from 1965 to 1979 to an unrecognised South African state, with the territory later changing its name to Zimbabwe?

answers on page 391

ROBERT GASCOYNE-CECIL
1830 – 1903, PM 1885 – 1886, 1886 – 1892 & 1895 – 1902

1. Robert Gascoyne-Cecil, a descendant of Queen Elizabeth I's advisor William Cecil, was born in 1830 at which Hertfordshire country house?

2. Gascoyne-Cecil entered politics as an MP in 1853. What title did he inherit from his father the following decade?

3. In 1888, Gascoyne-Cecil caused controversy by suggesting that British voters would not elect what type of MP?

4. For much of his time as prime minister, Gascoyne-Cecil unusually also occupied which position in government?

5. Which British policy, supported by Gascoyne-Cecil, saw Britain avoid permanent alliances?

6. In 1890, Gascoyne-Cecil's government issued an ultimatum to which country, concerning land claims in Africa?

7. In 1895, a crisis erupted between Britain and the United States over the border between British Guiana and which country?

8. At the end of the same year, which incident in the South African Republic presaged the Boer War?

9. Three years later, British control over Egypt was confirmed following which brief dispute with France?

10. Gascoyne-Cecil died in 1903. To date, he was the last prime minister to serve from which position?

answers on page 391

SIR EDWARD ELGAR
1857 – 1934

1. Edward Elgar was born in Worcestershire in 1857. Which 1908 set of suites was based on a composition that he'd originally composed when he was ten years old?

2. In 1882, Elgar was employed as a violin player in a Birmingham orchestra led by which organist and conductor?

3. One of his first major pieces, a concert overture from 1890, was inspired by the work of which 14th century French author?

4. Elgar's Variations on an Original Theme, Op. 36 is an orchestral work better known by what title?

5. Who wrote the poem that was used as the text for Elgar's 1900 piece The Dream of Gerontius, Op. 38?

6. The Pomp and Circumstance Marches take their title from a line in which William Shakespeare play?

7. Singer Clara Butt is widely credited with persuading Elgar to include lyrics for the trio theme from the Pomp and Circumstance March. How is this song now better known?

8. Which poet and academic wrote the lyrics for the afore-mentioned piece?

9. In 1924, Elgar was appointed to which position in the Royal Household?

10. Elgar was a fan of Wolverhampton Wanders F.C. What was the title of the anthem he composed for the club?

answers on page 391

W.S. GILBERT & ARTHUR SULLIVAN
1836 – 1911 & 1842 - 1900

1. William Schwenck Gilbert was born in 1836 in London. What's the title of the light verses that he wrote and illustrated in the 1960s for the magazine *Fun*?

2. Arthur Sullivan was born in 1842, also in London. In 1856, he was the first ever recipient of which scholarship from the Royal Academy of Music?

3. Starting in 1869, Gilbert worked with which figure, who was trying to raise London theatres from a state of disrepute?

4. In 1871, Gilbert and Sullivan were brought together by producer John Hollingshead. What was the title of their first collaboration, a Christmas piece about the Greek gods?

5. Gilbert and Sullivan are widely seen as two of the key practitioners of which popular 19th century musical style?

6. One of their early successes was based on Gilbert's story *The Elixir of Love*. What was the title of the resulting opera?

7. Nanki-Poo, Ko-Ko and Pooh-Bah feature in which opera?

8. Which company, still in existence today, staged Gilbert and Sullivan operas year-round during the 20th century?

9. What name is generally given to the disagreement that erupted between Gilbert and Sullivan over expenses in 1890?

10. What was the title of their final opera, which was released in 1896 shortly before their relationship permanently soured?

answers on page 392

THE LONDON UNDERGROUND

1. Opened in 1863 in London, what was the world's first underground railway line?

2. What name is given to the method, used early in the underground railway's construction, in which a trench is dug and then a roof section is place on top?

3. When it opened in 1900, the Central Line quickly gained what nickname?

4. Which American businessman founded a company in 1902 to take control of several Underground lines, including the Baker Street and Waterloo Railway?

5. What typeface, commissioned in 1913, is used on signs across the London Underground?

6. Who designed the famous diagrammatic tube map, which first appeared in 1933?

7. During the Second World War, many stations were used as air-raid shelters. In March 1943, 173 people died in a crowd crush incident at which station?

8. Which organisation was created in 2000 and is responsible for most public transport in London?

9. As of 2021, what's the deepest station on the London Underground?

10. A number of films, including the James Bond film *Skyfall*, have shot scenes on a disused platform at which station?

answers on page 392

EARLY BRITISH CINEMA

1. The oldest surviving film clip known to exist was recorded by French inventor Louis Le Prince in 1888. What's its title?

2. Which British inventor's work included an 1889 camera and an early colour film system he called Biocolour?

3. What's the title of Birt Acres and Robert W. Paul's 1895 film that is generally regarded as the first successful British film?

4. Which company was founded by Will Barker in 1902?

5. Who directed films such as *Alice in Wonderland* (1903), *Rescued by Rover* (1905) and *Comin' Thro the Rye* (1923)?

6. Which American-born film-maker was a key figure in early British cinema, expanding the Warwick Trading Company and creating shows such as the Unseen World series?

7. What name is generally given to many of the British films that were rapidly produced following the passage of the Cinematograph Films Act of 1927?

8. Which Hungarian-born British film-maker founded both London Films and British Lion Films, and in 1942 became the first in his profession to receive a knighthood?

9. Directors such as Humphrey Jennings, Alberto Cavalcanti and Norman McLaren all worked for which film production company, which was a subdivision of the Post Office?

10. The first successful European film with sound was the 1929 thriller *Blackmail*, which was directed by which film-maker?

answers on page 392

LEEDS

1. The name Leeds comes from an old Brythonic word, Ladenses. What did this word mean?

2. Which Leeds merchant, a key figure in the local cloth industry, was an important local benefactor who built and endowed St. John the Evangelist's Church?

3. In 1654, which former soldier became the first MP for Leeds?

4. Which antiquarian, who was born in the city in 1658, wrote the first history of Leeds?

5. Which architect, born in Leeds in 1764, subsequently emigrated to the United States and served as the second Architect of the Capitol?

6. The world's largest woollen mill opened in Leeds in 1788. What was its name?

7. Which brewery was founded in 1822 in Hunslet, which is now a suburb of Leeds?

8. In February 1865, a riot broke out following the imprisonment of a local woman named Eliza Stafford. What had she been accused of stealing?

9. In 1916, 35 women were killed in an explosion at which site?

10. In the 1920s, which Lithuanian-born businessman established the world's largest textile factory in the Harehills area of Leeds?

answers on page 393

THE BOER WAR
1899 - 1902

1. In Dutch and Afrikaans, the word 'boer' means what?

2. Although British and Dutch forces had long struggled for domination of southern Africa, matters came to a head in 1884 following the discovery of the Witwatersrand gold mines. The resulting gold rush led to the establishment of which city?

3. The first phase of the war saw several Boer victories. British prospects improved with the arrival of which military leader?

4. Who led the South African Republic during the conflict?

5. In October 1899, the British suffered a major defeat while trying to defend which city?

6. The ensuing siege lasted for more than three months. On December 25th, the Boers fired a carrier shell into the city. This shell had no fuse, and instead contained what gift?

7. In 1900, British soldiers captured which city?

8. As the Boers began to conduct guerilla warfare, which British leader adopted a scorched earth policy against the enemy?

9. Which Boer leader led a series of successful attacks from his base in the Orange Free State?

10. The war ended with a British victory in 1902. A memorial in Port Elizabeth, South Africa pays tribute to the deaths of 300,000 animals in the war. What type of animal?

answers on page 393

BUCKINGHAM PALACE

1. In the Middle Ages, the site of Buckingham Palace was known as part of which manor?

2. The land was acquired by John Sheffield, the Duke of Buckingham, in 1698 and he commissioned the construction of what would become Buckingham House. Who designed this house?

3. In 1761, George III purchased the site, intending for it to be used as a private retreat for who?

4. Under George IV, which architect was responsible for the refurbishment of the house, turning it into a palace with a new facade?

5. What did Buckingham Palace almost become in 1834?

6. Who was the first monarch to have the palace as their official London residence?

7. The landscape design of Buckingham Palace's garden was originally by which 18th century gardener?

8. Some of the rooms in the palace are named after particular events. The 1844 Room, for example, is named after a state visit by which foreign figure?

9. Which part of the palace was destroyed by German bombs during the Second World War?

10. What river still runs below the palace?

answers on page 394

EDWARD VII
1841 – 1910, reigned 1901 – 1910

1. Born in November 1841, the future king gained which lifelong nickname as a child?

2. In 1860, Edward became the first Prince of Wales to tour North America. While there, he watched acrobat Charles Blondin perform what feat?

3. Edward's father visited him in Cambridge in 1861 to reprimand him for a rumoured affair with which actress?

4. Who did Edward marry in Windsor in March 1863?

5. Edward is credited with having introduced what traditional Sunday activity in Britain?

6. In 1891, Edward appeared as a witness in court during a scandal over his part in an illegal round of what card game?

7. As king, Edward's interest in foreign affairs – and the fact that he was related to many other royal houses – earned him which nickname?

8. In 1908, new prime minister Sir Henry Campbell-Bannerman had to travel to Biarritz to meet the king and confirm his position by performing what act?

9. The king was drawn into a crisis in 1909, when the House of Lords refused to pass which piece of legislation?

10. Edward's final words before he died in 1910 were about his horse's win at Kempton Park. What was the horse's name?

answers on page 394

ARTHUR BALFOUR
1848 – 1930, PM 1902 – 1905

1. Born in 1848, Arthur Balfour entered politics in the 1870s. In 1887, his support of the Crimes Act earned him what nickname?

2. In 1891, Balfour became the last holder of which office who was not also at the time prime minster?

3. After becoming prime minister in 1902, Balfour secured what agreement that improved relations with France?

4. Which organisation, established while Balfour was prime minister, carried out research on issues of military strategy?

5. Along with Lord Randolph Churchill and others, Balfour was a member of which political group?

6. Balfour was a leading member of which social and intellectual group, which was formed by individuals who wanted to avoid discussing politics?

7. In the 1890s, Balfour was president of which organisation that studies paranormal phenomena?

8. What name is given to his 1917 attempt – as foreign secretary – to secure US assistance in the First World War?

9. In 1924, Balfour became the first president of which sporting organisation?

10. He died in 1930, having been immobilised by what medical condition?

answers on page 394

THE SUFFRAGETTES

1. Which country, in 1893, became the first to give the vote to all women over the age of 21?

2. Which philosopher and economist became an MP in 1865, and supported votes for women during his campaign?

3. In 1881, women living in which part of Britain were the first to be given the vote, provided they owned property in their own right?

4. Who founded the British Women's Social and Political Union (WSPU) in 1903, with the aim of organising direct action and civil disobedience?

5. The WSPU used a number of methods to raise money. Pank-a-Squith and Suffragetto were examples of what item?

6. In 1909, which suffragette at Holloway Prison in London became the first to be subjected to force-feeding?

7. What was the name of the suffragette who died after being hit by a horse at the 1913 Derby?

8. What was the informal name of the suffragette group that was formed in 1913, with the aim of protecting prominent leaders from physical attack or arrest?

9. Property-owning women over 30 were first allowed to vote in the 1918 election. Who was the first woman to win a seat?

10. The following year, following a by-election, who became the first woman to take a seat in the House of Commons?

answers on page 395

MARIE STOPES
1880 – 1958

1. Born in 1880, Marie Stopes was the daughter of palaeontologist Henry Stopes and which scholar and activist?

2. Early in her career, Stopes worked to prove the theories of Eduard Suess concerning the existence of which Paleozoic supercontinent?

3. As part of this effort, Stopes acquired the assistance of which explorer?

4. What was the title of her 1918 book that aimed to bring happiness to British couples?

5. While working on this book, Stopes met which American campaigner for birth control and sex education?

6. What was the title of the book about her life, credited to Alymer Maude, that was published in 1924?

7. What did Stopes and her second husband Humphrey Roe open on Marlborough Road, North London, in March 1921?

8. Which author, who wrote the 1922 book Birth Control: A Statement of Christian Doctrine Against the Neo Malthusians, was subsequently sued by Stopes for libel?

9. What was the title of Stopes's 1923 play about working class women?

10. Since November 2020, Marie Stopes International has been known by what new name?

answers on page 395

HERBERT ASQUITH
1852 – 1928, PM 1908 – 1916

1. Asquith was born in Yorkshire in 1952. Which constituency did he represent as an MP for more than thirty years?

2. He became prime minister in 1908. Which young MP did he appoint as President of the Board of Trade?

3. What measure, established in 1909 as part of the Trade Boards Act, initially applied to chain-making, dress-making, lace-making and the paper-box industry?

4. In 1910, Asquith persuaded King Edward VII to agree to do what in the event of the Liberals winning the next election?

5. A 1914 act was the first to give devolved government to part of the UK. What part of the UK did the act cover?

6. In 1911, Britain took the French side – against Germany – in which North African crisis?

7. Which crisis, in 1915, saw Asquith heavily criticised for failing to provide enough ammunition for British troops during the First World War?

8. Alfred Harmsworth, a powerful newspaper magnate during Asquith's time in office, is better known by what title?

9. After many more years involved in politics, Asquith died in 1928. He was buried in which cemetery?

10. As of 2021, Asquith remains the last prime minister from which political party?

answers on page 396

VIRGINIA WOOLF
1882 – 1941

1. Born in 1882, Virginia Woolf was the daughter of which well-known 19th century model and philanthropist?

2. Woolf was born at which location in London, which she later used as the title of an essay?

3. With her husband Leonard, she founded which publishing company in 1917?

4. A woman named Rachel Vinrace sets out for a trip to South America in which 1915 novel, which was Woolf's first?

5. What's the first name of the title character in Woolf's 1925 novel *Mrs. Dalloway*?

6. The first and third parts of Woolf's 1927 novel *To the Lighthouse* are set on which Scottish island?

7. *Orlando: A Biography* (1928) is said to have been inspired by the family history of which author, who was Woolf's close friend and lover?

8. In 1933, Woolf wrote *Flush: A Biography*, about the life of a cocker spaniel who was owned by which English poet?

9. What was the title of Woolf's final novel, published posthumously, about preparations for a pageant at an English country house?

10. In March 1941, Virginia Woolf drowned herself in which East Sussex river?

answers on page 396

THE BLOOMSBURY GROUP

1. Apart from painter Duncan Grant, all the male members of the Bloomsbury Group were educated at which university?

2. Which philosopher, though not a member of the group, was an influential figure thanks to books such as *Principia Ethica* (1903) and the 1925 essay *A Defence of Common Sense*?

3. Which painter and designer, the sister of Virginia Woolf, was a key member of the group along with her husband?

4. Which house in Firle, East Sussex, was one of the key focal points of the group outside London?

5. Another member of the group, E.M. Forster, wrote which 1924 novel about the British Empire?

6. Which member of the group taught at the Slade School of Fine Art and helped found The Burlington Magazine?

7. Which author is said to have coined the term Bloomsberries, and subsequently established another group called the Memoir Club?

8. The group gained national attention in 1910 when they were part of which infamous hoax, in which the Royal Navy was tricked into showing their flagship to fake Abyssinian royals?

9. Which author, whose novels included *Lady Into Fox* (1922) and *Aspects of Love* (1955), was a key member of the group?

10. Who wrote the 1930 novel *The Apes of God*, in which the Bloomsbury Group was criticised as elitist?

answers on page 396

JOHN MAYNARD KEYNES
1883 – 1946

1. Born in 1883, John Maynard Keynes studied at Cambridge University, before joining which Civil Service department?

2. What was the name of the weekly discussion group that Keynes founded upon his return to Cambridge?

3. Following the First World War, Keynes tried to stop Germany being burdened by huge payment demands. He was blocked by Lord Sumner and Lord Cunfliffe, who gained which nickname as a result?

4. In which 1919 book did Keynes argue for a more generous peace than the settlement that had been determined?

5. In 1921, Keynes published a key text in the development of which mathematical theory?

6. What was the title of his 1936 book, in which he argued in favour of interventionist economic policies?

7. In 1941, Keynes was appointed to serve a term as a director of which institution?

8. In 1944, Keynes was a delegate at which US conference, which aimed to regulate international finance?

9. What was the name of the theoretical global unit of currency, developed by Keynes and E.F. Schumacher?

10. In 1965, many years after Keynes died, which American economist coined the phrase 'We are all Keynesians now'?

answers on page 397

DOCTOR CRIPPEN
1862 - 1910

1. Hawley Harvey Crippen was born in 1862 in which American state?

2. What was the name of Crippen's second wife, who was also his victim?

3. In 1897, the Crippens moved to which part of London?

4. What was the name of the stage performer and 'strongwoman' who first reported Crippen's wife missing?

5. By this point, Crippen was engaged in an affair with which woman?

6. Fearful that he was to be arrested for murder, Crippen and his lover initially fled to which country?

7. The body of Crippen's wife was discovered buried in the basement of the couple's house. What was the name of the transatlantic liner that Crippen and his lover boarded as they tried to flee to Canada?

8. What was the name of the boat's captain, who recognised Crippen and sent a telegram to London warning them of the doctor's attempt to flee?

9. Who presided over Crippen's trial following his return to England?

10. Crippen was hanged in November 1910, at which location in London?

answers on page 397

GEORGE V
1865 – 1936, reigned 1910 – 1936

1. George was initially not expected to become king. At the age of 12, he joined which naval cadet training ship in Devon?

2. What was the name of the brother whose death from flu in 1892 left George second in line to the throne?

3. The following year, George married which minor member of the British royal family?

4. He became king in 1910. What event was held at Crystal Palace in London to mark his coronation the following year?

5. In 1917, George changed the name of the British royal house. Whereas previously the house had been Saxe-Coburg and Gotha, what did it now become?

6. Who wrote the 1922 poem *The King's Pilgrimage*, about George's tour that year of Belgium and France?

7. In 1932, George became the first British monarch to perform what act, which has since become an annual tradition?

8. Suffering ill health in his later years, George spent three months at Craigwell House, near which Sussex resort?

9. The king died January 1936. According to a myth that later became popular, what were his last words?

10. What was the name of the music, composed in six hours by Paul Hindemith, that was performed on the evening following the announcement of the king's death?

answers on page 398

ROBERT FALCON SCOTT & ERNEST SHACKLETON
1868 – 1912 & 1874 - 1922

1. Born in Devon in 1868, Robert Falcon Scott began a naval career at a young age. While stationed in the West Indies, he first encountered which explorer and geographer?

2. Ernest Shackleton was born in Ireland in 1874. In 1901, he became Scott's third officer on which vessel?

3. One of the many discoveries made by the expedition was which location, site of the South Pole?

4. What was the name of the ship used by Shackleton for his successful 1907-1909 expedition, which saw him come closer to the South Pole than any man had previously managed?

5. In 1910 Scott set off on his second trip to the Antarctic, this time on which vessel?

6. Scott reached the South Pole in January 1912. Which Norwegian explorer had already been there, a month earlier?

7. Two months later, on the return journey, what was the name of the army officer who left Scott's tent and – in an attempt to help his comrades – walked away to his death?

8. A memorial to the Scott expedition is located close to the McMurdo Station, at the top of which spot?

9. In 1914, Shackleton set out on the Endurance, with the aim of achieving what first in Antarctica?

10. Who eventually achieved this feat, in the late 1950s?

answers on page 398

THE OUTBREAK OF WORLD WAR ONE
1914

1. What name is generally given to the situation in the Balkans in the early 20th century, due to the overlapping influence of the major European powers in the region?

2. On 28th June 1914, Archduke Franz Ferdinand was assassinated in Sarajevo by which Bosnian Serb nationalist?

3. What name is used for the series of diplomatic events immediately after the assassination, which saw tensions begin to rise?

4. What name is generally given to the alliance that developed between Russia, France and the United Kingdom?

5. Who was the German Emperor (Kaiser) during the war?

6. On August 4th, the British Empire formally entered the war following the German invasion of which country?

7. What was the name of the German plan that aimed to defeat France before Russian troops could be mobilised?

8. What name is given to the divisions sent by the British Army early in the conflict?

9. This German plan failed in September 1914, when the Allies defeated Germany in which battle near Brasles in France?

10. What name is generally given to the late 1914 attempts by the Franco-British and German armies to overcome each other's northern flanks?

answers on page 398

THE WESTERN FRONT
1914 - 1918

1. In April 1915, at the Second Battle of Ypres, German forces used what type of gas for the first time on the Western Front?

2. What were used in battle for the first time in September 1916, at the Battle of Flers-Courcelette?

3. During the fighting, French pilot Louis Quenault became the first person to do what?

4. The longest battle in the war was which encounter, which lasted for nine months from February 1916?

5. What name is generally given to the (initially) all-volunteer part of the British forces?

6. What phrase refers to the spontaneous rise of non-aggressive behaviour that occurred occasionally during the war, most famously at Christmas 1914?

7. Which German defensive position was designed to give their forces respite following a series of massive losses?

8. Which Belgian village, the site of a 1917 British-led offensive, was almost completely destroyed during the war?

9. What name is given to the series of Allied offensives, starting with the Battle of Amiens in August 1918, that ultimately lead to the end of the war?

10. Who was buried at Westminster Abbey on 11th November 1920?

answers on page 399

THE NAVAL WAR
1914 - 1918

1. Which international crisis, that lasted from March 1905 to May 1906, is said to have led to the development of the major pre-war naval arms race between Britain and Germany?

2. Which First Sea Lord was a key figure in the build-up of Britain's naval forces in the years leading up to the war?

3. Who was First Lord of the Admiralty from 1911 to 1915?

4. On 5th September 1914, HMS Pathfinder became the first ship to be sunk by what method?

5. What was the name of the German warship that was sunk by the British during 1915's Battle of Dogger Bank?

6. Which ocean liner was torpedoed by a German U-boat in May 1915, with the loss of more than a thousand lives?

7. Which future Turkish leader was an Ottoman soldier in the Gallipoli campaign in 1915-1916, fighting against the British?

8. Which naval battle, fought in mid-1916 off the Danish coast, was the largest such battle in the war?

9. What name is generally given to the minefield, stretching from the Orkney Islands to Norway, that was laid by the United States Navy during the last year of the war?

10. Toward the end of the war, aircraft carriers were used in combat for the first time. HMS Furious launched what type of plane in 1918 raid?

answers on page 399

LORD KITCHENER & FIELD MARSHAL HAIG
1850 – 1916 & 1861 – 1928

1. Douglas Haig was born in Edinburgh in 1861. His family owned a company that manufactured which alcoholic drink?

2. Herbert Kitchener was born in Ireland in 1850. He joined the military, and in 1874 he was sent to assist in the mapping of which part of the world?

3. After joining the military, Haig served under Lord Kitchener in which late 19th century conflict in Africa?

4. Following service in the Boer War, Haig was sent to India. He was present in 1905 at which event, which was held to honour a visit by the future George V?

5. At the start of the Second World War, Kitchener was appointed to which government position?

6. Artist Alfred Leete created which wartime image?

7. What nickname did Haig gain in late 1916, due to the high number of casualties under his command?

8. Kitchener died in June 1916, in the sinking of which armoured cruiser off the coast of Orkney?

9. Following the war, Haig was captain of which golf club between 1920 and 1921?

10. Who created the Earl Haig Memorial sculpture, which is located on Whitehall?

answers on page 399

BRITISH LIFE DURING WORLD WAR ONE
1914 - 1918

1. Which piece of legislation, passed in August 1914, gave the British government wide-ranging powers over the country?

2. Which British builder was a key promoter of the idea of British Summer Time, which came into being in May 1916?

3. Which army units, first proposed in 1914, let army recruits serve alongside their friends and neighbours?

4. A Quaker, a clerk at a chocolate factory and a Sunderland footballer were among the members of which group?

5. Which marching song, first performed by Jack Judge in 1912, became popular during the war?

6. What name was given to the women who worked in TNT factories during the First World War, and who sometimes developed orange-yellow skin as a result?

7. Which organisation, established in 1915, was created to defend London from the threat of German airship attacks?

8. Scottish activist Helen Crawfurd and Glasgow rent campaigner Agnes Dollan were among the key figures of which organisation, which sought a peaceful end to the war?

9. In 1916, Field Marshal Sir John French was appointed as Commander-in-Chief of which military unit?

10. The Conscription Crisis of 1918 followed the government's attempt to impose conscription on which group of people?

answers on page 400

THE END OF WORLD WAR ONE
1918

1. Which English poet was killed on 4th November 1918, exactly a week before the signing of the armistice?

2. Who was the senior British representative at the signing of the armistice on 11th November 1918?

3. The war formally ended on 28th June 1919, following the signing of which agreement?

4. Which 1914 poem by Laurence Binyon contains, in its third and fourth stanzas, the lines that have become known as the Ode of Remembrance?

5. Prior to the end of the war, which secret deal had been struck between the UK and France with respect to the potential fall of the Ottoman Empire?

6. Which US president laid out fourteen points for peace that were to be used in the negotiations at the end of the war?

7. What organisation, founded the following year, was the world's first intergovernmental body dedicated to the maintenance of world peace?

8. In 1917, which commission was founded by Fabian Ware?

9. Which charity was founded in 1921, with Sir Thomas Lister as its first chairman?

10. Which English woman, the last known surviving veteran of the First World War, died in February 2012?

answers on page 400

DAVID LLOYD GEORGE
1863 – 1945, PM 1916 to 1922

1. Born in 1863, David Lloyd George was brought up speaking which language?

2. Lloyd George entered Parliament in 1890 and remained until 1945, as MP for which constituency?

3. In 1905, Lloyd George entered the cabinet of Sir Henry Campbell-Bannerman in which position?

4. In 1913, Lloyd George was involved in a scandal concerning the alleged purchase of shares in which company?

5. During the early years of the First World War, Lloyd George's reputation grew as he took on which position in government?

6. He became prime minister in 1916, but he swiftly lost support after backing which French General?

7. As the war ended in 1918, Lloyd George was one of many in Britain who fell ill during which event?

8. What name is generally given to the December 1918 election in which Lloyd George won a landslide after promising to make Germany pay the full costs of the war?

9. In 1933, Lloyd George warned that the fall of Adolf Hitler risked bringing about what condition in Germany?

10. Lloyd George died in 1945. His grave is marked by a monument that was designed by which Welsh architect?

answers on page 401

THE IRISH WAR OF INDEPENDENCE
1919 - 1921

1. Which Irish writer and journalist founded the republican political party Sinn Féin in 1905?

2. The British government granted Home Rule in 1912. Which group formed in the same year, aiming to block this plan?

3. Which activist, a leader of the 1916 Easter Rising, issued orders that were seen as a sign to begin the insurrection?

4. Refusing to take their seats in London after the 1918 election, Sinn Féin set up which rival parliament in Dublin?

5. Which May 1919 incident saw an IRA member rescued by comrades from a train on which he was being held?

6. In June 1919, which political body passed a resolution expressing sympathy for the idea of Irish self-governance?

7. More than thirty people were killed during which event in Dublin on 21st November 1920?

8. What name was given to constables recruited into the Royal Irish Constabulary at this time, many of whom were former British soldiers who had fought in the First World War?

9. A truce was signed in July 1921. Which Irish revolutionary figure was killed in an ambush in August 1922?

10. The Government of Ireland Act 1920 divided Ireland into Northern Ireland and Southern Ireland. Which organisation took over policing in Northern Ireland in June 1922?

answers on page 401

BRITISH COAL MINING

1. What type of fuel, crucial to the development of coal mining, was invented in the 18th century at Coalbrookdale in Shropshire?

2. In terms of tonnes produced, UK coal production peaked in which year?

3. Which organisation, founded in 1945, is based in Barnsley?

4. In 1953, aged fifteen, future mining activist Arthur Scargill began work at which Yorkshire pit?

5. In October 1966, 116 children and 28 adults were killed when a colliery spoil tip collapsed onto which Welsh village?

6. What measure was introduced by the Conservative government in 1974, to deal with energy problems arising from industrial action by coal miners and railway workers?

7. The miners' strike of 1984 – 1985 began with a local strike over the closure of which colliery?

8. During the strike, Betty Heathfield (nee Vardy) was a leading figure in which organisation?

9. Betteshanger, Chislet, Snowdown and Tilmanstone were the main collieries in which location?

10. Approved in 2020, Woodhouse Colliery (aka Whitehaven mine) is set to be the first new deep coal mine in England since which Leicestershire site opened in 1991?

answers on page 401

NEWCASTLE

1. The original Roman settlement on the site of Newcastle was called Pons Aelius. What did this name mean?

2. By what name was Newcastle known during the period of the Norman invasion, when much of the north of England was destroyed by the forces of William the Conqueror?

3. In 1080, who began construction of the 'New Castle Upon Tyne' that later gave the city its name?

4. Newcastle became England's northern fortress. What name was given to the group of businessmen who controlled the export of coal from the area during the Middle Ages?

5. Estimates suggest that during the mid-17th century, one third of the population of Newcastle died in which pandemic?

6. What phrase is first recorded in a 1679 letter by American legislator William Fitzhugh?

7. Which 19th century builder was a key figure in the redevelopment of Newcastle's centre, with his name now sometimes used to refer to the area around Grey Street?

8. Which famous steam locomotive was built in a Newcastle factory in the early 19th century?

9. Which well-known pottery moved to Newcastle in 1817 and was soon said to be the largest pottery in the world?

10. The Tyne Bridge, opened in 1928 by King George V, was designed by which engineering firm?

answers on page 402

SUNDERLAND

1. Which area to the west of modern Sunderland was a key Neolithic site in around 2,000 BC?

2. Which 7th-8th century English monk and writer spent much of his life at nearby Monkwearmouth-Jarrow Abbey?

3. John Lilburne, who's believed to have been born in Sunderland around the year 1614, is credited with coining which phrase regarding human rights?

4. Hartley Wood and Co Ltd., established in Sunderland in 1812, was a leading company in which business?

5. In 1883, 183 children died in a disaster at which Sunderland concert venue?

6. Which 19th century general, who was born in Sunderland, was a key figure in the Siege of Cawnpore during the 1857 Indian rebellion?

7. Which well-known Victorian stage actor, said to have been an inspiration for Count Dracula, spent a number of years working at Sunderland's (Royal) Lyceum Theatre?

8. Born in Sunderland in 1856, Sir William Mills is perhaps best known for having created what weapon?

9. Which local football stadium was the home of Sunderland A.F.C. From 1898 to 1997?

10. James Alfred Wight, born in Sunderland in 1916, wrote a series of books under which pen name?

answers on page 402

THE BBC

1. Which Australian opera singer featured in the BBC's very first live public broadcast, in June 1920?

2. Which Scottish executive was the organisation's first Director-General?

3. For the first two years of its existence, until 1925, the Radio Times was produced jointly by the BBC and which publisher?

4. In 1930, which play by Luigi Pirandello became the first piece of television drama ever produced in Britain?

5. The iconic Type A microphone used by the BBC between 1934 and 1959 was co-produced with which engineering company?

6. Delia Derbyshire, Daphne Oram, Dick Mills and Brian Hodgson were among the members of which BBC department?

7. The BBC was a founding member of which organisation, which was formed in Torquay in February 1950?

8. BBC Television Centre, which opened in White City in 1960, was designed by which London firm of architects?

9. Some 1960s TV idents featured the cartoon mascots Hullabaloo and Custard, with the former representing BBC1 and the latter representing BBC2. What type of animals were Hullabaloo and Custard?

10. What was launched on 23rd September 1974?

answers on page 403

MAIL

1. What position, renamed Postmaster General in 1710, was originally established in 1516 by Henry VIII?

2. Who established the first royal postal service between London and Edinburgh?

3. When the Royal Mail service was established by Charles I, the monopoly was given to which merchant?

4. The first mail coach, which began in 1784, operated between London and which city?

5. Rowland Hill is credited with which important change to the postal system, which was copied by many others around the world?

6. First issued in the United Kingdom on 1st May 1840, what name is generally used for the world's first adhesive postage stamp?

7. As of 2021, British stamps remain the only stamps in the world that are not required to feature what element?

8. Also in 1840, postal stationary letter sheets were introduced, featuring designs by which well-known artist?

9. What was first erected in Jersey in 1852, before arriving on the mainland the following year?

10. Postman Pat's fictional village Greendale was inspired by which valley in Cumbria?

answers on page 403

BONAR LAW
1858 – 1923, PM 1922 – 1923

1. Andrew Bonar Law was the first British prime minister to be born where?

2. His mother was an admirer of which Scottish minister?

3. In his twenties, Law secured a job working for which British ironmaster and Liberal politician?

4. What name was given to the election, held in 1900 following the events of the Boer War, in which Bonar Law first became an MP?

5. Within two years, Law had been given which junior ministerial position?

6. In 1911, Law became leader of the Conservative party after he beat which two other figures in a contest?

7. In 1915, under Asquith's coalition government, Law was given which cabinet role?

8. After just a year in office, Law resigned after being diagnosed with which illness?

9. Law was in office as prime minister for 211 days. As of 2021, who are the only two prime ministers to have served in the role for less time?

10. What was the title of Robert Blake's biography of Bonar Law?

answers on page 403

STANLEY BALDWIN

1867 – 1947, PM 1923 – 1924, 1924 – 1929, 1935 – 1937

1. Born in Worcestershire in 1867, Stanley Baldwin was the son of which 19th century writer?

2. Baldwin became prime minister in 1923, and then again in 1924. Which organisation called the ultimately unsuccessful General Strike of 1926?

3. Which organisation, formed in 1925, was designed to provide volunteer workers in the event of any strike action?

4. Baldwin's wife Lucy, née Ridsdale, was known for her activism in which area?

5. In 1935, Baldwin's government was criticised following the revelation of which secret agreement that aimed to end the Second Italo-Ethiopian War?

6. Baldwin resigned in 1937. He was criticised in which 1940 anti-appeasement book that was credited to 'Cato'?

7. In 1941, Baldwin's youngest daughter was badly injured in a bomb explosion at which London nightclub?

8. During the Second World War, Baldwin was criticised for not donating what item from his home to the war effort?

9. What was the name of Baldwin's country home from 1902 until his death 45 years later?

10. Stanley Baldwin died in 1947, and his ashes were buried in which location?

answers on page 404

RAMSAY MACDONALD
1866 – 1937, PM 1924, 1929 – 1931, 1931 – 1935

1. Born in 1866 in Moray, Scotland, MacDonald moved to London in 1886. A year later, he witnessed the Bloody Sunday demonstration in which part of London?

2. MacDonald studied science subjects at which institution?

3. In 1888, MacDonald became a private secretary to which merchant and Radical politician?

4. MacDonald became the first Labour prime minister in 1924. He's generally regarded as the first British prime minister to come from what background?

5. MacDonald's government swiftly fell following a decision to not prosecute which communist newspaper editor?

6. Which document, published before the 1924 election, was claimed to be a letter from Russia to the Communist Party of Great Britain?

7. Following the US stock market crash, MacDonald resigned and stood again as the head of which group?

8. In 1931 1,000 sailors in the British Atlantic Fleet mutinied over pay in which rebellion?

9. Which 1932 event saw British colonies seek to introduce tariffs as a means of dealing with the Great Depression?

10. MacDonald resigned in 1935, due to failing health. What cabinet role did he take until shortly before his death in 1937?

answers on page 404

GLASGOW

1. Glasgow has been settled since prehistoric times. Following the Roman withdrawal, the site was part of which kingdom?

2. Which 6th century figure is regarded as the founder and patron saint of Glasgow?

3. Opened in Glasgow in 1807, the oldest museum in Scotland is dedicated to the collection of which 18th century figure?

4. Which 18th century physicist and chemist, who was working at the University of Glasgow, discovered the concept of latent heat in 1761?

5. Which international youth organisation was founded in Glasgow in 1883 by businessman Sir William Alexander Smith?

6. What term was used to define an era of political radicalism that developed in Glasgow from the 1910s until the 1930s?

7. What name was given to the gangs that existed in Glasgow during the first half of the 20th century?

8. What name is usually used to refer to a 1919 confrontation between Glasgow police and striking workers from the city?

9. Which Scottish architect designed the main buildings of Glasgow School of Art, which opened in 1845?

10. What name is generally given to the 1945 report that laid out plans for the regeneration and rebuilding of Glasgow following the Second World War?

answers on page 405

THE JARROW MARCH
1936

1. One of the primary causes of the march was the closure in 1934 of the town's main employer, which was which local site?

2. Which organisation had organised a number of hunger marches to London since the 1920s?

3. Which figure, a founding member of the Communist Party of Great Britain, was one of the key figures in these marches?

4. In the 1931 general election, William Pearson won the Jarrow seat for the National Government. Who won the seat in the general election four years later?

5. The march to London set off on October 5th and took almost a month. The men of the Jarrow March preferred to be referred to by what name?

6. One of the speakers at the main event in London was the Rev. Canon Dick Sheppard, who was the founder of which pacifist organisation?

7. To the nearest thousand, how many people had signed the Jarrow marchers' petition?

8. What was the title of the book by the town's MP, published in 1939, that provided a history of the town?

9. Which English singer released *The Jarrow Song* in 1974?

10. What title was given to the 2011 event that served to mark the 75th anniversary of the Jarrow March?

answers on page 405

EDWARD VIII
1894 – 1972, king in 1936 but never crowned

1. Edward was born in London in 1894. When he was 16, he served as a midshipman on which Royal Navy vessel?

2. What was the name of Edward's younger brother, who died at the age of 13 after suffering a severe epileptic seizure?

3. In 1931, Edward met which American socialite, who was already married to her second husband?

4. In 1936, Edward became king following the death of his father. When he travelled to London for his Accession Council, he became the first British monarch to do what?

5. What was unusual about Edward's image on the coins that were produced when he became king?

6. What was the name of the American who was arrested in 1936 after producing a gun as he saw Edward in London?

7. In December, facing increasing opposition to his desire to marry, Edward abdicated in favour of his brother. He was subsequently given which royal title?

8. What controversial gesture did Edward give in 1937, while visiting Nazi Germany?

9. In 1940, possibly to avoid him playing any role in the Second World War, Edward was appointed to which role?

10. In June 1953, Edward watched the coronation of his niece Elizabeth on television, from which location?

answers on page 405

GEORGE VI
1895 – 1952, reigned 1936 – 1952

1. George VI was known to family and close friends by which nickname?

2. George wasn't expected to become king. During the First World War, he was a turret officer on HMS Collingwood during which 1916 naval battle?

3. During the 1920s, George saw which Australian-born speech therapist?

4. In 1927, during a visit to Jamaica, he played doubles tennis with which local sportsman?

5. The George Cross and the George Medal were launched to award civilian acts of courage. Who designed the George Cross?

6. Winston Churchill became prime minister in 1940, George is said to have preferred which other figure for the post?

7. What unusual honour did the king grant to both Neville Chamberlain before the war and Winston Churchill after?

8. Following the Second World War, George addressed the first assembly of which organisation, which met in London in January 1946?

9. In June 1948, George relinquished which title?

10. George VI died on 6th February 1952. His last public appearance had taken place six days earlier at which location?

answers on page 406

ELIZABETH, THE QUEEN MOTHER
1900 – 2002

1. Elizabeth Bowes-Lyon was born in 1900. Which Scottish castle was her childhood home?

2. When she married the future George VI in 1923, what did she do with her bouquet as she entered Westminster Abbey?

3. Elizabeth's husband became king in 1936. Which item, which had at one point been displayed at the Great Exhibition in 1851, was installed as part of her crown?

4. Which book, published in 1939, was written to raise funds for humanitarian causes during the Second World War?

5. Due to Elizabeth's popularity, Adolf Hitler is said to have referred to her by what title?

6. In 1947, Elizabeth became the last person to hold which title?

7. Following the death of her husband in 1952, Elizabeth continued to carry out royal engagements. She also oversaw the restoration of which castle on the north coast of Scotland?

8. In the 1956 Grand National, Elizabeth's horse Devon Loch fell just 40 yards from victory. Who was riding the horse?

9. Elizabeth died in March 2002, at the age of 101. What type of flower was placed on her coffin?

10. At her request, what was done with her funeral wreath following the ceremony?

answers on page 406

ART

1. Some of the earliest cave art in the world can be seen in which limestone gorge in Derbyshire?

2. Which English painter, best known for a series of portrait miniatures of the court of Elizabeth I and James I, has been described as the key artistic figure of Elizabeth England?

3. In 1768, Joshua Reynolds became the first president of which organisation?

4. Philanthropist Sir Henry Tate, who established the Tate Gallery in London, made his fortune in which industry?

5. Which artist, born in 1887, is best known for a series of paintings depicting life in northern industrial towns?

6. Eddie Chambers, Keith Piper, David Rodney and Marlene Smith established which 1980s British art movement?

7. In 1984, which British-American artist was the first winner of the Turner Prize?

8. The Singing Sculpture, The Pictures and Jack Freak Pictures are all series by which pair of British artists?

9. Artists such as Gillian Wearing, Damien Hirst, Sarah Lucas and Gavin Turk are often referred to as being part of which 1990s movement?

10. Rachel Whiteread, Antony Gormley, Yinka Shonibare and Heather Phillipson have all had work exhibited in which outdoor location near the National Gallery in Central London?

answers on page 407

BARBARA HEPWORTH & HENRY MOORE
1903 – 1975 & 1898 - 1986

1. In 1920, Barbara Hepworth and Henry Moore first met at which institution?

2. Moore's first public commission, for the headquarters of London Underground, was which late 1920s piece?

3. In 1933, Hepworth was involved with which art movement, along with Paul Nash and her partner Ben Nicholson?

4. Following the outbreak of the Second World War, Hepworth and her family moved to which Cornish town?

5. Moore and his family, meanwhile, moved to which Hertfordshire farmhouse, which became his home and workshop for the rest of his life?

6. Which sculpture by Moore, installed in Stevenage in 1949, shows a man and a woman holding a small child?

7. A cast of Moore's 1960s sculpture *Knife Edge Two Piece 1962-65* is located in which location in Westminster, London?

8. Which Hepworth sculpture can still be seen on the side of the John Lewis store in London's Oxford Street?

9. Barbara Hepworth died in 1972. A copy of which sculpture, which stood in London's Dulwich Park, was stolen in 2011?

10. Henry Moore died in 1986. A cast of his piece *Draped Seated Woman 1957-58* could be seen for many years in a park in London's Tower Hamlets, where it gained what nickname?

answers on page 407

OSWALD MOSLEY
1896 – 1980

1. Born in London in 1896, Oswald Mosley was a distant relative of which 20th century royal figure?

2. In his school days, Mosley was a champion in which sport?

3. Mosley's first wife Cynthia died in 1933. What was the name of his second wife, who he married three years later?

4. At the age of just 21, in 1918 Mosley became the Conservative MP for which constituency?

5. By 1924, he'd switched to become a member of which political group?

6. What was the name of the political party that Mosley formed in 1932?

7. Mosley found that many of his party's meetings faced disruption. He created the Fascist Defence Force, whose members were generally known by what nickname?

8. What event in October 1936 saw clashes between police officers and various groups of anti-fascist demonstrators?

9. Mosley and his wife were interned by the British government during the Second World War. He later formed a movement that aimed to establish what type of political system?

10. Mosley retired to France, where he died in 1980. What was the title of his autobiography?

answers on page 408

NEVILLE CHAMBERLAIN
1869 – 1940, PM 1937 - 1940

1. Born in 1869, Neville Chamberlain was eventually sent by his father to a sisal plantation in which country?

2. Although he was initially not interested in politics, by 1915 Chamberlain secured which position?

3. During the First World War, he briefly served under David Lloyd George in which role?

4. What was the title of a leaflet that he issued during the 1918 election, reflecting a change to the make-up of the electorate?

5. In the second general election of 1923, Chamberlain narrowly defended his seat against which Labour candidate?

6. He became prime minister in 1937. A new act suggested that companies should offer what benefit to their employees?

7. As Hitler gained power, what name was given to the plan in which Chamberlain would fly to Germany if war seemed inevitable?

8. Chamberlain ultimately resigned in May 1940, following which debate in the House of Commons?

9. What position in government did Chamberlain accept under new prime minister Winston Churchill?

10. Shortly before his death in 1940, Chamberlain supported Churchill in a dispute over war plans with which figure, who was the foreign secretary at the time?

answers on page 408

THE OUTBREAK OF WORLD WAR TWO
1939

1. What was the name of the German state that existed between the end of the First World War and the rise to power of Adolf Hitler?

2. Many in Germany were angry at what they saw as the country's harsh punishment after the First World War. This punishment had been established in which 1919 agreement?

3. Which 1930s event, which began in the US, caused economic hardship in many countries?

4. In 1933, which law gave Adolf Hitler 'temporary' power to act without parliamentary consent?

5. In 1938, Hitler claimed that which region – formally part of Czechoslovakia – would represent his final territorial claim?

6. The same year, Neville Chamberlain claimed that peace had been secured following which arrangement?

7. In 1939, Hitler's Germany announced that they were laying claim to which Polish port?

8. What name was given to the non-aggression pact signed between Germany and the Soviet Union around this time?

9. What word, related to a desire for more 'living room', was used by the Germans to describe their need for more territory?

10. On 3rd September 1940, the United Kingdom and France declared war after Germany invaded which country?

answers on page 408

WINSTON CHURCHILL
1874 – 1965, PM 1940 – 1945, 1951 – 1955

1. Winston Churchill was born in 1874 at which location in Oxfordshire?

2. After joining the army, Churchill saw action in British India and the Boer War. In the Sudan he served under which figure?

3. He became a Conservative MP in 1900, but four years later he 'crossed the floor' to join the Liberal Party following the proposal of which immigration legislation?

4. Churchill once again became a Conservative MP in 1924. As Chancellor of the Exchequer under Baldwin, he restored which monetary system in his first budget?

5. Churchill became prime minister in 1940. What phrase is used to describe his speech in May of that year, in which he insisted that Britain faced a long road to victory?

6. Despite victory in the war, he lost the 1945 election. A year later, he used which phrase in a speech about the USSR?

7. Churchill became prime minister again in 1951, but by this time he was in poor health. What was he awarded in 1953?

8. Upon his retirement in 1955, Churchill was offered – but declined – which title?

9. In 1963, John F. Kennedy gave Churchill which title?

10. Churchill died in January 1965. What name was given to the operation that had been established to plan for his funeral?

answers on page 409

DUNKIRK
26ᵗʰ May - 4ᵗʰ June 1940

1. What name is given to the period at the start of the war in which land operations on the Western Front were limited?

2. What was the code name of the German operation that saw them invade France and the Low Countries in mid-1940?

3. What was the name of the fortified French line, constructed in the 1930s, that was designed to deter a German invasion?

4. British forces were trapped following the German invasion. What code name was given to the evacuation plan?

5. Which Royal Navy officer was in charge of planning the Dunkirk evacuation?

6. The operation was coordinated from a military base at which location in Kent?

7. As German forces advanced, they were temporarily slowed by British soldiers who were trapped in which French city?

8. What name is given to the small vessels, including fishing boats and pleasure craft, that were also involved in the evacuation?

9. What phrase is used to refer to a speech by Winston Churchill, given in the House of Commons on 4ᵗʰ June 1940, that referred to the events of Dunkirk and the Battle of France?

10. What name is given to the flag that features the St. George's Cross along with the arms of Dunkirk?

answers on page 409

DOVER

1. Dover was known by what name during the Roman occupation?

2. Which hospital was founded in 1203 to take care of pilgrims who arrived in Dover on their way to Canterbury Cathedral?

3. What's the name of the chalk stream, flowing through Dover, that once had a wide estuary?

4. What occurred near Dover in 1580, and is believed to have been one of the largest in the history of Britain?

5. What was built in the early 19th century to facilitate movement between forts on the Western Heights and the harbour below?

6. Footballer Cuthbert Ottaway, who was born in Dover in 1850, was the first person to hold what title?

7. Which author, whose work included the *Breezie Langton* series, was born in Dover in 1833?

8. During the Second World War, Dover and much of the Kent coast gained which nickname?

9. What was the name of the luxury boat train that ran between 1929 and 1972, connecting Dover to London?

10. Walter Kent's song *(There'll Be Bluebirds Over) The White Cliffs* of Dover was popularised by a 1942 recording from which singer?

answers on page 409

THE BATTLE OF BRITAIN & THE BLITZ
1940 - 1941

1. What was the name of the Nazis' aerial warfare branch?

2. Who was in charge of the RAF during the Battle of Britain?

3. What code name was given to the ring of coastal early warning radar stations that aimed to detect enemy aircraft?

4. By mid-1940, Hitler was planning for an invasion of the United Kingdom. What code name was used for this plan?

5. The Supermarine Spitfire became a symbol of the Battle of Britain, but which fighter aircraft was credited for more than half the losses sustained by the Germans during this period?

6. Who is credited as the most successful Allied pilot during the Battle of Britain, having shot down 21 German aircraft?

7. What phrase, coined by Winston Churchill but originating in the works of William Shakespeare, is generally used to describe the pilots who fought in the Battle of Britain?

8. What name did the Germans use for their attempt to destroy RAF Fighter Command in 1940?

9. Which New Zealand officer, a key figure in the Battle of Britain, was given the nickname 'Defender of London' in Germany?

10. Which British commander, appointed as head of Bomber Command following the Blitz, was put in charge of plans to carry out bombing attacks on Germany?

answers on page 410

COVENTRY

1. Which saint is believed to have founded a Saxon nunnery in Coventry, around the year 700 AD?

2. Which Anglo-Saxon noblewoman is said to have ridden naked through Coventry's streets in the 11th century?

3. Which phrase, referring to a voyeur, comes from later retellings of the story in the previous question?

4. What type of cloth, woven and dyed with woad, was a product of the city until the recipe was lost in the 17th century?

5. What phrase is believed to have arisen from the 17th century practice of Royalist prisoners being transported to the city?

6. Which 17th century horologist, who was Sheriff of Coventry in 1682, is credited with having made the first stopwatch?

7. Which 19th century inventor was a founder of the Coventry Sewing Machine Company, and later invented the differential gear for bicycles?

8. Which company began building cars in Coventry in 1897, and provided cars to the British monarch until the 1950s?

9. What words were inscribed on the wall behind Coventry Cathedral's altar, following the building's destruction in an air raid in November 1940?

10. Which architect oversaw the redevelopment of the city's bombed centre in the late 1940s and 1950s?

answers on page 410

THE AFRICAN CAMPAIGN
1940 - 1943

1. In September 1940, Italian forces invaded Egypt. What name was given to the British military operation, launched in December 1940, that saw the Italian advance halted?

2. Which German military leader, who commanded the Afrika Korps, gained the nickname 'desert fox'?

3. Which Mediterranean island – of strategic importance to the African campaigns – endured an Axis siege for two years?

4. Which 1941 operation saw German troops head to North Africa following British victories over the Italians?

5. During the Western Desert Campaign, the British Army's 7th Armoured Division gained which nickname?

6. Between April and November 1941, Allied forces were besieged at which Libyan port city?

7. Field Marshal Bernard Montgomery led British forces into a crucial victory in which battle in Egypt in late 1942?

8. What name was given to the late 1942 Allied invasion of French North Africa?

9. In November and December 1942, Allied forces raced to capture which city on the north coast?

10. Which 1943 battle, which saw Allied forces overcome the Italians and Germans, was one of the final confrontations of the war in Africa?

answers on page 411

THE ITALIAN CAMPAIGN
1943 - 1945

1. What code name was given to the Allied plan to invade Sicily in July 1943?

2. What role was played by a tramp named Glyndwr Michael, in the build-up to the invasion of Sicily?

3. The Allies prepared for the invasion from a base in tunnels beneath which European city?

4. Which Italian dictator was dismissed on 25th July 1943, and was ultimately executed two years later?

5. On September 3rd 1943, Allied forces had moved from Sicily to mainland Italy. That same day, Italy signed an armistice with the Allies at which location in Sicily?

6. German forces in Italy still fought back against the Allies. What name was given to the defensive fortifications that were designed to defend Rome against an Allied attack?

7. In early 1944, Allied forced were involved in four costly assaults on which site – home of an abbey – near Rome?

8. What defensive line, located in the Apennine Mountains, formed Germany's last line of defence in Italy?

9. What was the name of the final Allied attack during the Italian campaign, which saw soldiers enter Lombardy?

10. What name is given to the agreement, signed in April 1945, that saw German forces formally surrender in Italy?

answers on page 411

BRITISH LIFE DURING WORLD WAR TWO

1. When the Second World War began, what was the first commodity to be rationed?

2. In September 1939, W.S. Morrison was appointed to which revived government position?

3. Artist Ernest Wallcousins is credited with designing which five-word motivational poster?

4. What name was given to the operation, beginning in September 1939, that evacuated millions of schoolchildren from the areas of Britain most at risk of bombing?

5. The Local Defence Volunteers later became known by which name?

6. What was the name of the MI5 agent who, under the alias Jack King, infiltrated fascist groups in the UK by posing as a Gestapo agent?

7. In 1940, ARP warden Thomas Alderson was the first person to be awarded what decoration?

8. From 1942, who served as the Official War Artist, producing posters such as *Join the ATS* (1941) and some of the *Careless Talk* images?

9. Which report, published in 1942, is generally considered to be the basis for the reforms that resulted in the Welfare State?

10. In 1944, which singer served four weeks in prison for misusing petrol coupons?

answers on page 411

ALAN TURING & BLETCHLEY PARK

1. Born in London in 1912, Alan Turing studied at Cambridge. In 1936 he developed which mathematical model of computation?

2. In 1938, Turing began to work part-time with which codebreaking organisation?

3. Turing was involved in the analysis and deciphering of which device, which was used extensively by Nazi Germany?

4. At the outbreak of the Second World War, Turing joined the codebreaking team at Bletchley Park in Buckinghamshire. What informal name was given to this group?

5. What code name was given to the intelligence obtained by the Bletchley Park operators?

6. What name is given to the spy ring that worked for Soviet intelligence during the war, with one of their members believed to have infiltrated Bletchley Park?

7. The Turing test, created by Alan Turing in 1950, aims to test a machine's ability to do what?

8. Turing died in 1954 at his home in Wilmslow, having ingested a fatal dose of which chemical?

9. The 'Alan Turing law', part of the Policing and Crime Act 2017, offered pardons to men who had previously been convicted of what offences?

10. What does CAPTCHA stand for?

answers on page 412

THE WAR IN THE PACIFIC
1941 - 1945

1. Since 1937, Japan had been engaged in a military conflict with which other country?

2. In December 1941, Japan launched a surprise attack on the US Pacific Fleet at which location in Honolulu?

3. The next day, Japan invaded which country?

4. What name was given to the special-operations units – the Long Range Penetration Groups – of the British and Indian armies during the 1943-1944 Burma campaign?

5. Who commanded the British Fourteenth Army, aka the 'Forgotten Army', during most of its operations in Burma?

6. What was the name of the 1943 – 1944 operation that saw the Allies attempt to destroy a Japanese base at Rabaul?

7. Which 1945 naval battle, which saw Allied forces gain a staging area close to Japan, is sometimes referred to as the 'typhoon of steel'?

8. Operation Oboe was part of a 1945 campaign to liberate which island, which had been occupied by Japan since 1941?

9. Following the atomic bombings of Hiroshima and Nagasaki in August 1945, Japan swiftly surrendered and accepted which the terms of which Allied statement?

10. What happened to Japanese soldier Teruo Nakamura at the end of the war in the Pacific?

answers on page 412

D-DAY
6th June 1944

1. The Normandy landings were part of the Battle of Normandy, which was given which code name?

2. What name was used for the rehearsal landings that took place on Slapton Sands in Devon, in April 1944?

3. D-Day was originally set for 1st May. Who was appointed as the commander of the Supreme Headquarters Allied Expeditionary Force?

4. Who was commander of the 21st Army Group, which comprised the land forces involved in D-Day?

5. What name was given to the operation that aimed to trick German intelligence into expecting an attack on Calais?

6. What was the name of the coastal defences, built by the Nazis between 1942 and 1944, that aimed to prevent an invasion?

7. The first action of D-Day occurred in darkness, as Allied forces secured two key bridges, which spanned which waterways?

8. What were the code names for the five beaches targeted for landings on D-Day?

9. Who was the only woman to land at Normandy on D-Day?

10. What nickname was given to the modified tanks that were specifically designed to support troops during the landings?

answers on page 413

THE END OF WORLD WAR TWO
1945

1. Which event, in early February 1945, saw the Allied leaders meet to discuss the postwar reorganisation of Europe?

2. Adolf Hitler committed suicide on 30th April 1945. Who briefly succeeded him as Germany's head of state?

3. In London, crowds sang which song in the presence of Winston Churchill?

4. Which policy, considered between 1945 and 1947, would have removed much of Germany's industrial capability?

5. What term is used to describes a secret agreement between Churchill and Joseph Stalin, whereby Eastern European countries were to be divided into 'spheres of influence'?

6. What name is given to countries such as Latvia, Estonia and Lithuania, which were controlled by communist regimes in the immediate aftermath of the war?

7. In 1948, the UK was one of the countries that voted in favour of which international document?

8. What name was given to plans, drawn up by the British, that considered a fresh conflict with the Soviet Union?

9. In an essay in October 1945, titled *You and the Atomic Bomb*, which English writer popularised the term 'cold war'?

10. Construction of what structure began on 13th August 1961 in Germany?

answers on page 413

CLEMENT ATTLEE
1883 – 1967, PM 1945 – 1951

1. Born in Putney in 1883, Clement Attlee studied at Oxford and then worked in London as a secretary for which historian, socialist and social reformer?

2. Attlee entered politics and in 1919 he became the mayor of which deprived inner-city London borough?

3. He became an MP in 1922, and from 1931 to 1935 he was the deputy to which leader of the Labour Party?

4. In 1939, Attlee joined Winston Churchill's war cabinet along with which other Labour member?

5. Attlee became prime minister in 1945 and began a program of sweeping nationalisation. Which organisation took over the country's collieries on 'vesting day', the 1st of January 1947?

6. Attlee's government supported which American initiative that provided foreign aid for post-war Western Europe?

7. What was the title of the pamphlet, published in 1947, that tried to influence Attlee into relying less on the United States?

8. In 1951, Attlee's government attempted to bring in cuts in order to pay for the country's participation in which conflict?

9. Attlee lost the 1951 election. In 1958, he was one of the founding figures of which campaign group?

10. Attlee died in October 1967. Which sculptor created the statue of him that stands in the Houses of Parliament?

answers on page 413

ANEURIN BEVAN & THE NHS

1. Born in South Wales in 1897, 'Nye' Bevan left school at the age of 13 and took up what job?

2. Bevan became an MP in 1929. Five years later he married which Scottish politician, who also became an MP in 1929?

3. Which figure, head of the Socialist Medical Association, proposed the establishment of a state health service at the 1934 Labour Party Conference?

4. Following the 1945 election, Bevan became Health Minister. The NHS is said to have been partially modelled on which organisation, which was founded in South Wales in 1890?

5. What was the title of Bevan's 1952 book, which asked how workers can obtain power in Great Britain?

6. Bevan died in 1960. By this point a group of left wing Labour Party members had become known as the Bevanites. Which MP, who represented Coventry East, was one of the key figures in this group?

7. Which British soap opera, set in an English hospital, was first broadcast on ITV between 1957 and 1967?

8. Which London hospital was occupied for several months in 1977, by workers protesting against plans for its closure?

9. The TV series *Casualty* is set in which fictional hospital?

10. In July 2021, during the COVID-19 pandemic, what award did Queen Elizabeth II give to the NHS?

answers on page 414

THE WINDRUSH GENERATION

1. HMT Empire Windrush, which became known for bringing West Indian immigrants to London, was built in the 1920s and was originally given what name?

2. The Windrush set sail for Britain from which Jamaican port?

3. Arrivals were initially housed in a deep shelter at which London station?

4. Calypsonian Aldwyn Roberts, who arrived on the Windrush in 1948, was better known by which stage name?

5. Which Trinidad-born writer wrote the 1956 novel *The Lonely Londoners*?

6. The West Indian Gazette, generally considered to have been the first major British black newspaper, was founded in 1958 by which journalist?

7. Which 1959 novel by E.R. Braithwaite tells the story of a London teacher who comes from British Guiana?

8. Which annual London event can be traced back to a Caribbean Carnival that took place in Camden in 1959?

9. Windrush Square, which was given its name in 1998 to mark the 50th anniversary of the Windrush's arrival, is located in which London district?

10. What was the name of the activist who helped draw media attention to the Windrush scandal in the 2010s, and who died in 2020 after settling her own case with the Home Office?

answers on page 414

THE COMMONWEALTH

1. Which South African statesman is believed to have coined the phrase 'British Commonwealth of Nations' in 1917?

2. The Commonwealth was formalised by which 1931 act of the British parliament?

3. In a speech in 1959, Elizabeth II noted that which nation had been the first independent country within the British Empire?

4. What name was given to the idea, floated in the mid 1950s, that France and other European nations might be invited to join the Commonwealth?

5. Which London mansion is the headquarters of the Commonwealth Secretariat?

6. In 1965, Arnold Smith of Canada became the first person to hold which position?

7. Although the British Empire Games had a long history, the first event with the title Commonwealth Games was held in 1970 in which country?

8. Which country was suspended from the Commonwealth between 1995 and 1999, following the execution of writer and activist Ken Saro-Wiwa?

9. In 2009, who was commissioned to write *The Commonwealth Anthem*?

10. As of 2021, which African country is the most recent to have joined the Commonwealth?

answers on page 414

GAMES & TOYS

1. The Hamley's toy retailer began life in High Holborn, London in 1760, when the first store opened under what name?

2. What was invented by London engraver John Spilsbury around the year 1760?

3. In 1893, what process – invented by the British toy company William Britain – revolutionised the production of toy soldiers by making them cheaper and lighter?

4. A company called J.K. Farnell is credited with creating the first British example of what toy, in 1906?

5. What company was established by Frank Hornby in 1908?

6. Which British company, established in 1939 by Hungarian businessman Nicholas Kove, initially sold inflatable rubber toys before becoming better-known for model kits?

7. What board game was invented by Anthony E. Pratt from Birmingham during the Second World War?

8. In 1947, a Hampshire man named Fred (B.F.) Francis invented which racing game?

9. Starting in the 1960s, which British toy manufacturer licensed the American GI Joe toys and sold them in the United Kingdom as Action Man?

10. Which hit 1996 video game focuses on the adventures of British archaeologist Lara Croft?

answers on page 415

MOTOR RACING

1. The first British Grand Prix was held in 1926, at which Surrey race circuit?

2. In 1916, Dario Resta became the first British driver to win which race?

3. In 1958, which driver narrowly beat Stirling Moss to become the first British F1 world champion?

4. Which British driver won four 500cc motorcycle titles, and the F1 title in 1964, and as of 2021 remains the only person to win World Championships on both two and four wheels?

5. Which British driver was nicknamed Red Five by commentator Murray Walker?

6. In 1995, who became the first British winner of the World Rally Championship?

7. Opened in 2003, the McLaren Technology Centre – home of the F1 team – is located close to which Surrey town?

8. Who scored his first F1 podium in the 2007 Australian Grand Prix?

9. As of 2021, the 2011 Canadian Grand Prix holds the record for the longest ever F1 race, having lasted for more than four hours (including a red flag period). Which British driver won the race?

10. Which team won its first Formula E race at the 2019 Rome ePrix, with Mitch Evans behind the wheel?

answers on page 415

ELIZABETH II
b. 1926, reigned from 1952

1. Elizabeth I was born in April 1926 at which location in London?

2. Elizabeth and her sister Margaret were supervised as children by their governess, Marion Crawford. What was the title of the book that Crawford later published about the girls?

3. Although she stayed in Britain during the Second World War, consideration was given to sending Elizabeth and Margaret to safety in which country?

4. Later in the war, Elizabeth served in which branch of the army?

5. Where was Elizabeth when she was informed of her father's death in 1952?

6. Who designed Elizabeth's coronation gown?

7. In 1991, Elizabeth became the first British monarch to address which body?

8. What term did Elizabeth use to describe the year 1992?

9. In 2011, Elizabeth made the first state visit by a British monarch to which country?

10. In 2017, Elizabeth became the first British monarch to reach which jubilee?

answers on page 416

PRINCE PHILIP
1921 - 2021

1. What's the name of the Greek villa where Philip was born on 10th June 1921?

2. As a child, Philip was evacuated from Greece along with his family on which British naval vessel?

3. In 1939, Philip met the future Queen Elizabeth during a tour of which naval facility?

4. By 1947, Philip had adopted which surname from his mother's side of the family?

5. Following their marriage in 1947, Philip and Elizabeth spent their honeymoon at which house in Hampshire?

6. What was the highest rank achieved by Philip during his active military career?

7. The Duke of Edinburgh's Award scheme was launched in 1956. The scheme is modelled on which set of beliefs set down by Kurt Hahn?

8. In a 1960 speech, Philip is said to have coined which phrase, which refers to the act of putting your foot in your own mouth?

9. What name was given to the national plan that was set up for publicly handling Philip's death?

10. Philip died in 2021. His last will and testament will remain sealed for how long?

answers on page 416

PRINCE CHARLES
b. 1948

1. Born in 1948, Charles is the longest-serving heir apparent to the British throne in history. Who previously held that record, until April 2011?

2. In November 1956, Charles became the first heir apparent to do what?

3. In 1966, Charles spent two terms at which school in Australia?

4. Which 2000 book, written by Charles and illustrated by Sir Hugh Casson, tells the story of a man who lives in a cave?

5. What's the name of the organisation, founded by Charles in 1976, that aims to help vulnerable young people?

6. Following his marriage to Diana in 1981, Charles set what precedent when his son William was born a year later?

7. In 1993, construction began on which experimental new town, designed by Leon Krier and endorsed by Charles?

8. In 2000, Charles made a cameo appearance in which British soap opera?

9. What tradition was revived by Charles in 2000, having previously fallen out of fashion since the days of John Thomas in the 19th century?

10. When Charles married Camilla Parker Bowles in April 2005, what title did she receive?

answers on page 416

BRITISH TELEVISION

1. Which Scottish inventor demonstrated his first working television set in January 1926?

2. Which event in 1953 is generally regarded as having helped to massively increase sales of television sets in Britain?

3. Which series, which ran from 1954 to 1957, is generally regarded as the first British soap opera?

4. In September 1955, which company became the first ITV contractor to start broadcasting?

5. ITV and its news provider ITN swiftly introduced Britain's first female newsreader. What was her name?

6. On the night of ITV's first broadcast, who died in a fire in a dramatic episode of the BBC's radio soap *The Archers*?

7. What was the name of the 1963 review that examined the future of television in Britain, and which led to the launch of BBC2?

8. In July 1967, BBC2 became Europe's first colour TV broadcaster with live coverage of which event?

9. What was the first programme shown on Channel 4, when the new station launched in November 1982?

10. As of 2021, what is the most-watched broadcast in the history of British television, when figures for all channels are counted?

answers on page 417

ANTHONY EDEN
1897 – 1977, PM 1955 to 1957

1. Born in County Durham in 1897, Anthony Eden was related on his mother's side to which figure in the history of tea?

2. Eden became an MP in 1923. What pseudonym did he use for a series of articles that he wrote for The Yorkshire Post?

3. In the run-up to the Second World War, Eden led a group of Conservative dissenters that were known by what name?

4. In 1955, Eden became prime minister. As of 2021, what distinction does he have in terms of employment statistics?

5. Which Royal Navy frogman disappeared in 1956 while examining a Soviet cruiser docked in Portsmouth?

6. What name was used to describe the idea, which Eden rejected in 1956, of Britain and France merging to form a unified state with common citizenship?

7. Eden resigned in 1957, following the Suez Crisis. He moved to Wiltshire and began to breed what type of animal?

8. Which figure, who served as both Lord Keeper of the Privy Seal and Chancellor of the Exchequer under Eden, was at one point widely tipped to succeed him as prime minister?

9. In the 1970s, Eden was an interviewees in which TV series about the Second World War, produced by Jeremy Isaacs?

10. Before he died in January 1977, Eden was the last surviving member of which body?

answers on page 417

THE SUEZ CRISIS
1956

1. The Suez Canal opened on 17th November 1869. Which French diplomat was a key figure in the canal's development?

2. Which Egyptian president nationalised the Suez Canal Company in 1956?

3. Which country was the first to invade Egypt following this declaration, in October 1956?

4. What name was given to the secret agreement that was designed to topple the Egyptian leader and occupy the canal?

5. Who was the French prime minister at the time, a key figure in securing an alliance with the UK for the invasion?

6. Who, as First Sea Lord at the time, was in charge of the British naval forces?

7. Several battles occurred in which northern Egyptian town, which was established on the coast when the canal was built?

8. The conflict lasted for nine days. The lack of a peace settlement is widely regarded as having been a key factor in which later conflict, which occurred in 1967?

9. Which Canadian statesman won the 1957 Nobel Prize for Peace, for his role in ending the Suez crisis?

10. Which American policy from 1957 meant that Middle Eastern countries would be able to request American assistance in the face of armed aggression?

answers on page 418

HAROLD MACMILLAN
1894 – 1986, PM 1957 – 1963

1. Born in 1894, Maurice Harold Macmillan served in the First World War and spent twelve hours – badly wounded – in a shell hole following which 1916 battle?

2. In the 1920s, Macmillan began to work for which publishing company?

3. He became an MP in 1924. What position in government did he hold during the Suez War of 1956?

4. Following Eden's resignation in 1957, Macmillan became prime minister. What name was given to the 1957 investigation into allegations of government insider trading?

5. In 1957, the first successful British hydrogen bomb was tested at which location in the Pacific Ocean?

6. Which organisation, founded in 1957, included figures such as Bertrand Russell, Peggy Duff and Canon John Collins?

7. What nickname was given to Macmillan in 1958, due to an Evening Standard cartoon by Victor 'Vicky' Weisz?

8. What name was given to Macmillan's major Cabinet reshuffle, which took place in July 1962?

9. Who was Macmillan's Secretary of State for War in 1963, causing a scandal that damaged the government's credibility?

10. Macmillan resigned in October 1963. In 1977, nine years before his death, he became president of which London club?

answers on page 418

BRITISH ANIMALS

1. A mid-18th century pug named Trump features in numerous paintings by which artist?

2. What was the name of the grizzly bear that was given to George III in 1811, by the Hudson's Bay Company of North America?

3. What was the name of the 19th century cow that gained fame for its huge size, weighing 1,132kg and with a length of 3.4m?

4. What was the name of Edward VII's Wire Fox Terrier, who walked in the king's funeral procession in 1910?

5. What was the name of the racing pigeon that won a 1,000-mile race from Rome to Derby in 1913?

6. What was the name of the gorilla who featured on numerous television shows while living at London Zoo between 1947 and 1978?

7. Petra, Shep and Bonnie are among the many dogs to have featured on which British children's television series?

8. Which carp, once described as the most famous fish in Britain, was around fifty years old when she died in 2010?

9. Between 1999 and 2002, a cat named Catmando (aka Cat Mandu) was named joint leader of which British political party?

10. Cats named Treasury Bill, Nelson and Larry have all held which position in the London political world?

answers on page 418

KITCHEN SINK REALISM

1. What name is usually given to the playwrights and novelists who, from the 1950s, began to create work that reflected disillusionment with British society?

2. Which 1947 film, directed by Robert Hamer, is considered to be a precursor to the kitchen sink realism of the 1950s?

3. Which 20th century artist, whose work included paintings of domestic scenes, is widely credited as a key early figure in the 'kitchen sink' movement?

4. In the 1950s and 1960s, Joan Littlewood was a key director of which influential organisation?

5. Who wrote the 1956 play *Look Back in Anger*?

6. A girl named Jo and her mother Helen feature in which play (later a film) by Shelagh Delaney, first performed in 1958?

7. Which author's novels, often associated with the 'kitchen sink' style, included *Saturday Night and Sunday Morning* (1958) and *The Death of William Posters* (1965)?

8. The style also proved popular on television. Who directed the 1966 BBC play Cathy Come Home, about a young couple's descent into poverty and homelessness?

9. Which 1966 novel by Bill Naughton, also a 1963 play and a 1966 film, tells the story of a womanising Cockney man?

10. Which actor has been playing Ken Barlow in *Coronation Street* since the show began in 1960?

answers on page 419

MANCHESTER

1. Prior to the Roman invasion of Britain, Manchester is believed to have been occupied by which tribe?

2. During the construction of a second runway at Manchester Airport, remains of an early neolithic community were discovered at which farm?

3. What was the name of the Roman fort established on the site in around 79 AD?

4. By the 11th century, Manchester was part of which administrative region?

5. Which item, preserved in Manchester Cathedral, is believed to offer evidence of a much earlier Anglo-Saxon church?

6. A Manchester linen weaver named Richard Percival is said to have been the first casualty of which event?

7. Which 36-mile waterway links Manchester to the Irish Sea and was crucial to the city's expansion during the Industrial Revolution?

8. As the city's textiles industry grew, Manchester gained what nickname in the 19th century?

9. Which event in August 1819 saw soldiers charge into a crowd that had gathered to demand parliamentary reform?

10. Which British daily national newspaper began life in 1821, and was founded by Manchester cotton merchant John Edward Taylor?

answers on page 419

THE SWINGING SIXTIES

1. Which Chelsea boutique, opened in 1966 and taken over by Freddie Hornik in 1969, was a key location in the London psychedelic scene?

2. *England Swings* is a hit 1965 song by which US singer?

3. English model Lesley Lawson is better known by what nickname?

4. What was the name of the boutique run by Vivienne Westwood and Malcolm McLaren at 430 King's Road between 1974 and 1976?

5. Which model, actress and singer was named the Face of 1966 by the Daily Express?

6. What was the name of the London nightclub that opened in the mid-1960s above the Prince Charles Cinema, and which was known as a favourite haunt of The Beatles?

7. Which 60s British figure, a pioneer of mass marketed menswear, was known as The King of Carnaby Street?

8. Cathy Gale, Emma Peel and Tara King were all characters in which 60s British television series?

9. Which Italian film-maker directed the 1966 film *Blow-Up*, about a London photographer who believes that he's caught a murder on film?

10. What's the title of Peter Whitehead's 1967 documentary about London culture during the Swinging Sixties?

answers on page 420

FASHION

1. Thomas Burberry, who founded the Burberry brand in 1856, is also credited with the invention of which tough fabric?

2. What name is generally given to the coats, made of hard-wearing material such as leather or PVC, pioneered by 19th century Staffordshire draper George Key?

3. Which 19th century English designer moved to Paris in his 30s and established an influential fashion house?

4. Sutherland Macdonald, who operated a salon in London in the early 20th century, is said to have been the first person to offer what service from an identifiable premises in Britain?

5. Which area of London is named after the wife of the 3rd Earl of Burlington?

6. Which 20th century British hairstylist was known for helping to repopularise the bob cut?

7. Which Polish immigrant founded a textile company in Leeds in 1891 and is credited with providing the first ready-to-wear clothing in the UK?

8. Which English model and actress, also known as Jordan Mooney, was a key figure behind the W10 London punk look?

9. In 1964, the so-called Second Battle of Hastings took place between members of which two groups?

10. Which English fashion designer was chief designer at Givenchy from 1996 to 2001?

answers on page 420

MUSIC

1. *My Ladye Nevells Booke* is a late 16th century piece by which English composer?

2. Which folk song index, running to around 25,000 entries, includes elements of earlier indexes such as the work of Francis James Child?

3. Which 18th century folk song, about the joy of poaching, was also included in the broadcasts of a well-known 'numbers station' in the 20th century?

4. Who wrote the 20th century piece *Fantasia on a Theme by Thomas Tallis*?

5. Which composer's work included the 1945 piece *The Young Person's Guide to the Orchestra*, which was originally commissioned for an educational documentary film?

6. Which band, formed in London in 1972, featured a number of musicians who would go on to be members of The Sex Pistols?

7. *Pink Flag* (1977) was the first album by which band?

8. Which record label was founded in Manchester by Tony Wilson and Alan Erasmus?

9. In 1996, the Midland Grand Hotel, now the St. Pancras Renaissance Hotel, was the location for which music video?

10. Who was the first ever winner of the British talent show *The X Factor*?

answers on page 420

THE BEATLES

1. What was the name of John Lennon's first band, a skiffle group that later changed its name to the Quarrymen?

2. Having changed their name to the Silver Beetles, the band toured Scotland in 1960 as the backing group for which Liverpudlian singer?

3. Who became the band's manager in January 1962?

4. The band's first single was *Love Me Do*, released in the UK in October 1962. What was the B-side track?

5. What term, first used in 1963, was used to describe the fanatical support that quickly developed for the band around the world?

6. Which American film-maker, who went on to work on the *Superman* movies, directed the Beatles in *A Hard Day's Night* (1964) and *Help!* (1965)?

7. What was the title of the song released in 1965 by John Lennon's father Alfred 'Freddie' Lennon?

8. In 1968, the Beatles travelled to an ashram in India that was run by which guru?

9. Which American musician is co-credited on the song *Get Back*?

10. The Beatles broke up in 1970. Seven years later, what was the title of their first officially sanctioned live album?

answers on page 421

LIVERPOOL

1. Liverpool's name comes from two Old English words, 'liver' and 'pol'. What did these words mean?

2. The area around Liverpool was sparsely inhabited until 1207, when which king announced the establishment of a new port and borough?

3. Liverpool benefited from increased trade with the Americas. Which political figure, who served as the local MP from 1790, was a key defender of the slave trade?

4. Which shipping company, founded in Liverpool in 1845, owned the Titanic?

5. Jesse Hartley and Philip Hardwick designed which structure, which opened in 1846?

6. What occurred in Liverpool on November 7th 1865, following the arrival of the CSS Shenandoah sailing ship?

7. In 1892, Liverpool F.C. was founded by which businessman?

8. A memoir by Bridget Dowling claims that which infamous figure lived in Liverpool between 1912 and 1913?

9. Adrian Henri, Brian Patten, Pete Brown and Roger McGough were members of which influential 1960s group, which helped give rise to the Merseybeat movement?

10. During the 1981 Toxteth Riots, what was used by police in England for the first time?

answers on page 421

HAROLD WILSON
1916 – 1995, PM 1964 – 1970 & 1974 - 1976

1. Harold Wilson was born in Huddersfield in 1916. His father James was once deputy election agent for which politician?

2. Wilson became an MP in 1945. Two years later, aged 31, he became the youngest member of a British Cabinet in the 20th century when he was appointed to which position?

3. Wilson is credited with coining which phrase, which refers to Swiss bankers?

4. Wilson became Labour prime minister in 1964. What was legalized by the Sexual Offences Act 1967?

5. In 1965, Wilson was given which award?

6. In 1967, Wilson sued which pop group for libel, following the publication of a promotional postcard for their single *Flowers in the Rain*?

7. What was launched in 1968, allowing many working-class people to obtain their first bank accounts?

8. Comprehensive education was expanded, and which organisation was established in 1969?

9. In 1975, Wilson secretly offered £14 million to which foreign dictator, in the hope that he would stop providing arms to the IRA?

10. Wilson resigned in 1976. What satirical name was given to his resignation honours list?

answers on page 422

FOOTBALL

1. In 1863, the Football Association first met at which location on Great Queen Street in London?

2. What name is given to the medieval game, originating in at least the 12th century, that is still played annually in Ashbourne, in Derbyshire?

3. What name was given to Scottish football players who moved south to play for English teams in the late 19th century?

4. What did solicitor Llewelyn Kendrick establish in 1876?

5. Which Scottish administrator is credited with having established the English Football League in 1888?

6. England left which organisation in 1928, before rejoining in 1946?

7. In 1946, who became the first manager of the English national team?

8. Which company, from 1949 to 1954, was the first supplier of the English kit?

9. England's first game in a World Cup was a 1950 defeat to which country?

10. What was the final score in England's 1966 World Cup Final victory over West Germany?

answers on page 422

DERBY

1. Derby was originally part of the Danelaw. In 917 AD, it was captured by which figure, who was ruler of the Mercians and a daughter of Alfred the Great?

2. Which clergyman, who was born in Derby in 1585, later moved to the New World and became one of the leading ministers and theologians of the Massachusetts Bay Colony?

3. Who arrived in Derby in 1745, demanding billets for 9,000 troops?

4. Who opened the first water-powered silk mill on an island in the River Derwent in 1721?

5. What device, patented by Jedediah Strutt in 1759, revolutionised the production of stockings?

6. Which 18th century Derby artist was one of the key painters of the Industrial Revolution?

7. Which 19th century Derby MP introduced a key maritime safety measure (despite Derby being far from the sea)?

8. LMS No. 10000 and 10001, which were built at the Derby Works manufacturing site, were the first examples of what type of rolling stock in Britain?

9. Which 20th century British farmer is often credited with developing the concept of 'pick your own' strawberries?

10. In 1977, what did Elizabeth II give to the Mayor of Derby on the steps of the Council House?

answers on page 422

ENOCH POWELL
1912 – 1998

1. During his childhood, John Enoch Powell was given which nickname due to his interest in a collection of stuffed birds?

2. After serving in the army during the Second World War, Powell joined the Conservative Party. Until 1947, he is said to have aspired to which foreign position?

3. In 1959, Powell criticised fellow MPs for using the term 'sub-human' in relation to which event in Kenya?

4. The following year, he was appointed to which government position, which he held until 1963?

5. What name is generally given to Powell's controversial 1968 speech about immigration?

6. During the speech, Powell quoted from a letter written by a woman living in which city?

7. In the aftermath of the speech, Powell was sacked from which political position?

8. Later in the same year, Powell gave a speech in which he laid out an alternative, free-market economic policy. What name is generally given to this speech?

9. In the 1974 general election, Powell became MP for South Down, representing which political party?

10. Powell lost his seat in 1987, and subsequently turned down which honour?

answers on page 423

BIRMINGHAM

1. Dating from around 500,000 years ago, what paleolithic artefact was found in Birmingham in 1890?

2. What was the name of the Roman fort that existed in what is now Edgbaston in Birmingham?

3. Who, in 1166, purchased from King Henry II a royal charter allowing him to hold a market on the site of the modern city?

4. Erasmus Darwin, James Watt and Josiah Wedgwood were just some of the members of which 18th and 19th century dinner club, which met in the city?

5. Opened in 1740, what was the name of Birmingham's first regular theatre?

6. What was the name of the world's first mechanised cotton mill, opened in Birmingham in 1741?

7. Which 1791 riots took place in Birmingham, with the main targets being religious dissenters?

8. 19th century inventor Alexander Parkes, who came from Birmingham, is credited with which 1856 invention?

9. Which popular font is based on a design by a Birmingham printer?

10. Which popular food item was invented by a Birmingham chemist in 1837 because his wife was allergic to eggs?

answers on page 423

GOLF

1. Established in the 15th century, the Old Course at which location is generally considered to be the oldest golf course in the world?

2. As of 2021, the oldest known instructions for playing golf feature in the diary of which Edinburgh medical student?

3. After his arrest during the 1745 Jacobite Rising, golfer John Rattray was set to be hanged. How was he saved?

4. Which Scottish golfer, born in 1821, is often referred to as The Grand Old Man of Golf?

5. In 1860, the first Open Championship (or British Open) was played at which Scottish club?

6. Who became the first English-born player to win the Open Championship, when he triumphed in 1890?

7. The Professional Golfers' Association, established in 1901, is based at which Warwickshire golf resort?

8. The first Ryder Cup between Britain and American, played in 1927, was named after the English businessman Samuel Ryder. How had Ryder made his money?

9. The fictional Royal St. Marks golf course, which features in Ian Fleming's 1959 James Bond novel *Goldfinger*, is based on which real Kent course?

10. In 1994, wich English golfer, born in October 1963, became the first non-American to top the LPGA Money list?

answers on page 424

EDWARD HEATH
1916 – 2005, PM 1970 – 1974

1. Born in Broadstairs, Kent in 1916, Edward Heath went on to study at Oxford University, where he won which scholarship in his first term?

2. He became an MP in 1950. In 1968, he sacked which MP from the Shadow cabinet following a controversial speech?

3. During the 1970 election, Heath was given which nickname by his rival Harold Wilson?

4. What nickname was given to Heath by the magazine *Private Eye*, following his fight to abolish resale price maintenance?

5. What occurred on 15th February 1971?

6. Also in 1971, while still prime minister, Heath captained Britain's winning team in which sporting event?

7. In 1972, which comedy group released a sketch titled Teach Yourself Heath, based on the prime minister's peculiar accent?

8. What name was given to the British Army operation in August 1971 that saw suspected IRA members arrested and then imprisoned without trial?

9. What slogan did Heath's Conservative Party use when they sought re-election in 1974?

10. The Conservatives lost, and Heath was defeated in a leadership election by Margaret Thatcher. He remained as an MP, and between 1992 and 2001 he held which title?

answers on page 424

BRITAIN IN THE EU

1. Which event in 1948 is regarded by many historians as the first 'federal moment' in European history?

2. In May 1949, the Treaty of London saw the UK become one of the ten founding members of which organisation?

3. Two years later, the UK declined to join which organisation that was designed to regulate economic activities?

4. Who vetoed the UK's attempts to join the European Economic Community (EEC) in 1963 and 1967?

5. A 1972 treaty provided for the accession of the UK to the European Communities, along with Denmark and Ireland. Which other country signed, but then didn't ratify the treaty?

6. In 1975, the first referendum concerning the UK's membership of the European Communities took place. What were the only two parts of the country that voted against continued membership?

7. In 1979, the UK opted out of which agreement that is widely regarded as having led to the creation of the euro currency?

8. In 1983, which Labour leader said in the general election that he'd immediately withdraw the UK from the EEC?

9. Which 1992 treaty oversaw the transition from the European Communities to the European Union?

10. Which Anglo-French businessman founded the Referendum Party in 1994?

answers on page 424

PORTSMOUTH

1. There have been settlements on the site of Portsmouth since before the Roman invasion. Which Norman lord is credited with having founded the modern city of Portsmouth in 1180?

2. In 1204, King John was staying at Portchester Castle when he heard of which loss?

3. What vessel sank off Southsea Island in 1545?

4. What nickname was once given to Portsmouth Point, due to its seedy reputation?

5. Which author, who worked as a doctor in Portsmouth, was a goalkeeper for Portsmouth A.F.C. in the late 20th century?

6. Which actor and comedian was born in Portsmouth in September 1925, and went on to feature in films by directors such as Stanley Kubrick, Blake Edwards and Hal Ashby?

7. A quarter of a million people gathered in Portsmouth in 1968 to witness the return of Alec Rose, who had single-handedly circumnavigated the world in which boat?

8. Which architect was responsible for designing more than twenty local pubs, as well as the early Fratton Park stadium?

9. What was the name of the building, which included a nightclub and a shopping centre, that was built in the Brutalist style and was finally demolished in 2004?

10. What's the name of the observation tower, opened in 2005, that's designed to reflect the city's maritime history?

answers on page 425

JAMES CALLAGHAN
1912 – 2005, PM 1976 – 1979

1. Leonard James Callaghan was born in Portsmouth in 1912. As of 2021, he's the only British prime minister to have ever served in which branch of the armed forces?

2. Aged 17, Callaghan went to work in Maidstone as a clerk for which organisation?

3. Callaghan was a key figure in which 1972 policy concerning relations between the government and the trade unions?

4. Callaghan became prime minister in 1976. What name is given to the discussion that he started with a speech on education at Ruskin College, Oxford?

5. In 1977, lacking a majority, Callaghan agreed a pact with the Liberal Party, which at the time was led by which figure?

6. In 1978, Callaghan ridiculed the idea of an early election by singing which old music hall song?

7. What phrase was commonly used to describe Callaghan's ability to maintain close ties to the trade unions?

8. In the 1979 election, what slogan was used by Margaret Thatcher's Conservatives to criticize Callaghan's government?

9. In 1988, Callaghan and his wife helped secure the copyright of *Peter Pan* for which London hospital?

10. As of 2021, James Callaghan is the only person to have held all four examples of which title?

answers on page 425

THE WINTER OF DISCONTENT
1978 - 1979

1. Which report, prepared for the Conservatives in 1977, set out problems with trade union power in the country?

2. In September 1978, thousand of workers – mostly from the Transport and General Workers Union (TGWU) – went on strike after a pay offer from which car company?

3. At this time, what level of pay increase was the government encouraging companies to offer to their employees?

4. In January 1979, a strike of which workers led to major pickets across the country?

5. After refuge collectors went on strike, the media used what term to refer to rats and rubbish in Leicester Square?

6. The use of the term 'Winter of Discontent', which refers to a quote from Shakespeare, is credited to which journalist?

7. Members of which profession went on strike in Liverpool and Tameside toward the end of January?

8. What famous newspaper headline in The Sun referred to Callaghan's insistence that there was no chaos in the country?

9. In the run-up to the 1979 general election, the Conservative Party worked with which British advertising agency?

10. James Callaghan lost a vote of no confidence in March 1979, leading to a general election. Which three smaller parties voted with Labour?

answers on page 426

THE CONSERVATIVE PARTY

1. The modern Conservative Party's history is generally traced back to which political manifesto launched by Sir Robert Peel in 1834?

2. In 1909, the Conservative Party formally took what new name?

3. Between 1911 and 1916, Arthur Steel-Maitland was the first person to hold which position?

4. Gervais Rentoul was the first chairman of which Conservative parliamentary group?

5. Who became the first British actor to win an Academy Award, for his lead role in the 1929 film *Disraeli*?

6. What was the title of the Conservative Party's 1947 pamphlet that included elements such as a 'Pledge to the Consumer' and a 'Woman's Charter'?

7. Since 1983, the Conservative Party has been a member of which international political alliance based in Germany?

8. What political group was founded by Michael Spicer in July 1993, and over the years has counted the likes of Suella Breverman, Jacob Rees-Mogg and Steve Baker as chairman?

9. Faith, Flag and Family is the motto of which group, founded in 2005?

10. Which party leader established the Conservative Future youth movement in 1998?

answers on page 426

MARGARET THATCHER
1925 – 2013, PM 1979 to 1990

1. Margaret Roberts was born in October 1925. Her father Alfred Roberts later held which position from 1945 to 1946?

2. From 1943 to 1947, she studied what subject at Oxford University?

3. In both 1950 and 1951, she stood (unsuccessfully) as the Conservative candidate for Dartford. From 1959 until 1992, she was the MP for which constituency?

4. Between 1970 and 1974, Thatcher served in what position under Edward Heath?

5. What name is generally given to her 1976 speech in which she warned that the British government was ignoring the threat posed by the Soviet Union?

6. What nickname was given to her by a Soviet journalist?

7. Thatcher resigned from her position as prime minister in November 1997, following a leadership challenge by which former minister?

8. In 1998, Thatcher called for the release of which former Chilean dictator, who was under house arrest in London?

9. In February 2007, Thatcher became the first living prime minister to receive which honour in the Houses of Parliament?

10. Margaret Thatcher died in April 2013. For the last few months of her life, she'd been living at which London hotel?

answers on page 426

THE FALKLANDS WAR
1982

1. Which country was the first to establish a permanent colony in the Falkland Islands, in 1764?

2. Britain first claimed the islands in 1765. What was the name of the first British settlement in the Falklands?

3. Which 1952 incident saw an Argentine attempt to stop the British rebuilding a damaged base on the Antarctic Peninsula?

4. The first significant incident in the 1982 conflict came when an Argentine flag was raised on South Georgia Island. What name was given to the Argentine invasion of the islands, which followed a few weeks later?

5. Who was Argentina's president during the Falklands War?

6. Who was governor of the islands during the war?

7. What was the name of the Argentine vessel that was sunk by the British in May 1982, with the loss of over 300 lives?

8. Two days later, which British vessel was sunk after being struck by a missile, resulting in 20 deaths and a number of severe injuries?

9. Which battle in late May 1982 saw the British suffer losses and damage while successfully landing troops?

10. What's the name of the Falklands capital, which fell to British control near the end of the war on 14th June 1982?

answers on page 427

PRINCESS DIANA
1961 – 1997

1. Born in 1961, Diana Spencer was the step-granddaughter of which British novelist?

2. What was Diana's job when she became engaged to Prince Charles?

3. Who designed Diana's dress for her 1981 wedding?

4. Queen Elizabeth II gave Diana which item of jewellery as a wedding present?

5. In November 1985, Diana famously danced with which American actor at the White House?

6. Which actor and voice coach is said to have helped Diana develop her public speaking voice in the early 1990s?

7. Which journalist interviewed Diana in 1995 for a controversial edition of the BBC's current affairs show *Panorama*?

8. Following her divorce from Charles, Diana worked with a number of charities. In 1997, she was criticised by a Ministry of Defence official for her involvement in a campaign against what type of weapon?

9. She was also patron of which British charity that provides support and accommodation to homeless people?

10. Diana was killed in a car crash in 1997, and was buried on an island within the grounds of which country house?

answers on page 427

PRINCE WILLIAM
b. 1982

1. Born in June 1982, William is said to have been given which nickname by his mother following a trip to Australia?

2. In 1991, William gained a permanent scar on his forehead after being accidentally hit by what object?

3. William met his future wife, Catherine Middleton, while studying at which university?

4. Aged 21, William was appointed to which position, which lets the monarch delegate functions to him through letters patent?

5. In 2006, William became President of which English sporting organisation?

6. What did William do in December 2009, as part of an initiative organised by the Centerpoint charity?

7. In 2010, after transferring to an RAF base in Anglesey, William became the first member of the British royal family since Henry VII to do what?

8. From July 2015, William spent two years as a full-time pilot with which organisation?

9. Which charity, initially established with his brother Harry, supports the work of the Duke and Duchess of Cambridge?

10. Which dog, owned by William and his wife, featured in a number of official photographs before his death in 2020?

answers on page 427

PRINCE HARRY
b. 1984

1. Henry Charles Albert David (Prince Harry) was born in 1984 at which London hospital?

2. After training at Sandhurst, in April 2006 Harry was commissioned in which Household Cavalry regiment?

3. In February 2008, Harry was confirmed to have spent time serving in which role in Helmand Province, Afghanistan?

4. He returned to Afghanistan in 2012, this time serving in what role based at Camp Bastion?

5. Which Paralympic-style sporting event, launched by Harry in 2014, features injured servicemen and women?

6. Before leaving the Armed Forces in mid-2015, Harry spent time seconded to which organisation?

7. In December 2017, Harry succeeded his grandfather Prince Philip as Captain General of which organisation?

8. What name was used by the media to describe the decision by Harry and his wife Meghan Markle to step back from senior Royal service?

9. In March 2020, Harry's last solo engagement as a senior royal was at the opening of a museum at which Northamptonshire sporting venue?

10. What's the title of the TV series, hosted by Harry and Oprah Winfrey, that focuses on mental health issues?

answers on page 428

NORWICH

1. Norwich gained its name from the Anglo-Saxon name Venta Icenorum. What did that name mean?

2. What was the name of the 12th century boy whose death was attributed by locals to Norwich's Jewish population?

3. Norwich's importance as a centre of the wool trade led to it being confirmed, in the 14th century, as what type of port?

4. Which local tanner led a Protestant rebellion in 1549, with the support of the city's poorest inhabitants?

5. What name was given to the Dutch and Flemish migrants who moved to Norwich in the 16th century, fleeing persecution in their home countries?

6. What animal is believed to have been introduced to England by these migrants?

7. Which local newspaper, published between 1701 and 1713, is believed to have been one of the first of its kind?

8. In 1797, a banker named Thomas Bignold founded which financial institution?

9. Which food manufacturer was established in Bawburgh, near Norwich, in 1814 and has since gone on to become one of Britain's oldest existing food brands?

10. Norwich flower vendor William Cullum, who became famous for racing against pleasure boats in the area, was known by which nickname?

answers on page 428

JOHN MAJOR
b. 1943, PM 1990 – 1997

1. Born in 1943, John Major was the son of which circus and music hall performer?

2. Major famously left school before his 16th birthday with which qualifications?

3. After working in banking, Major became an MP in 1979 and joined which informal dining club of Conservative MPs?

4. He became Chancellor of the Exchequer in 1989, and was the first person to deliver what type of budget?

5. Following the resignation of Margaret Thatcher, Major became prime minister. What scheme did he launch a year later, with the aim of improving public services?

6. What name is given to the event in 1992 in which the pound crashed out of the European Exchange Rate Mechanism?

7. Which organisation was privatised under Major, following an act introduced in 1993?

8. In 1993, Major struggled to gain ratification of which European treaty?

9. Two years later, in an attempt to silence his critics within the Conservative party, Major fought a leadership contest and beat which challenger?

10. After leaving politics, in 2007 Major published a book about the history of which sport?

answers on page 429

CRICKET

1. The first generally accepted reference to 'creckett' is found in a 16th century legal dispute in which English county?

2. *The Laws of Cricket*, which lays out the game's rules, has been owned and maintained since 1788 by which club?

3. By the late 18th century, which Hampshire social club was the main English cricket club until its closure in 1796?

4. What name was given to the long-running series of games between amateur and professional cricketers, first played in 1806?

5. Lord's, the cricket venue founded in 1814, was backed by members of which London club?

6. In 1817, which Surrey-born cricketer became the first player known to have scored two centuries in the same match?

7. Who wrote the 1832 memoir (originally serialised in a London newspaper) *The Cricketers of My Time*, which is generally regarded as one of the first books about the sport?

8. Which 19th century cricketer, who played for Kent County Cricket Club between 1850 and 1875, was a key figure in the legalisation of overarm bowling?

9. John Wisden launched his famous cricket almanac in 1864, as a rival to *The Guide to Cricketers* by which writer?

10. Which cricketer, who played for 44 seasons from 1865, is regarded as one of the greatest figures in the sport's history?

answers on page 429

BOLTON

1. Which Roman general is believed to have built a fort at Blackrod in the 1st century AD?

2. Following William the Conqueror's invasion, Bolton was granted to which Norman aristocrat?

3. Which 16th century manor house was, at various times, occupied by industrialists such as Samuel Crompton and William Lever?

4. Which Protestant martyr, executed in 1555, left behind the so-called 'footprint of faith' while being interrogated at Smithills Hall?

5. Up to a thousand locals were killed in 1644, when which Royalist English Civil War leader led an assault on the town?

6. Which 19th century doctor and philanthropist established an ear, nose and throat ward at Bolton Hospital?

7. Which company, founded in Bolton in 1833 at the Soho Ironworks, was known for a number of steam locomotives, some of which were exported to the United States?

8. Which Bolton-born industrialist and politician established one of the world's most successful soap manufacturers?

9. Which stadium was the original home of Bolton Wanderers F.C. from their formation in 1895?

10. Which steeplejack, born in Bolton in 1938, became famous in the 1970s following a BBC documentary about his work?

answers on page 429

TONY BLAIR
b. 1953, PM 1997 – 2007

1. As a student, Tony Blair was a member of which rock band?

2. Blair became leader of the Labour Party in 1994, and swiftly announced that he was planning to replace which clause of the party's constitution?

3. In 1997, Blair became prime minister. Who was his press secretary and official spokesman from 1997 until 2003?

4. One of the first acts of the Blair government was to give which organisation the power to set the UK base rate of interest?

5. The Belfast Agreement, signed in April 1998, is generally known by which other title?

6. Which 2000 act allows the public to request access to information held by public authorities in the UK?

7. In 2000, Operation Barras resulted in the rescue of hostages in which country?

8. In 2003, Blair became the first Briton since Winston Churchill to receive which American honour?

9. After leaving office, Blair became Special Envoy of the Quartet on the Middle East. Who are the four members of this organisation?

10. What was the title of the 2016 report that covered the Iraq War?

answers on page 430

EDINBURGH

1. Which Celtic-speaking people are believed to have built a hillfort named Din Eidyn prior to the 7th century BC?

2. Following the establishment of the Danelaw in the 9th century, the northern tip of Northumbria was cut off and became part of the Kingdom of Scotland. In 973 AD, Edgar the Peaceful granted the area to which Scottish king?

3. Which palace was constructed in Edinburgh in the early 16th century, by the order of James IV of Scotland?

4. Princes Street, named after the future George IV was, before the king's objection, going to be given what name?

5. Which 18th century Scottish architect was responsible for the layout of Edinburgh's New Town?

6. Which 18th century philosopher and historian, born in Edinburgh, is known for works such as *A Treatise of Human Nature* (1739-40)?

7. What did Sir Walter Scott discover in a sealed room at Edinburgh Castle in 1818?

8. In November 1824, what started in an engraving workshop just off Edinburgh's High Street?

9. In the 19th century, which part of Edinburgh was often referred to as Little Ireland?

10. *There's Something About a Soldier*, in 1949, was the first public example of what event in Edinburgh?

answers on page 430

THE LABOUR PARTY

1. Which organisation, founded in 1884, is now primarily a think tank and remains affiliated with the Labour Party?

2. The modern Labour Party traces its origin back to the 1900 foundation of which socialist alliance?

3. Which Scottish trade unionist was a founder of the Labour Party and served as its first parliamentary leader between 1906 and 1908?

4. In the 1920s, the Labour Party overtook which other party to become the main opposition to the Conservatives?

5. Which 1924 act, introduced by the first Labour government, increased government subsidies to enable local authorities to build municipal housing?

6. Who was leader of the party between 1955 and 1963?

7. Which Labour party figure was leader of the Greater London Council (GLC) from 1981 until it was abolished in 1986?

8. Between 1994 and 2002, the Labour Party was based in offices in which London skyscraper?

9. Which former Labour MP was known as the Beast of Bolsover?

10. Which left-wing grass-roots organisation was co-founded by Jon Lansman in 2015, following the election of Jeremy Corbyn as the Labour Party's leader?

answers on page 431

GORDON BROWN
b. 1951, PM 2007 – 2010

1. Gordon Brown was accepted by the University of Edinburgh at the age of sixteen. What subject did he study?

2. Brown became an MP in 1983, initially representing which constituency?

3. In 1986, Brown published a biography of which pacifist politician who had once led the Independent Labour Party?

4. Brown became Chancellor in 1997. He changed the inflation measure from the Retail Price Index to what other measure?

5. Another early move was to transfer banking supervision to which organisation?

6. Brown became prime minister in 2007. The Labour party launched which advertising campaign around this time?

7. What name was used for a 2008 event in which a number of MPs called for Brown to resign?

8. What name was given to the new towns announced by the Labour government, which were intended to provide new standards of sustainability?

9. Which 2008 act, passed by the Brown government, concerned attempts to reduce greenhouse gas emissions?

10. What name was generally given to an event in Rochdale during the 2010 election campaign, in which Brown's comments about a voter were accidentally recorded?

answers on page 431

RUGBY

1. The remains of which Roman town can be found just outside Rugby, on the road known as Watling Street?

2. Which 16th century merchant left provision in his will for the foundation of Rugby School?

3. In November 1605, members of which plot waited at an inn near Rugby to find out whether their plan had been successful?

4. Who wrote the 1857 novel *Tom Brown's School Days*, which is set at Rugby School?

5. Which Rugby schoolboy is credited with inventing the modern game of Rugby by picking up a football and running with it?

6. 19th century Rugby leatherworker Richard Lindon is said to have developed which sporting item?

7. Which 19th century educator introduced a number of influential reforms during his time as headmaster of Rugby School?

8. What name is given to the 1895 event in which rugby league and rugby union went their separate ways?

9. In the following season, which West Yorkshire team became the first winners of the Challenge Cup?

10. What did Frank Whittle develop in Rugby in the 1930s?

answers on page 431

DAVID CAMERON
b. 1966, PM 2010 to 2016

1. After leaving university, David Cameron joined the Conservative Research Department. What was the name of the group formed by Cameron and colleagues such as Edward Llewellyn and Rachel Whetstone?

2. Cameron became prime minister in 2010. Who became his deputy?

3. Which former newspaper editor was Cameron's director of communications from 2007 to 2011?

4. What name is given to the fiscal policy adopted by the Cameron government in 2007?

5. What code name was given to the UK's participation in 2011 military strikes in Libya?

6. In May 2011, Cameron became the first British prime minister in over a century to not also serve as patron of which non-profit organisation?

7. The 2011 England riots, which followed a police shooting, started in which part of London?

8. What was the name of the main 'No' campaign group during the 2014 Scottish independence referendum?

9. Cameron resigned in 2016, after the Brexit referendum. He later became an adviser to which financial services company?

10. In 2017, Cameron became president of which charity?

answers on page 432

BREXIT

1. Which speech, delivered in January 2013, saw David Cameron announce that he would hold an in-out referendum on the UK's future in the European Union?

2. The UK Independence Party (UKIP) started out in 1991 under what name?

3. Which Labour MP served as chairman of the Vote Leave campaign?

4. Which UK region saw 59.26% support for leaving the EU, the highest in the country?

5. Nigel Farage stood down as leader of UKIP following the referendum. Who replaced him?

6. On 29th March 2017, PM Theresa May triggered the UK's withdrawal from the EU in a letter that triggered what mechanism?

7. Which French politician was appointed as the EU's chief Brexit negotiator in May 2017?

8. What name was given to the British government's planning for the possibility of a no-deal Brexit?

9. When the UK left the EU in 2020, it had been a member of the bloc for how many years?

10. What name was given to the arrangement for post-Brexit handling of customs and immigration issues at the British-Irish border?

answers on page 432

THERESA MAY
b. 1956, PM 2016 – 2019

1. Between 1977 and 1983, Theresa May worked for which financial organisation?

2. In a 2002 speech at the Conservative Party Conference, May suggested that people often referred to the party by which nickname?

3. After becoming an MP in 1997, May became a government minister in 2010 when she was given which two roles?

4. In 2005, May co-founded which political pressure group?

5. What name is generally given to the Home Office policy, launched under May in 2012, that encouraged people to voluntarily leave the UK if they lacked leave to remain?

6. May introduced the Investigatory Powers Act 2016, which is often referred to by which nickname?

7. After losing seats in the 2017 general election, May entered into an arrangement with the Democratic Unionist Party (DUP). What name is given to this type of arrangement?

8. Shortly after winning the election, May ordered a public inquiry into which 1970s and 1980s scandal?

9. In a 2017 interview, May said that one of the 'naughtiest' things she'd ever done was to run through what?

10. In December 2018, May's government became the first in British history to be declared as what?

answers on page 432

THE ENGLISH CHANNEL & THE NORTH SEA

1. Which islet off the coast of Brittany marks the south-western limit of the English Channel?

2. What's the narrowest part of the English Channel, at which point Britain and France are only 20.7 miles (33.3km) apart?

3. In the 19th century, geologist Charles Lyell claimed (probably incorrectly) that the Goodwin Sands were the remains of which supposed ancient island?

4. What name is generally given to a group of deep trenches in the North Sea, approximately 125 miles east of Dundee?

5. 19th century French engineer Aimé Thomé de Gamond was ridiculed, and died penniless, after spending much of his life promoting which idea?

6. In July 1988, which oil platform in the North Sea was destroyed by an explosion and fire?

7. In the 1904 Dogger Bank Incident, British fishing ships were fired on by naval vessels from which country?

8. Which unrecognised micronation claims HM Fort Roughs, an offshore platform in the North Sea, as its territory?

9. In 1875, which English steamship captain became the first person to complete an observed, unassisted swim across the English Channel?

10. In 1909, which French aviator made the first crossing of the English Channel by airplane, landing near Dover?

answers on page 433

BOXING

1. In 1681, the 2nd Duke of Abemarle organised the first recorded boxing match in Britain, which was between which two people?

2. What title did James Figg hold between 1719 and 1730?

3. Early boxing in England was chaotic and sometimes fatal. Which 18th century boxer established a set of rules, which later evolved to become the London Prize Ring rules?

4. What contribution to boxing was made by John Sholto Douglas in 1867?

5. The same year, the first amateur boxing matches played to these rules took place at which Fulham sports ground?

6. What phrase was coined by writer Pierce Egan to describe prizefighting in the 19th century?

7. Which 20th century Welsh boxer had nicknames such as The Mighty Atom and The Tylorstown Terror?

8. Which British journalist, who worked for newspapers such as the Daily Herald and the News of the World, wrote a number of books about boxing and later became an honorary steward of the British Boxing Board of Control?

9. Which Welsh boxer held the WBO super-middleweight title for over a decade from 1997?

10. In 2012, which British boxer became the first person to win an Olympic women's boxing gold medal?

answers on page 433

KINGSTON UPON HULL

1. Which wealthy wool merchant became the first mayor of Kingston upon Hull in 1332, and founded a family that went on to become influential across the country?

2. During the Middle Ages, Hull enjoyed strong trade with a number of Baltic nations as part of which confederation?

3. In 1773, the first example of what type of company was formed in the city?

4. Which British anti-slavery campaigner was MP for Kingston upon Hull from 1780 to 1784?

5. Which businessman, born in Hull in 1862, owned a shipping company and was for a while the richest man in England?

6. Which architect, who served as the City Architect of Kingston upon Hull from 1900 to 1926, designed many of the city's best-known buildings?

7. Hull was heavily bombed during the Second World War. What name was given to the practice whereby people would sleep in the countryside when bombing raids were expected?

8. Which poet became a librarian at the University of Hull in 1955 and held the position until his death thirty years later?

9. In the 20th century, Hull's economy was damaged by which conflict over fishing rights between the UK and Iceland?

10. In 2017, Hull was awarded which title, which is given out once every four years?

answers on page 434

BORIS JOHNSON
b. 1964, PM from 2019

1. Alexander Boris de Pfeffel Johnson was born in New York in 1964. The 'de Pfeffel' part of his name comes from a part of the family originating in which German state?

2. While studying at Oxford, Johnson joined which private dining club?

3. In 1987, Johnson secured work as a graduate trainee at which British newspaper?

4. Johnson's first wife was which author and journalist?

5. Johnson achieved national fame in 1998 after appearing on which British quiz show?

6. Between 1999 and 2005, Johnson edited which British magazine?

7. After an unsuccessful attempt to become MP for Clwyd South in 1997, Johnson finally entered the House of Commons in 2001 as MP for which constituency?

8. As Mayor of London, Johnson oversaw a ban on what activity on public transport?

9. What's the title of Johnson's 2004 comic novel about an attempt to assassinate a visiting US president?

10. He became prime minister in July 2019. Who did he appoint as his chief adviser?

answers on page 434

TENNIS

1. The world's first tennis club was founded in 1872 in which English town?

2. Which 19th century Welsh inventor and army officer is generally regarded as one of the key pioneers of lawn tennis?

3. In 1877, which English player won the first Wimbledon tournament?

4. In 1888, which seven-time Wimbledon champion was elected the first president of the Lawn Tennis Association?

5. The Davis Cup, which has pitted British and American tennis players against each other since 1900, is named after which American player and politician?

6. Established in 1902, Wimbledon has (as of 2021) the world's longest-running sports sponsorship deal with which company?

7. Fred Perry, the first tennis player to win a Career Grand Slam, was the 1929 World Champion in which other sport?

8. Which female player's victories include the 1955 French Championships, the 1958 Australian Championships, and the 1961 Wimbledon Championship?

9. Aorangi Terrace, a banked area at Wimbledon, is now better known by what name?

10. Before Emma Raducanu won the US Open in 2021, who was the last British woman to win a Grand Slam singles title?

answers on page 434

COVID-19

1. What's the full name of the virus that causes COVID-19?

2. The first death of a British resident from COVID-19 is believed to have occurred in January 2000 at which Kent hospital?

3. On 31st January 2020, the first UK COVID-19 cases were confirmed in which city?

4. What code name was used for the British military operation, launched in March 2020, that was designed to help tackle COVID-19 in the UK and its Crown Dependencies?

5. Who was the Chief Scientific Adviser to the UK government when the COVID-19 pandemic started?

6. One of the key government bodies offering advice during the pandemic was SAGE. What does this acronym stand for?

7. Between March and April 2020, who deputised for Boris Johnson while he was ill with COVID-19?

8. What was the name of the scheme, in August 2020, that offered UK customers a discount on food and drink?

9. What happened to Margaret Keenan in December 2020?

10. Who became head of the NHS Test and Trace service in April 2021?

answers on page 435

THE FUTURE...

1. By what name is Great Britain known in George Orwell's *1984* (1949)?

2. As of 2021, Shetland, Sutherland and Newquay in Cornwall are the three proposed British locations for what type of site?

3. Which British comic book hero, created by Frank Hampson, is described as a 'pilot of the future'?

4. The first stage of the High Speed 2 (HS2) rail project – due for completion in 2029 – will connect London to a new station in which city?

5. Which English author's novels include *The Drowned World* (1962), *High Rise* (1975) and *Kingdom Come* (2006)?

6. In *The Hitchhiker's Guide to the Galaxy*, what's the name of the alien race responsible for destroying Earth?

7. Who wrote the dystopian novel *The Children of Men*, set in a future version of England in which mass infertility has left the world in turmoil?

8. According to a 1966 film starring Peter Cushing and Bernard Cribbins, what alien race is supposed to invade Earth – with London as its primary target – in the year 2150 AD?

9. In *The Time Machine* by H.G. Wells, by the year 802,701 AD London is inhabited by which race of childlike creatures?

10. What is expected to happen to Britain in approximately 7.5 billion years?

answers on page 435

ANSWERS

IN THE BEGINNING...

1. 13.8 billion years ago
2. 4.5 billion years ago
3. 3.7 billion years ago
4. The last universal common ancestor, from which all life on Earth is descended
5. The Cambrian explosion
6. Tetrapods
7. The Triassic period
8. Sauropods
9. Pangaea
10. Upright man

GEOLOGY

1. Around 17 to 22 miles (27 to 35km). Globally, the crust's thickness ranges from 5 to 70km
2. Volcanic eruptions
3. The Jurassic Coast
4. 12 miles west of the Scottish coast
5. Lewisian gneiss, which is around 3 billion years old and can be found on the Isle of Lewis
6. Lava (or magma)
7. Avalonia
8. Chalk
9. The Weald
10. The coastline

PALAEOLITHIC BRITAIN (THE OLD STONE AGE)

1. Humans using stone tools
2. Homo
3. Norfolk
4. The English Channel
5. Swanscombe

6. Kents Cavern
7. The Red Lady of Paviland
8. The Creswellian culture (or sometimes Late Magdalenian)
9. The Younger Dryas
10. Acheulean

MESOLITHIC BRITAIN (THE MIDDLE STONE AGE)

1. The north of Germany
2. Wild reindeer
3. Barbs
4. The dog (canis familiaris)
5. Howick
6. Star Carr
7. The Holocene
8. Doggerland
9. Bouldnor Cliff
10. Gough's Cave in Cheddar Gorge, Somerset

NEOLITHIC BRITAIN (THE NEW STONE AGE)

1. Hunter-gatherer
2. Deforestation
3. The Post Track
4. Flagstones
5. Avebury
6. The Altar Stone
7. The River Avon
8. The Ness of Brodgar
9. The Westray Wife (sometimes the Orkney Venus)
10. The Meldon Bridge Period

BRONZE AGE BRITAIN

1. Tin
2. The sword or dagger

3. The Mount Pleasant Phase
4. Seahenge
5. A horse
6. The Sea Peoples
7. Stonehenge
8. The Hallstatt culture
9. The Bell Beaker culture
10. The Wessex culture (not to be confused with the later Saxon kingdom of the same name)

IRON AGE BRITAIN

1. The Trinovantes
2. Pytheas
3. tin
4. Phoenicia
5. The Celtic religion, or Celtic paganism
6. Maiden Castle
7. Vespasian's Camp
8. Colchester
9. Gaul
10. Wine (particularly from Italy)

ROMAN BRITAIN

1. Caratacus
2. Pegwell Bay (although the site could still have been Walmer or Deal instead)
3. Claudius
4. The Battle of the Medway
5. Anglesey
6. Cartimandua (or Cartismandua)
7. The Battle of Mons Graupius
8. The London Wall
9. The Caledonians
10. Honorius

EARLY RELIGION & THE ARRIVAL OF CHRISTIANITY

1. Druids
2. Anglesey
3. Sulis (or Sulis Minerva), and the Romans called the spa baths Aquae Sulis (the waters of Sulis)
4. King Lucius
5. St. Alban, who lived in the 3rd century BC
6. The Edict of Milan
7. Saint Patrick
8. St. Ninian
9. Wodan
10. Augustine of Canterbury

BATH

1. Aquae Sulis
2. The frigidarium
3. The Aching Man's City
4. A Sally Lunn
5. John Wood, the Elder
6. Ralph Allen
7. Pulteney Bridge
8. Beau Nash
9. Haile Selassie of Ethiopia
10. Mary Berry

EARLY LITERATURE

1. Cædmon
2. Grendel
3. Scandinavia
4. Wiglaf
5. The Wanderer
6. Walter of Aquitaine
7. The Mabinogion

8. Tristan and Iseult (or Tristan and Isolde), and the story is believed to have influenced the story of Lancelot and Guinevere
9. The Tremulous Hand of Worcester
10. Julian of Norwich

BOUDICA

1. The Iceni
2. Norfolk
3. Prasutagus
4. Gaius Suetonius Paulinus
5. A hare
6. St. Albans
7. Nero
8. The Battle of Watling Street (although the exact location is uncertain)
9. He says that she poisoned herself once she saw that defeat was inevitable
10. The western end of Westminster Bridge, facing Big Ben and the Palace and Westminster

ROMAN LONDON

1. Lud
2. Londinium
3. The Devil's Highway
4. King's Cross
5. London Stone
6. The River Fleet
7. An amphitheatre
8. Londiniensi
9. Carausius
10. Alfred the Great

ROADS

1. Shrewsbury
2. The A2, or the Dover Road
3. Old Hell Road
4. Pavage
5. The Rebecca Riots
6. He was convicted of speeding, after driving through Paddock Wood at 8mph (four times the limit). He was fined 1 shilling plus costs
7. Seventeen
8. The first automatic traffic lights (earlier manual lights, operated by police constables, had first been installed outside the Houses of Parliament in 1868)
9. The cat's eye road safety device
10. It's a speed camera

SAINT GEORGE

1. Turkey
2. The Roman army
3. Diocletian
4. Alexandra
5. Silene
6. Apollo
7. Gelasius I
8. Lod
9. Edward VI
10. April 23rd

THE END OF THE ROMAN ERA

1. The Germanic tribes
2. Magnus Maximus
3. Stilicho
4. Niall 'Noigiallach' (aka Niall of the Nine Hostages)

5. The Crossing of the Rhine
6. Constantine III
7. Civitas
8. Honorius
9. The Visigoths
10. The Saxons

ANGLO-SAXON BRITAIN

1. Vortigern
2. Hengist and Horsa
3. The Battle of Badon, or the Battle of Mons Badonicus
4. Ætheling
5. The Witenaġemot, or Witan
6. Æthelberht
7. Whitby
8. Ceawlin
9. Gildas
10. Sutton Hoo

THE HEPTARCHY

1. Henry of Huntingdon (although the term 'heptarchy' was not used for another five hundred years)
2. The Dark Ages
3. Tamworth
4. Penda
5. Oswald
6. Cædwalla
7. The Wuffingas (or Uffingas)
8. Essex
9. Bretwalda
10. Ecgberht (or Egbert)

THE LEGEND OF KING ARTHUR

1. Uther Pendragon

2. Tintagel
3. Annwn (also written as Annwfn or Annwfyn)
4. Lancelot
5. The Siege Perilous
6. The Fisher King
7. Morgan le Fay
8. Brocéliande
9. Sir Thomas Malory
10. The Battle of Camlann

OFFA OF MERCIA

1. Pybba
2. Æthelbald
3. Islamic (the coin copies many features of a coin minted by an Abbasid ruler)
4. The Mercian Supremacy
5. Kent
6. Cynethryth
7. Charlemagne
8. Offa's Dyke (although recent studies suggest that it might have been begun before his time)
9. The Kingdom of Powys
10. Ecgfrith

THE VIKING AGE

1. The Isle of Portland, the southernmost point of Dorset
2. Lindisfarne
3. Great Heathen Army
4. The Danelaw
5. A raven
6. Danegeld
7. Berkserker (from the word for bear)
8. Odin
9. Valhalla

10. Rollo

KENNETH MACALPIN, KENNETH I OF SCOTLAND

1. Iona
2. Dál Riada
3. He supposedly got them drunk, and then dropped them onto spikes that had been hidden beneath their seats
4. Forteviot
5. The Conqueror (An Ferbasach)
6. The Stone of Scone
7. His brother, Donald I
8. High King of Ireland
9. The Prophecy of Berchán
10. Malcolm II

ORKNEY & SHETLAND

1. Brochs
2. Dwarfie Stane
3. Thule
4. Norn
5. Henry Sinclair
6. Robert Stewart
7. The Shetland Bus
8. The Ayre
9. HMS Royal Oak
10. The Yellow Cake Revue

ALFRED THE GREAT

1. Æthelwulf
2. Chippenham
3. Wessex
4. Guthrum
5. The Somerset Levels

6. The Battle of Edington (sometimes referred to as The Battle of Ethandun)
7. Ealhswith
8. The Burghal Hidage
9. The Doom Book
10. Either Chron's disease or haemmorhoids

WINCHESTER

1. Venta Belgarum
2. The Clarendon Way
3. St. Swithun (or Swithin)
4. Henry of Blois, brother of King Stephen
5. Simon de Montfort
6. The Winchester Round Table, created around the mid-13th century, mostly likely during the reign of Edward I
7. Queen Mary and Philip II of Spain
8. The City Cross, or Buttercross. He was stopped by the locals
9. Edward Young
10. Jane Austen

ÆTHELSTAN

1. Edward the Elder
2. Mercia
3. Scandinavian York (also known as Jórvik)
4. Scotland
5. The Battle of Brunanburh
6. Ealdormen
7. There wasn't one. Anglo-Saxon kings held their councils at various locations around the country
8. Tithing
9. King of the Whole of Britain
10. Malmesbury Abbey, in Wiltshire

ÆTHELRED THE UNREADY

1. Edward the Martyr
2. Dunstan
3. The Battle of Maldon
4. J.R.R. Tolkien
5. St. Brice's Day (November 13th)
6. Sweyn Forkbeard
7. Normandy
8. Olaf II (also known as Saint Olaf)
9. Edmund Ironside
10. Poorly advised

OXFORD

1. Gunhile (or Gunnhild)
2. Emo of Friesland
3. Sweating sickness
4. They were burnt at the stake for heresy, and are now referred to as the Oxford Martyrs
5. Magdalen Bridge
6. Blackwell's
7. Henry Hare
8. William Morris (the company was Morris Motors)
9. Hitler is believed to have planned to make it the new capital city
10. Roger Bannister

CNUT THE GREAT

1. Harald Bluetooth
2. Denmark, England & Norway
3. Sandwich
4. The Battle of Helgeå, in Sweden
5. Henry of Huntingdon
6. Emma of Normandy

7. Wulfstan
8. Conrad II
9. Winchester
10. Harthcnut

MACBETH OF SCOTLAND

1. Malcolm II
2. Cnut the Great
3. Mormaer of Moray (a semi-autonomous lordship centred on the Spey valley and the area around Inverness, not the modern area of Moray)
4. Tanistry
5. Rome
6. Thorfinn Sigurdsson
7. Edward the Confessor
8. The Battle of Lumphanan
9. Iona
10. Three witches (or 'weird sisters')

EDWARD THE CONFESSOR

1. The House of Wessex
2. Normandy (France)
3. He was blinded by red hot pokers, inserted into his eyes
4. Macbeth
5. To continue the laws of Cnut
6. Westminster Abbey
7. Harold Godwinson, later (briefly) King Harold
8. Rhys ap Rhydderch
9. William of Normandy, later William I
10. Alexander III

WESTMINSTER ABBEY

1. Aldrich
2. King Edgar
3. The Romanesque style
4. William the Conqueror (although his predecessor, Harold II, might have been crowned there as well)
5. Henry III
6. Technically, neither. It's a church, having lost its abbey status following the reign of Henry VIII, when Catholics were driven out
7. Nicholas Hawksmoor
8. Benedict XVI, in 2010
9. King (or sometimes Saint) Edward's Chair
10. Geoffrey Chaucer

WILLIAM I & THE BATTLE OF HASTINGS

1. Robert I (aka Robert the Magnificent)
2. Matilda of Flanders
3. Odo of Bayeux
4. The Battle of Stamford Bridge
5. Pevensey Bay
6. Battle
7. Edgar Ætheling (grandson of Æthelfred the Unready)
8. The Harrying of the North
9. The Revolt of the Earls
10. The Tower of London

EXETER

1. Isca Dumnoniorum (which translates as Watertown of the Dumnonii, a reference to a local tribe)
2. Gytha Thorkelsdóttir, the mother of former king Harold
3. Sir Thomas Bodley (founder of the Bodleian Library)
4. Northernhay Gardens

5. The Bideford (or Exeter) Witch Trial, with some sources claiming that they were the last witches to be hanged in England
6. Romany Rye
7. Henry Chadwick
8. Harry Hems
9. The Baedeker Blitz
10. Princesshay (which was subsequently demolished and rebuilt)

A BRIEF HISTORY OF THE ENGLISH LANGUAGE

1. The West Germanic branch
2. Via the Anglo-Saxon settlers who migrated to Britain following the end of Roman rule
3. A British Celtic language
4. Brittonic
5. Futhorc
6. Old Norse, which was descended from a North Germanic language
7. Anglo-Norman
8. Norman French
9. Henry IV, who ruled in the early 15th century
10. 1604

EARLY SCOTLAND

1. Alba
2. Egypt (via a princess named Scota)
3. The Picts
4. The Gaels
5. The Caledonians
6. Fergus Mor
7. Saint Columba
8. Bernicia
9. Robert II

10. The Scottish Marches

ABERDEEN

1. William the Lion
2. The Common Good Fund
3. Bon Accord
4. The Aberdeen Doctors
5. The Granite City
6. The Great North of Scotland Railway (GNSR)
7. William Dyce
8. The Gordon Highlanders
9. Typhoid
10. Annie Lennox

EARLY WALES

1. Pentre Ifan (John's Village)
2. Bryn Celli Ddu
3. The Silures
4. Tydfil
5. Saint David
6. Cadwaladr
7. Rhodri the Great
8. The Kingdom of Gwynedd
9. Gruffydd ap Llywelyn
10. Edward I

THE DOMESDAY BOOK

1. Medieval Latin
2. Little Domesday
3. Edward the Confessor
4. 10%
5. Hides
6. Exon Domesday (or Liber Exoniensis)

7. The Book of Winchester
8. Richard FitzNeal
9. Nonsuch Palace
10. The National Archives at Kew

WILLIAM II

1. William Rufus (Rufus is Latin for 'the Red', and William is said to have had red hair)
2. The Rebellion of 1088
3. Anselm
4. The Holy Face of Lucca
5. Malcolm III
6. Westminster Hall (the oldest surviving part of what is now Westminster Palace)
7. Carlisle Castle
9. Brockenhurst
9. Walter Tirel
10. The Rufus Stone

HENRY I

1. Winchester
2. Matilda, daughter of King Malcolm III
3. The Treaty of Alton
4. The Marcher Lords
5. The White Ship
6. The crew and passengers were all said to be drunk
7. Maredudd ap Bleddyn
8. Adeliza of Louvain
9. Lampreys
10. Matilda

STEPHEN, MATILDA & THE ANARCHY

1. Blois
2. Hugh Bigod
3. Wales
4. She was the daughter of the previous king, Henry I
5. Geoffrey V of Anjou, from whom the name Plantagenet is derived
6. The Battle of Lincoln
7. Oxford Castle
8. Henry FitzEmpress
9. The Treaty of Winchester
10. Dover Priory

DAVID I OF SCOTLAND

1. Malcolm III
2. The Pearl of Scotland, or St. Margaret
3. The House of Dunkeld
4. King Henry I of England
5. Prince of the Cumbrians
6. The Battle of Clitheroe
7. The Battle of the Standard
8. Kinloss Abbey
9. His grandson, Henry's son, who became Malcolm IV
10. Carlisle Castle

WINDSOR CASTLE

1. William I
2. Motte-and-bailey
3. Henry I
4. The Order of the Garter
5. John II
6. Squatters and paupers
7. The Queen's Beasts

8. A Windsor Castle guidebook
9. Frogmore
10. The Queen's Private Chapel

HENRY II

1. The House of Plantagenet
2. Eleanor of Aquitaine
3. The Angevin Empire
4. Malcolm IV
5. Henry the Young King
6. Louis VII
7. Diarmait Mac Murchada (aka Dermot MacMurrough)
8. The Great Revolt
9. The Glanvill Treatise (or the Treatise on the Laws and Customs of the Kingdom of England)
10. Fontevraud Abbey

THE ASSASSINATION OF THOMAS BECKET

1. Theobald of Bec
2. Lord Chancellor
3. The Constitutions of Clarendon
4. Winchester
5. The north-west transept
6. They were told to serve in the Holy Lands for fourteen years. It's believed that none of them ever returned to England, although some rumours suggest otherwise
7. Alexander III
8. St. Dunstan's
9. Arbroath Abbey
10. 29th December

CANTERBURY

1. Durovernum Cantiacorum (Kentish Durovernum)
2. Dunstan
3. Westgate
4. Huguenots
5. The Crab and Winkle Way
6. Henry Willis
7. Rupert Bear
8. Soft Machine
9. Princess Marina, the Duchess of Kent
10. Smallfilms (set up by Oliver Postgate and Peter Firmin)

DOVER CASTLE

1. The Cinque Ports
2. St. Mary in Castro (or St. Mary de Castro)
3. Around £10,000
4. Constable's Gate
5. A windmill
6. Thomas Becket
7. He led a group of 10 men who obtained the keys to the castle and took the site for the Parliamentarian side in the Civil War
8. A large, working pair of wings
9. The Dover Castle Clock
10. Admiral of the Fleet Michael Boyce, Baron Boyce

RICHARD I

1. Beaumont Palace
2. Aquitaine
3. Three lions
4. They were stripped and flogged, leading to a series of mob attacks on Jews across the country
5. Cyprus

6. The Battle of Jaffa
7. Henry VI
8. John (later King John)
9. A crossbow
10. Very little, possibly only six months

THE CRUSADES

1. Atsiz
2. The Council of Clermont
3. Peter the Hermit
4. Kilij Arslan
5. Godfrey of Bouillon
6. The Knights Templar
7. Saladin (or Salah ad-Din)
8. Acre
9. Constantinople
10. Nine

JOHN

1. Lord of Ireland
2. Lackland
3. Philip II
4. Isabella of Angoulĕme
5. Normandy
6. Runnymede, near Windsor Castle
7. The First Barons' War
8. Louis (later Louis VIII of France, also known as The Lion)
9. The Crown Jewels
10. The Treaty of Lambeth

MAGNA CARTA

1. The Battle of Bouvines
2. Great Charter of Freedoms
3. Stephen Langton
4. That the barons could seize the king's assets if he failed to conform to the charter
5. The Charter of the Forest
6. The first mechanically printed edition of Magna Carta
7. The divine right of kings
8. The U.S. Capitol
9. Sir Edward Maufe
10. The right to due legal process

THE LEGEND OF ROBIN HOOD

1. Piers Plowman
2. He was a yeoman, which meant that he was somewhere between a knight and a peasant
3. Guy of Gisbourne
4. May Games
5. Lincoln green
6. The Sheriff of Nottingham
7. Howard Pyle
8. James Woodford
9. A fox
10. Locksley Castle, near Sheffield

NOTTINGHAM

1. The Place of Caves
2. Snot
3. Ye Olde Trip to Jerusalem
4. The Nottingham Goose Fair
5. John Boot, the founder of Boots the Chemist
6. Trent Bridge

7. John Player, the founder of John Player & Sons
8. Carrington Street Station
9. The lace industry
10. The Raleigh Bicycle Company

HENRY III

1. Nine
2. William Marshal
3. The Battle of Sandwich (sometimes referred to as the Battle of Dover)
4. Parliament
5. The Statute of Jewry
6. The Provisions of Oxford
7. Simon de Montfort
8. The Battle of Lewes
9. The Battle of Evesham
10. His heart, which was taken to be reburied at Fontevraud Abbey in France

EDWARD I

1. Edward the Confessor
2. Longshanks
3. He was in Sicily, while part of the Ninth Crusade
4. Llywelyn ap Gruffudd
5. The Eleanor crosses (including the one at Charing in London, which led to the name Charing Cross)
6. Jews (anti-Jewish sentiment had been building for many years and had become particularly virulent during the reign of Edward's father Henry III)
7. The Great Cause
8. John Balliol
9. The Stone of Destiny
10. Robert the Bruce

WILLIAM WALLACE

1. Alexander III
2. William de Heselrig
3. Ettrick Forest
4. The Battle of Stirling Bridge
5. The Battle of Falkirk
6. John de Menteith
7. A garland of oak
8. He was hung, drawn and quartered
9. Blind Harry
10. The Abbey Craig, to the north of Stirling

ROBERT THE BRUCE

1. Robert de Brus (grandfather of the later figure Robert the 1. Bruce)
2. John Cornyn
3. Christina of the Isles
4. St. Andrews
5. The Battle of Bannockburn
6. The Treaty of Edinburgh-Northampton
7. Leprosy
8. Dunfermline Abbey
9. David II
10. The Elgin Marbles

EDWARD II

1. Caernarfon Castle (hence his nickname Edward of Caernarfon)
2. Piers Gaveston
3. The Ordinances of 1311
4. Stirling Castle, leading to the Battle of Bannockburn
5. The Great Famine
6. Hugh Despenser

7. Thomas, Earl of Lancaster
8. Contrariants
9. Berkeley Castle
10. That he'd actually survived and had gone to live as a hermit in mainland Europe, although this claim is viewed with great scepticism by most modern historians

CHESTER

1. Deva Victrix
2. Minerva's Shrine
3. Æthelfrith of Northumbria
4. Edgar the Peaceful
5. The Chester Rows
6. Westchester
7. William Lawes
8. *There Was a Jolly Miller Once* (also known as *The Miller of the Dee*)
9. The Dee Bridge disaster
10. John Douglas

EDWARD III

1. Edward of Windsor (because he was born at Windsor Castle)
2. He became Earl of Chester
3. Roger Mortimer
4. Nottingham Castle
5. The Battle of Crécy
6. The Round Table from Arthurian legend
7. Treason (the act is the Treason Act)
8. William Wykeham
9. The Good Parliament
10. John of Gaunt

THE HUNDRED YEARS' WAR
PART I: THE EDWARDIAN WAR

1. The House of Valois
2. The dead king, Charles IV, was his uncle
3. Philip, Count of Valois, became Philip VI
4. Hastings
5. The Battle of Sluys
6. David II
7. He insisted that he was worth more, so he had his own ransom doubled
8. The Jacquerie
9. Black Monday
10. Aquitaine

THE BLACK DEATH

1. Bubonic plague
2. Weymouth, in Dorset
3. Bristol
4. The Oriental rat flea
5. Joan of England, daughter of Edward III
6. *Ring a Ring o' Roses* (or *Ring Around the Rosie* in the US)
7. Plague Doctor
8. Daniel Defoe
9. Sir John Lawrence
10. New Churchyard, better known as the Bedlam or Bethlem burial ground

BRISTOL

1. Brycg Stowe (which meant, place by the bridge)
2. William Canynge
3. The New Room in Broadmead
4. Edward Colston
5. Edmund Burke

6. Cigarettes
7. The second Reform Bill, which was designed to give cities such as Bristol greater representation in the House of Commons
8. The Bristol L
9. The refusal to employ Black or Asian bus crews
10. The last operational Concorde made its final landing

EDWARD THE BLACK PRINCE

1. Woodstock (hence his name Edward of Woodstock)
2. The Duchy of Cornwall
3. Nottingham Castle
4. Caen
5. The Order of the Garter
6. The Battle of Winchelsea
7. Carcassonne
8. Joan, Countess of Kent (also known as the Fair Maid of Kent)
9. An ostrich
10. Canterbury Cathedral

CORNWALL

1. Tin
2. Common Brittonic
3. The Dumnonii or Dumnones
4. A Knocker
5. The Cornovii
6. Donyarth or Dungarth (although he was most likely an under-king who paid tribute to Alfred the Great)
7. The Battle of Deptford Bridge, near London
8. The Lisbon earthquake
9. A stannary
10. Jamaica Inn

THE HUNDRED YEARS' WAR
PART 2: THE CAROLINIAN WAR

1. Castille (part of modern Spain)
2. Peter the Cruel
3. Charles V of France
4. Avignon
5. The Eagle of Brittany and The Black Dog of Brocéliande
6. The Battle of La Rochelle
7. The Great Chevauchée
8. The Treaty of Bruges
9. The Butcher
10. The Truce of Leulinghem

RICHARD II

1. Bordeaux
2. 10
3. Henry Bolingbroke (later Henry IV)
4. The Lords Appellant
5. The Merciless Parliament
6. Geoffrey Chaucer
7. A white hart (deer)
8. Flint Castle
9. The Epiphany Rising
10. Pontefract Castle

THE PEASANTS' REVOLT

1. Wages were fixed at pre-plague levels, contracts had to be upheld, and refusing to work became a criminal offence
2. Essex
3. Wat Tyler
4. Lady Joan, the Countess (or Fair Maid) of Kent
5. Blackheath
6. John Ball

7. Greenwich

8. The Savoy Palace (now the site of the Savoy Hotel)

9. John Wrawe

10. Serfdom

HENRY IV

1. Bolingbroke Castle, hence his nickname Henry Bolingbroke
2. John of Gaunt, a son of Edward III
3. The Teutonic Knights
4. Thomas Arundel
5. In Ireland, on a military campaign
6. Edmund Mortimer
7. The longbow
8. Jerusalem
9. The Jerusalem Chamber at Westminster Abbey
10. Thomas Becket

OWAIN GLYNDŴR AND THE WELSH REVOLT

1. The Inns of Court, where he most likely worked as a legal apprentice
2. David Hanmer
3. Scrope v Grosvenor, which involved two different families who were using the same coat of arms
4. Iolo Goch, aka Iolo the Red
5. The Battle of Mynydd Hyddgen
6. Machynlleth
7. The Tripartite Indenture
8. Prince of Wales
9. Jack of Kent, aka Siôn Cent
10. Hippo, now part of Algeria

CARDIFF

1. Womanby Street
2. Llewelyn Bren
3. The Battle of St. Fagans
4. John Crichton-Stuart, the 2nd Marchess of Bute
5. Ivor Novello
6. Riverside A.F.C.
7. City status
8. Billy the Seal
9. Shirley Bassey
10. Richard Rogers

GEOFFREY CHAUCER & THE CANTERBURY TALES

1. They were vintners (wine-makers)
2. The Inner Temple (one of London's four Inns of Court)
3. Blanche of Lancaster (the wife of Edward III's son John of Gaunt)
4. A gallon of wine daily, for the rest of his life
5. The Tabard Inn in Southwark
6. A free meal at the pub, upon their return
7. *The Decameron*
8. An astronomical instrument that contained a handheld model of the entire universe, used to identify stars and planets
9. *Troilus and Criseyde*
10. Speaker of the House of Commons

HENRY V

1. Henry of Monmouth
2. An arrow hit him in the face, and he was left with permanent scars
3. Sir John Falstaff
4. A snowstorm, which was seen as either a good omen or a bad omen by different observers

5. Saint Crispin
6. Glass
7. The Order of the Dragon
8. Rouen
9. The Lollards
10. King of France (he had been named heir to Charles VI, who survived him)

SOUTHAMPTON

1. Hamwic, or Hamtun
2. God's House Tower
3. Italy
4. Henry V
5. William Capon, with the school being King Edward VI 6. School
6. Isaac Watts
7. Walter Taylor
8. RMS Titanic
9. Benny Hill
10. Spitfire planes

THE HUNDRED YEARS WAR
PART 3: THE LANCASTRIAN WAR

1. Harfleur
2. Calais
3. Around 15,000 men (or up to 25,000 if armed servants are included)
4. He had all French prisoners executed, most likely because they outnumbered their captors
5. The Battle of Verneuil
6. The Maid of Orléans (or the Maid of Lorraine)
7. Philip the Good, also known as Philip III of Burgundy
8. The Battle of Castillon, which resulted in an English defeat
9. The Treat of Picquigny

10. George III, who dropped the claim out of respect to the exiled King Louis XVIII, who lived in England after the French Revolution

HENRY VI

1. King of France (after the death of his grandfather Charles VI)
2. Owen Tudor
3. The Great Bullion Famine
4. Margaret of Anjou
5. The Great Slump
6. Jack Cade
7. Calais
8. Jackanapes
9. Richard, Duke of York
10. Loveday (or the Annunciation Loveday)

THE WARS OF THE ROSES

1. The House of York had a white rose, while the House of Lancaster had a red rose
2. He was captured by the House of York
3. The Battle of Wakefield
4. The Tower of London
5. Robin of Redesdale
6. Norham Castle, in Northumberland
7. Richard Neville, the Earl of Warwick
8. The Battle of Tewkesbury
9. Melancholy
10. Migraines

EDWARD IV

1. Earl of March
2. Elizabeth Woodville

3. The Sun in Splendour
4. John Neville, the Marquess of Montagu
5. Flemish merchants
6. He would gorge himself, then leave so he could vomit, then return to continue eating
7. Eltham Palace
8. The first printing press in England
9. The Medici Bank
10. His brother Richard, Duke of Gloucester

LANCASTER

1. The River Lune
2. Henry III
3. John of Gaunt, the 1st Duke of Lancaster (son of Edward III and father of Henry IV)
4. The Pendle witches
5. The Lancaster Martyrs
6. Dodshon Foster
7. A printed cardboard train ticket
8. Dinosaur (or Dinosauria originally, meaning 'terrible reptile')
9. George Pike England
10. *Missing You*

YORK

1. Saint Paulinus of York
2. The Kingdom of Jorvik
3. Edmund I
4. The wooden Ouse Bridge, which was subsequently replaced
5. Josce (or Joceus)
6. Edmund of Langley, the first Duke of York (a son of Edward III, and brother of John of Gaunt)
7. The York Mystery Plays (or the York Corpus Christi Plays)

8. John Nevison (this story, which should possibly refer instead to Samuel Nicks, is believed to have inspired a similar tale about Dick Turpin)
9. An open-air slaughterhouse or meat market
10. George Hudson

EDWARD V

1. The Princes in the Tower
2. President of the Council of Wales and the Marches
3. Ludlow Castle
4. Their uncle Richard, Duke of Gloucester
5. Titulus Regius
6. Smothered with their pillows
7. Sir Christopher Wren
8. Perkin Warbeck
9. He was executed on the order of Henry VII
10. Elizabeth of York

RICHARD III

1. Scoliosis
2. The Council of the North
3. The Court of Requests
4. A white boar
5. Henry Stafford, 2nd Duke of Buckingham
6. The Battle of Bosworth Field
7. The Plantagenets
8. Greyfriars in Leicester
9. A car park
10. Leicester Cathedral

LEICESTER

1. The Jewry Wall
2. *King Lear* (with the city supposedly founded by the real-life King Leir)
3. Leicester Forest
4. Daniel Lambert
5. Robert Stephenson
6. The Chartists
7. Sir Edwin Lutyens
8. Bishop of Leicester
9. Arnold George Dorsey, aka Engelbert Humperdinck
10. James Walter Butler

BRITISH SCHOOLS & EDUCATION

1. The King's School at Canterbury
2. Eton College
3. Sir Roger Manwood
4. The Sunday School Movement
5. Redbrick
6. Bedford College
7. Ragged Schools
8. That it should be non-denominational
9. The Sandon Act
10. The Butler Act

DEAL

1. Addelam
2. Perkin Warbeck
3. The Goodwin Sands
4. James Cook
5. Sir John Rennie
6. The Nora, a Dutch vessel that had been mined
7. A time ball

8. The Royal Naval School of Music (or Royal Marines School of Music)

9. Hoodening (the horse is known as a hooden horse)

10. The F.A. Vase

HENRY VII

1. His mother was the great-granddaughter of John of Gaunt, a son of Edward III

2. The Duchy of Brittany

3. To win the crown on the field of battle

4. Lambert Simnel

5. Morton's Fork

6. The Mad War

7. The Auld Alliance

8. The Star Chamber

9. As a royal residence

10. Richmond Palace

HENRY VIII

1. Arthur

2. Seventeen

3. The Holy League

4. Clement VII

5. The English Reformation

6. Alien priories

7. Jousting

8. Thomas Cromwell

9. John Blanke

10. Two (Anne of Cleeves and Catherine Parr)

HENRY'S 1ST WIFE:
CATHERINE OF ARAGON

1. Edward I
2. Spain
3. The House of Trastámara
4. The sweating sickness
5. Durham House, in London
6. An ambassadorship (she was given the role of Spanish ambassador)
7. Mary (later Queen Mary I)
8. A nunnery
9. Thomas Wolsey
10. Kimbolton Castle

HENRY'S 2ND WIFE:
ANNE BOLEYN

1. Hever Castle
2. Queen Claude of France
3. Mary
4. St. Edward's Crown
5. Elizabeth Barton, the Nun of Kent
6. Sir Thomas More
7. Elizabeth (later Queen Elizabeth I)
8. The Tower of London
9. *O Death Rock Me Asleep*
10. An expert swordsman was brought in from France

HENRY'S 3RD WIFE:
JANE SEYMOUR

1. Needlework
2. Maid-of-honour
3. The Pacific
4. Quail

5. Bound to obey and serve
6. Mary, the king's daughter with Catherine of Aragon, and the future Mary I
7. The Pilgrimage of Grace
8. A male heir, who went on to become Edward VI
9. Hampton Court Palace
10. A queen's burial

HENRY'S 4TH WIFE:
ANNE OF CLEVES

1. Germany
2. William of Cleves, a prominent Protestant figure
3. Hans Holbein the Younger
4. Rochester Abbey
5. The marriage was not consummated
6. Thomas Cranmer
7. The King's Beloved Sister
8. She asked the king to remarry her, but he refused
9. Chelsea Old Manor
10. She was the last of them to die, surviving until 1557

HENRY'S 5TH WIFE:
CATHERINE HOWARD

1. Anne Boleyn
2. Agnes Howard, the Dowager Duchess of Norfolk
3. Henry Mannox
4. Francis Dereham
5. No other will but his
6. Ulcerous legs
7. Thomas Culpeper, a distant cousin
8. Syon Abbey
9. How to lay her head upon the executioner's block
10. He became the last person known to have been executed on the order of Henry VIII

HENRY'S 6TH WIFE: CATHERINE PARR

1. Sir Thomas Seymour (the brother of Jane Seymour)
2. *Prayers or Meditations*
3. The Third Succession Act, restoring his daughters Mary and Elizabeth to the line of succession to the throne
4. Katherine Brandon, the Duchess of Suffolk
5. A warrant for her arrest. She swiftly reconciled with the king, who had been turned against her by advisers
6. Four (Henry was her third husband)
7. *The Lamentation of a Sinner*
8. Sudeley Castle in Gloucestershire
9. Protestantism
10. Sir George Gilbert Scott

EDWARD VI

1. Jane Seymour (Henry VIII's third wife)
2. Margaret Bryan
3. The Antichrist
4. The Rough Wooing
5. Hertford
6. Edward Seymour, the Duke of Somerset
7. The Battle of Pinkie (sometimes referred to as the Battle of Pinkie Cleugh)
8. The Prayer Book Rebellion (concerning the introduction of the unpopular Book of Common Prayer)
9. John Dudley, the Earl of Warwick (and subsequently Duke of Northumberland)
10. Lady Jane Grey

LADY JANE GREY

1. Henry VII
2. Catherine Parr

3. Protestantism
4. Nine
5. The Privy Council
6. Burning
7. Wyatt's Rebellion
8. Lord Guildford Dudley
9. She was beheaded at Tower Green, in the Tower of London
10. A proven contemporary portrait

MARY I

1. Catherine of Aragon (Henry VIII's first wife)
2. Ludlow Castle
3. The Princess of Wales
4. Queen Regent
5. Prince Philip of Spain
6. The Marian exiles
7. Reginald Pole
8. Portlaoise
9. St. James's Palace
10. Bloody Mary

ELIZABETH I

1. Anne Boleyn (Henry VIII's second wife)
2. The Tower of London, before being moved to Woodstock
3. Robert Dudley
4. William Cecil
5. The Babington Plot
6. Sir Francis Walsingham
7. Plymouth
8. Tilbury
9. The Golden Speech
10. Mary I, her half-sister

THE EARLY AMERICAN COLONIES

1. John Cabot
2. The Northwest Passage between the Atlantic and Pacific oceans
3. Jamestown
4. Tobacco
5. Bermuda
6. The Eleutheran Adventurers
7. The Pequot
8. The Netherlands
9. The Darien Scheme
10. Thirteen

SIR FRANCIS DRAKE

1. William Hawkins
2. The Judith
3. The Cimarrons of Panama
4. The Rathlin Island massacre
5. He led a circumnavigation of the world (a previous circumnavigation didn't count, since its captain had died halfway)
6. The Golden Hind (or Golden Hinde)
7. Buckland Abbey
8. Singeing the King of Spain's Beard
9. Playing bowls
10. He was buried at sea in a lead coffin

PLYMOUTH

1. Mount Batten
2. Sir John Hawkins
3. Pocahontas
4. The Pilgrim Fathers
5. Henry Winstanely

6. William Cookworthy (although the factory moved to Bristol two years later)
7. Plymouth Gin
8. Napoleon Bonaparte
9. Robert Hawker
10. Sir Francis Chichester

SIR FRANCIS BACON

1. Lord Keeper of the Great Seal
2. Anthony Cooke
3. Queen Elizabeth I
4. The Queen's Counsel designate (her legal counsel)
5. Baron Verulam
6. His long-time enemy, Sir Edward Coke
7. The scientific method
8. Alice Barnham
9. The use of freezing as a method of preserving meat
10. Thomas Jefferson (the other two men were Sir Isaac Newton and philosopher John Locke)

CAMBRIDGE

1. Duroliponte
2. Gog Magog Hills
3. St. Bene't's Church, dedicated to St. Benedict of Nursia (the founder of the Benedictine order of monasticism)
4. The Round Church
5. Peterhouse
6. Hobson's Conduit, or Hobson's Brook
7. Oxford
8. Douglas Adams
9. Jim Ede
10. The Garden House riot

SIR WALTER RALEIGH

1. The Huguenots
2. The Desmond Rebellions
3. The Roanoke Colony
4. The Ark Royal
5. Elizabeth 'Bess' Throckmorton (sometimes written as Throgmorton)
6. Madre de Deus (Mother of God)
7. El Dorado
8. The Angel Falls waterfall
9. The Main Plot
10. He was beheaded at the Palace of Westminster, on the king's orders, to appease Spain

ELIZABETHAN LITERATURE

1. John Lyly
2. Tamburlaine the Great
3. Jack Wilton
4. Elizabeth I
5. Philip Sidney
6. Every Man in His Humour
7. Mary Sidney
8. Thomas Campion
9. The Faerie Queene
10. The War of the Theatres

CHRISTOPHER MARLOWE

1. A spy against Catholics
2. Virgil's Aeneid
3. Tamburlaine the Great, loosely based on the life of Timur
4. The University Wits
5. Barabas
6. Mephistophilis

7. Henry VI
8. Edward II
9. The School of Night
10. Deptford

WILLIAM SHAKESPEARE

1. He was a glover and leather worker
2. Anne Hathaway
3. The Lord Chamberlains Men (later The King's Men)
4. The Globe
5. Hamlet
6. The unity of time, i.e. taking place over 24 hours
7. Henry V
8. Richard Burbage
9. The Church of the Holy Trinity in Stratford-upon-Avon
10. The First Folio

MARY, QUEEN OF SCOTS

1. She was his great-niece, since her paternal grandmother Margaret Tudor was Henry VIII's sister
2. The House of Stuart
3. James V of Scotland
4. Edward Tudor, later Edward VI
5. Francis II
6. Henry Stuart, Lord Darnley
7. The Rising of the North
8. Edinburgh
9. The Casket Letters
10. Fotheringay Castle

JAMES I OF ENGLAND / VI OF SCOTLAND

1. Thirteen months
2. Stirling Castle

3. The Treaty of Berwick
4. *Daemonologie*
5. The Isle of Lewis, in the Outer Hebrides
6. The Hampton Court Conference
7. Infanta Maria Anna, daughter of King Philip III of Spain
8. Ulster. This was the largest of a number of 16th and 17th century attempts to forcibly colonise Ireland with British settlers
9. Robert Cecil
10. The Addled Parliament

GUY FAWKES & THE GUNPOWDER PLOT

1. The Bye Plot
2. Robert Catesby
3. The State Opening of Parliament
4. An outbreak of bubonic plague
5. His daughter Elizabeth
6. William Parker, Lord Monteagle, a member of the House of Lords
7. 36
8. John Johnson
9. Holbeche House
10. Pope Night

CHARLES I

1. Anne of Denmark
2. The Caroline era (from the Latin Carolus, for Charles)
3. Henrietta Maria
4. The Thirty Years' War
5. George Villiers, the Duke of Buckingham
6. Darnell's Case, or the Five Knights' Case
7. The Bishops' Wars
8. Three weeks
9. The Root and Branch Petition

(maybe change this to the War of the Three Kingdoms)
10. High treason (for allegedly colluding with the Scots)

THE ENGLISH CIVIL WAR

1. The New Model Army
2. John Pym
3. Clubmen
4. A battle where the time and place are agreed beforehand
5. Pride's Purge
6. The Battle of Marston Moor
7. The Putney Debates
8. The Engagement
9. Sir Thomas Fairfax
10. Banqueting House

OLIVER CROMWELL

1. Puritans
2. Cambridge
3. Old Ironsides
4. The Rump Parliament
5. The Levellers
6. Ireland
7. Wexford
8. Lord Protector
9. Praise-God Barebone
10. "Warts and all" - he wanted the portrait to be true to life, rather than flattering

PURITANISM

1. The Vestments Controversy, which saw Puritans holding their own services for the first time
2. Protestantism
3. Presbyterianism

4. John Foxe
5. The Genevan Book of Order
6. Martin Marprelate
7. The Mayflower
8. The Fifth Monarchists or Fifty Monarchy Men
9. The Great Ejection
10. Nonconformists

RICHARD CROMWELL & THE RESTORATION

1. Almost nine months
2. Tumbledown Dick
3. George Monck
4. The Convention Parliament
5. The Good Old Cause
6. The Spanish Netherlands
7. The Declaration of Breda
8. Oak Apple Day
9. Regicide, in relation to the death of Charles I
10. He was exhumed, posthumously put on trial, and then had his head placed on a pole outside Westminster Hall for twenty years

CHARLES II

1. Dover
2. The Royal Society
3. Dunkirk and Fort-Mardyck, parts of France that were a drain on his finances
4. The Royal Observatory
5. The East India Company
6. The Clarendon Code
7. The Great Plague (bubonic plague)
8. Pudding Lane
9. James was a Catholic
10. Mercury

ART & LITERATURE DURING
THE RESTORATION

1. Samuel Pepys
2. George Etherege
3. Christopher Wren, with the result being St. Paul's Cathedral
4. John Milton
5. John Dryden
6. Nell Gwyn
7. *The Country Wife*
8. Aphra Benn
9. John Locke
10. Rose Tremain

JAMES II

1. Duke of York
2. Anne Hyde
3. The Test Acts
4. James Scott, the Duke of Monmouth
5. The Battle of Sedgemoor
6. The Glorious Revolution
7. They were charged with seditious libel and taken to the Tower of London. Their subsequent acquittal damaged James's authority
8. His wife gave birth to a son, James Frances Edward, who replaced his Protestant daughter Mary as heir to the throne
9. The Great Seal of the Realm (a new one was quickly made)
10. Jacobites

SIR ISAAC NEWTON

1. Christmas Day
2. Gottfried Leibniz
3. A reflecting telescope
4. An apple

5. *The Principia* (or, to give it its full title, *Philosophiæ Naturalis Principia Mathematica*, or *Mathematical Principles of Natural Philosophy*)
6. The Philosopher's Stone
7. Cambridge University
8. Master of the Mint (at the Royal Mint)
9. Mercury, most likely from his experiments
10. Force

WILLIAM & MARY

1. In the south of modern-day France
2. Mary, Queen of Scots
3. The Hague, in the Netherlands
4. The Bill of Rights
5. The Battle of the Boyne, in Ireland (the Orange Order still exists, its name a tribute to William)
6. Smallpox
7. The Nine Years' War
8. Spain
9. Sophia, Electress of Hanover
10. A mole's burrow

ANNE

1. Henrietta Maria (the former wife of Charles I)
2. George, Prince of Denmark
3. Sarah Churchill (nee Jennings)
4. The Duke of Marlborough
5. Gout
6. William, Duke of Gloucester
7. The War of the Spanish Succession
8. An extratropical cyclone, estimated to have been a Force 2 hurricane
9. The Acts of Union
10. George of Hanover

GEORGE I

1. Ernest Augustus, Duke of Brunswick-Lüneberg
2. 56
3. The Ottoman Empire
4. Rushing to escape a rainshower
5. James Francis Edward Stuart (aka The Pretender, the son of James II)
6. Spain
7. She was imprisoned in the Castle of Ahlden, in Germany
8. The South Sea Company
9. Robert Walpole
10. The Order of the Bath

EDWARD TEACH, AKA BLACKBEARD

1. New Providence
2. Henry Jennings
3. Benjamin Hornigold
4. Queen Anne's Revenge
5. A man known only as Richards
6. Charles Town
7. Charles Eden
8. Mary Ormond (or Osmond)
9. Alexander Spotswood
10. Ocracoke Island

SIR ROBERT WALPOLE

1. The Whigs
2. King's Lynn
3. The Tower of London
4. The Screen, or Screenmaster-General
5. First Lord of the Treasury
6. The Patriot Whigs, later the Patriot Party
7. Sir Bluestring

8. Houghton Hall
9. Earl of Orford
10. Paintings, particularly Old Masters from around Europe

10 DOWNING STREET

1. A brewery
2. Sir George Downing
3. Sir Christopher Wren
4. George II
5. He was supposedly the last private occupant of the houses that became 10 Downing Street, and had to be persuaded to move
6. Number 5
7. Electric lighting
8. Arthur Balfour
9. SW1A 2AA
10. Yellow (it's since been painted black)

THE WHIG PARTY

1. They believed in constitutional monarchism, with a strong role for parliament
2. A cattle driver
3. They were vehemently opposed to a Catholic king
4. Many French goods being imported into England (the Whigs were protectionists and, in many cases, anti-French)
5. Rotten (or pocket) boroughs
6. Slavery
7. The Reform Club
8. Henry John Temple
9. The Liberal Party
10. Herbert Butterfield

GEORGE II

1. He was born outside Great Britain (in Germany)
2. Monsieur de Busch
3. The Theatre Royal, on Drury Lane in London
4. Leicester House (formerly to the north of Leicester Square, but now demolished)
5. George Frideric Handel
6. The royal library
7. The War of Jenkins' Ear (referring to Robert Jenkins)
8. The Battle of Dettingen, in a part of the Holy Roman Empire that is now in Bavaria
9. Minorca
10. He wanted the sides removed, so that their remains could mingle

DICK TURPIN

1. The Blue Bell Inn (later renamed the Rose and Crown)
2. Butchery
3. Elizabeth Millington
4. The blackening of faces for disguise while in the forest
5. The Gregory (or Essex) Gang
6. Holland
7. John Palmer (or Parmen)
8. Knavesmire
9. William Harrison Ainsworth
10. Black Bess

HENRY PELHAM

1. Seaford, in Sussex
2. Secretary at War
3. The Norfolk Congress (they met at Houghton Hall in Norfolk)
4. The Broad Bottom Ministry

5. The War of the Austrian Succession (which finally ended in 1748)
6. William Pulteney, Lord Bath
7. The Gin Act
8. Britain adopted the Gregorian calendar, which it has used ever since
9. Jews (although the act was repealed the following year)
10. His brother, Thomas

BONNIE PRINCE CHARLIE
& THE JACOBITE UPRISING OF 1745

1. James II, former king of England
2. Rome, where his father had been given a residence
3. France
4. *Johnnie Cope*
5. The Battle of Culloden
6. Prince William, Duke of Cumberland
7. *The Skye Boat Song*
8. The Prince's Cairn
9. Protestantism
10. St. Peter's Basillica in the Vatican

THE HEBRIDES

1. The Callanish Stones
2. Dál Riata (or Dál Riada), which eventually became the Kingdom of Alba
3. King Magnus III of Norway
4. Somerled (aka Somhairle)
5. The Treaty of Perth
6. Donald Monro (or sometimes Munro)
7. The Flannan Isles
8. Iain Mac Fhearchair (aka John MacCodrum)
9. The Battle of the Braes
10. William Lever, Viscount Leverhulme

ROBERT CLIVE, AKA CLIVE OF INDIA

1. Brazil
2. The Carnatic Wars
3. Warren Hastings
4. The Siege of Arcot
5. Calcutta
6. The Battle of Plassey
7. He became Mayor of Shrewsbury
8. The title of Bengal, making the company the sovereign rulers of the region
9. A penknife
10. His pet giant tortoise, Aldwaita, which was believed to have been up to 255 years old

GEORGE III

1. Frederick, Prince of Wales, whose death in 1751 left George as heir apparent
2. Weymouth
3. The Crown Estate
4. Frederick, aka Lord, North
5. A tree
6. James Hadfield
7. Emperor of the British Isles
8. Princess Amelia, his youngest (and favourite) daughter
9. Windsor Castle
10. Arsenic, the source of which is unknown

THE INDUSTRIAL REVOLUTION

1. Friedrich Engels
2. Richard Arkwright
3. The Flying Shuttle
4. The Bridgewater Canal
5. The Puddling Process

6. Horsepower
7. Thomas Savery
8. The Spinning Mule
9. The Combination Act
10. The Luddites

SHEFFIELD

1. The Urn People
2. Dore
3. Hallun, or Hallam
4. Beauchief Abbey
5. The Company of Cutlers in Hallamshire (Sheffield was known for the production of cutlery)
6. Mary, Queen of Scots
7. Stainless Steel
8. Little Chicago
9. *Threads*
10. The Republic

CANALS

1. The Stour
2. The Oxford-Burcot Commission
3. The Sankey Canal
4. The Worcester Bar, which was eventually removed and replaced by the Gas Street Basin
5. Canal Mania
6. The Llangollen Canal
7. Roses and Castles
8. Edward Leader Williams
9. The Tuel Lane Lock
10. The Union Canal

TRAINS

1. Wollaton Wagonway
2. Lake Lock Rail Road
3. Salamanca
4. Crown Street Station, which connected the city with Manchester
5. George Stephenson
6. London Bridge Station
7. The Romney, Hythe and Dymchurch Railway
8. The Great Western Railway (GWR), the London and North Eastern Railway (LNER), the London, Midland (LMS) and Scottish Railway and Southern Railway (SR)
9. Dr. Richard Beeching
10. Puffing Billy

THE AMERICAN REVOLUTION

1. The Stamp Act
2. The fact that they were being asked to pay tax while having no representation in the British parliament
3. The Sons of Liberty
4. John Dickinson
5. The Boston Massacre
6. The Gaspee
7. The Boston Tea Party
8. The Intolerable Acts
9. The Suffolk Resolves
10. The Battles of Lexington and Concord

THE AMERICAN WAR OF INDEPENDENCE

1. Thomas Paine
2. The Battle of Bunker Hill
3. The Olive Branch Petition

4. Thomas Jefferson, John Adams, Benjamin Franklin, Robert Livingston and Roger Sherman
5. George Washington
6. Sir Thomas Gage
7. Roderigue Hortalez and Company
8. The Battle of Quebec
9. Yorktown
10. The Treaty of Paris

CAPTAIN JAMES COOK

1. The Freelove
2. The transit of Venus across the Sun
3. HMS Endeavour
4. Terra Australis
5. The Māori of New Zealand
6. Botany Bay
7. Hawaii
8. Lono, a Hawaiian god associated with fertility, music and peace
9. They disembowelled him and baked his remains
10. Melbourne, Australia

ADAM SMITH

1. Kirkcaldy
2. *The Theory of Moral Sentiments*
3. David Hume
4. Benjamin Franklin
5. The Wealth of Nations
6. Division of labour
7. A tax on man-servants
8. Absolute advantage
9. *Essays on Philosophical Subjects*
10. The Father of Capitalism (or the Father of Economics)

MARY PRINCE

1. Bermuda
2. The Moravian Church
3. John Adams Wood
4. Rheumatism
5. Daniel James
6. Somerset vs. Stewart
7. Thomas Pringle
8. Susanna Strickland
9. James MacQueen
10. Camden

THE FRENCH REVOLUTIONARY WARS

1. Louis XVI
2. Napoleon Bonaparte
3. The Glorious First of June, aka the Fourth Battle of Ushant
4. The Vendée, in the west of the country
5. Italy
6. Spithead
7. The Directory
8. The Coup of 18 Brumaire (Brumaire was a month in the short-lived French Republican Calendar)
9. The First Battle of Copenhagen
10. The Treaty of Amiens

WILLIAM PITT THE YOUNGER

1. Hayes
2. George Grenville
3. Chatham
4. Chancellor of the Exchequer
5. The East India Company
6. New South Wales

7. Prime Minister of the United Kingdom of Great Britain and Northern Ireland (he'd previously been Prime Minister of Great Britain until the Acts of Union)
8.The Saviour of Europe
9. Westminster Abbey
10. The Ministry of All the Talents

THE NAPOLEONIC WARS

1. The Continental System
2. The Golden Cavalry of St. George
3. The Battle of Austerlitz
4. Spain
5. Portugal
6. Russia
7. Nathan Mayer Rothschild
8. Elba, off the coast of Tuscany
9. It's now in Belgium, although at the time it was part of the Netherlands
10. Saint Helena, in the South Atlantic

ADMIRAL HORATIO NELSON

1. Robert Walpole (the distant relative was Horatio Walpole)
2. HMS Raisonnable
3. Malaria
4. Little Lucy
5. Frances 'Fanny' Nisbet
6. The Invasion of Corsica
7. Rear Admiral of the Blue
8. The Battle of the Nile
9. Vice-Admiral Sir Thomas Hardy
10. William Railton

THE WAR OF 1812

1. The Jay Treaty
2. The Little Belt Affair
3. James Madison
4. The Battle of Lake Erie (aka the Battle of Put-in-Bay)
5. Tecumseh
6. The Creek War
7. The Battle of Niagara Falls, aka the Battle of Lundy's Lane
8. Washington City (now known as Washington D.C.)
9. Andrew Jackson
10. The Treat of Ghent

ARTHUR WELLESLEY, THE DUKE OF WELLINGTON

1. Dublin (he was Anglo-Irish)
2. The Maratha Confederacy
3. Rye, in East Sussex
4. The Battle of Vitoria
5. Lord Warden of the Cinque Ports
6. Catholics
7. He challenged him to a duel, which ended with both men unharmed
8. The Iron Duke
9. He assembled an army to protect London, although ultimately there was no major unrest in the country
10. Commander-in-Chief

THE ROYAL NAVY

1. Henry VIII
2. The Age of Sail
3. HMS
4. Pax Britannica
5. The combined strength of the next two largest navies in the world

6. HMS Holland 1 (or Torpedo Boat No 1)
7. HMS Dreadnought
8. The Grand Fleet
9. Trident
10. HMS Raleigh

MEDWAY

1. The Hoo Peninsula
2. Rochester
3. Shouting as he led his army into battle, hence his name Gyllingas, which comes from an Old English word which means 'to shout'
4. Bishop of Rochester
5. The Pilgrims' Way
6. The Pett family
7. Upnor Castle
8. The Second Anglo-Dutch War
9. Anne Pratt
10. Submarines

GEORGE IV

1. Carlton House
2. She was a Roman Catholic, which meant that the marriage was technically void
3 Princess Caroline of Brunswick
4. Laudanum
5. Ireland
6. The Royal Pavilion
7. George 'Beau' Brummell
8. The First Gentleman of England
9. Robert Jenkinson, Lord Liverpool
10. Sir Henry Halford

BRIGHTON

1. Someone named Beorhthelm
2. Hollingbury Castle
3. Whitehawk Camp
4. The future Charles II, who left the country via Brighton (and nearby Shoreham-by-Sea) toward the end of the English Civil War
5. The Great Storm of 1703
6. Magnus Volk
7. Eugenius Birch
8. Rex Whistler
9. The Chattri
10. Ken Fines

SPENCER PERCEVAL

1. He's the only British prime minister to have been assassinated
2. Harrow
3. Warren Hastings
4. Northampton
5. That she'd had given birth to an illegitimate child (a claim that was found to be untrue)
6. The Walcheren Campaign
7. John Bellingham
8. He believed he was entitled to compensation, having been unjustly imprisoned in Russia
9. The Cat and Bagpipes
10. He was found guilty, and despite evidence suggesting that he was insane, he was hanged in public a few days later

J.M.W. TURNER

1. The Royal Academy of Arts

2. *Fishermen at Sea*
3. Walter Ramsden Fawkes
4. Sarah Danby
5. *The Fighting Temeraire* (full title: *The Fighting Temeraire, tugged to her last berth to be broken up, 1838*)
6. John Linnell
7. Liber Studiorum
8. Inclusion in that year's census, since being on the boat meant that he was not inside any property
9. Tate Britain
10. The new £20 note (the first to be printed on polymer)

JOHN CONSTABLE

1. The corn business, since his father was a corn merchant
2. Wivenhoe Park
3. Maria Bicknell
4. *The White Horse*
5. The Six-Footers
6. *The Hay Wain*
7. Salisbury Cathedral (the painting is Salisbury Cathedral from the Bishop's Grounds)
8. The Barbizon school of painting
9. St John-at-Hempstead Church, in Hempstead
10. Constable Country

JANE AUSTEN

1. Steventon
2. Typhus
3. The Juvenilia
4. *Lady Susan*
5. *Northanger Abbey*
6. By a Lady
7. Fitzwilliam
8. Sanditon

9. Richard Bentley
10. Her nephew, James Edward Austen-Leigh

WILLIAM IV

1. The Sailor King
2. Lord High Admiral
3. Dorothea Bland, also known as Mrs. Jordan
4. Clarence House (at the time, he was the Duke of Clarence)
5. Princess Adelaide of Saxe-Mainingen
6. A Half Crown-nation
7. Women were explicitly barred from voting
8. Slaves were still allowed in Ceylon (Sri Lanka) and Saint Helena, and in territory controlled by the East India Company
9. He went against the will of Parliament, by dismissing William Lamb
10. Victoria, the Duchess of Kent, mother of his niece and heir

THE BRONTË SISTERS

1. Gondal
2. Glass Town
3. Branwell (Patrick Branwell Brontë)
4. Bell (Charlotte was Currer Bell, Emily was Ellis Bell and Anne was Action Bell)
5. Mr. Lockwood
6. Gateshead Hall
7. She calls herself Helen Graham, but her real name is later revealed to be Helen Huntingdon
8. Keeper
9. Elizabeth Gaskell
10. Haworth

SIR ROBERT PEEL

1. Textiles
2. Lord Byron
3. Orange Peel (since orange is the colour of the Protestant Orange Order)
4. The Bedchamber Crisis
5. Bobbies and Peelers
6. Ten
7. Income tax
8. Insanity
9. The Great Irish Famine
10. The Conservatives

THE METROPOLITAN POLICE

1. The Bow Street Runners
2. Constable Joseph Grantham
3. Flintlock pistols
4. Fingerprints
5. The Queen's (or King's, at the time) Medal, for gallantry or distinguished service
6. The Siege of Sidney Street
7. She became the first female police officer and the first commander of the Metropolitan Police's Women Patrols
8. Scotland Yard (or New Scotland Yard)
9. Operation Countryman
10. Cressida Dick

THE ISLE OF MAN

1. King Orry's Grave
2. The Ronaldsway Culture
3. Manannán
4. Magnus Olafsson, aka Magnus Barefoot
5. Alexander III

6. Tynwald
7. King of Mann
8. The Dukes of Atholl
9. Castletown
10. The Bee Gees

THE RNLI

1. Sir William Hillary
2. Lord Liverpool, the prime minister at the time
3. Algernon Percy, the Duke of Northumberland
4. He came up with the self-righting lifeboat
5. The Tower of Refuge
6. SS Suevic
7. Whitby
8. The Mary Stanford, based on Ballycotton in Ireland
9. The Dunkirk evacuation
10. The Mumbles lifeboat disaster

THE ISLE OF WIGHT

1. Arwald
2. The Battle of Bonchurch (although some sources suggest that the French might in fact have won the battle)
3. King Charles I
4. J. Samuel White
5. The Needles Batteries
6. Alexander Graham Bell
7. A Marconigram, after the inventor Guglielmo Marconi
8. Percy Stone
9. Operation Pluto
10. Richie Havens

VICTORIA

1. Alexandrina
2. Lady Flora Hastings
3. The Grandmother of Europe
4. Mrs. Melbourne
5. Edward Oxford
6. The Widow of Windsor
7. John Brown
8. Abdul Karim
9. The House of Hanover
10. Sir Thomas Brock

PRINCE ALBERT

1. Schloss Rosenau
2. The House of Saxe-Coburg and Gotha
3. King Consort
4. The House Dragon
5. The Isle of Wight
6. Chancellor of the University of Cambridge
7. That he'd been arrested for treason and taken to the Tower of London
8. The Trent affair, which was caused by alleged British interference during the American Civil War
9. Typhoid fever
10. Sir George Gilbert Scott

CHARLES DICKENS

1. Landport, which is now part of Portsmouth
2. Warren's Blacking Warehouse, near Charing Cross station, where he pasted labels onto pots of boot blacking
3. *A Dinner at Poplar Walk*
4. Boz
5. *The Pickwick Papers*

6. Ellen Ternan
7. Phiz
8. They were crows
9. Staplehurst
10. Rochester Cathedral

CHARLES BABBAGE & ADA LOVELACE

1. Father of the computer
2. Lord Byron
3. The Analytical Society
4. Mary Somerville
5. The Royal Astronomical Society (initially called the Astronomical Society of London)
6. The Babbage principle
7. The Difference Engine
8. The Analytical Engine
9. The first algorithm
10. GameStop

ISAMBARD KINGDOM BRUNEL

1. Abraham-Louis Breguet
2. The shipworm, which was well known at the time for boring through wood
3. The Royal Society
4. The Clifton Suspension Bridge
5. The Great Western Railway
6. London Paddington
7. He opted for a broad (7ft0.25in) gauge, instead of the standard British gauge (4ft8.5in)
8. Hungerford Bridge (Brunel's bridge has since been replaced by a newer design)
9. Renkioi Hospital
10. Kensal Green Cemetery

THE GREAT EXHIBITION OF 1851

1. Henry Cole
2. The Crystal Palace, in Hyde Park. The palace was destroyed by fire in 1936
3. Sir George Smart
4. Public pay toilets
5. It was the largest diamond
6. A voting machine, possibly the first in the world
7. Samuel Colt
8. A fax
9. Majolica
10. Albertopolis

BLACKPOOL

1. The Carleton Elk (also known as Horace)
2. Henry Banks
3. John Isaac Mawson
4. Wakes weeks
5. W.H. Cocker
6. Blackpool Pleasure Beach
7. The Bass Brewery, with the holidays known as Bass Excursions
8. Railway Queen of Great Britain
9. Littlewoods
10. No. 303 Squadron, also known as one of the Polish Fighter Squadrons

THE CRIMEAN WAR

1. The Concert of Europe
2. The Eastern Orthodox Church
3. Tsar Nicholas I
4. The Danubian Principalities (roughly the location of Romania today)

5. The Battle of Sinop
6. The Battle of the Alma (sometimes The Battle of the Alma River)
7. Sevastopol
8. Lord Cardigan
9. Alfred, Lord Tennyson
10. It was to become neutral, closed to all warships and with no military presence on its shores

FLORENCE NIGHTINGALE

1. Florence, hence her first name
2. Selimiye Barracks in Scutari, now part of Istanbul
3. Eliza Roberts
4. The Sisters of Mercy
5. The Lady with the Lamp
6. Notes on Nursing
7. St. Thomas's Hospital in Central London (the school is now called the Florence Nightingale School of Nursing and Midwifery and is part of King's College London)
8. Linda Richards
9. The Freedom of the City of London
10. Lytton Strachey

MARY SEACOLE

1. The Doctress
2. Scotland
3. Lord Nelson, and his mistress Emma Hamilton
4. The British Hotel
5. *Wonderful Adventures of Mrs. Seacole in Many Lands*
6. Florence Nightingale
7. Prince Victor, aka Count von Gleichen
8. Princess Alexandra, the Princess of Wales and wife of the future Edward VII
9. The Jamaican Order of Merit

THE GREAT STINK OF 1858

1. Cholera
2. Edwin Chadwick
3. Michael Faraday
4. The Miasma theory
5. *Little Dorrit*
6. Lime chloride
7. Joseph Bazalgette
8. The Victoria, Chelsea and Albert embankments
9. Crossness Pumping Station
10. SS Bazalgette

THE RIVER THAMES

1. 'Dark'
2. Isis
3. Seven Springs (which is the farthest location from the mouth)
4. Westminster Abbey and the Palace of Westminster
5. Eel Pie Island
6. Lake Havasu City in Arizona
7. Frost fairs
8. Old Father Thames
9. It's part of the East London railway line, a line on the London Overground network
10. *Three Men in a Boat*

THE BRITISH EMPIRE

1. The Mongol Empire in the late 13th / early 14th centuries
2. The Age of Discovery
3. Britain's Imperial Century
4. The Suez Canal

5. Metropole
6. Malta, but the plans were never fully implemented
7. The Wind of Change Speech
8. Zimbabwe
9. Canada
10. Hong Kong, which was given to China

THE EAST INDIA COMPANY

1. Queen Elizabeth I
2. Sir Thomas Smythe
3. The Battle of Swally
4. Leadenhall Street, in the City of London
5. Captain Henry Every
6. The Boston Tea Party
7. Hong Kong Island
8. Honourable Company's Service, or Honourable Company's Ship
9. St. James's Square, in Westminster
10. The British Raj

THE BRITISH RAJ

1. Charles Canning
2. Princely states
3. The Indian National Congress
4. Pandita Ramabai
5. The untouchables
6. Lord Curzon
7. Mahatma Gandhi
8. Bengal
9. Direct Action Day, aka the 1946 Calcutta Killings
10. India and Pakistan

CHARLES DARWIN

1. The Mount
2. Zoonomia
3. HMS Beagle
4. Sir Charles Lyell
5. Emma Wedgwood
6. That the human population, unchecked, doubles every twenty-five years, thereby potentially exceeding the supply of food
7. The Galápagos Islands
8. *On the Origin of Species* (full title: *On the Origin of Species by Means of Natural Selection, or the Preservation of Favoured Races in the Struggle or Life*)
9. The Descent of Man, and Selection in Relation to Sex
10. Chagas disease, which is mostly spread by insects

BIG BEN

1. St. Stephen's Tower (although it was officially called the Clock Tower)
2. Augustus Pugin
3. 334
4. He was the last person (to date) to be imprisoned in the tower's Prison Room
5. The Ayrton Light (named after Acton Smee Ayrton, who was in charge of the tower at the time)
6. Pennies
7. London Victoria
8. The Cambridge (or Westminster) Chimes, supposedly a variation on part of Handel's Messiah
9. Benjamin Gaunt
10. The Elizabeth Tower (to mark the Diamond Jubilee of Elizabeth II)

BENJAMIN DISRAELI

1. Judaism
2. *Vivian Grey*
3. The Who? Who? Ministry
4. The Church of Ireland
5. The Suez Canal
6. Empress of India
7. The Earl of Beaconsfield
8. The Congress of Berlin
9. One-nation conservatism
10. Primroses, which she claimed had been his favourite flowers

WILLIAM EWART GLADSTONE

1. Slavery, since he owned a number of large plantations that were worked by African slaves
2. The Railways Act
3. Tree felling
4. The concept of the free breakfast table
5. The People's William
6. The Midlothian Campaign
7. *Bulgarian Horrors and the Question of the East*
8. Alexandria, thereby starting a short war with Egypt
9. The Home Rule Bill
10. Archibald Primrose, Lord Rosebery

JACK THE RIPPER

1. Whitechapel
2. Mary Ann Nichols
3. Frederick Abberline
4. Leather Apron (the nickname of an early suspect in the case)
5. The Goulston Street graffito

6. The From Hell letter
7. George Lusk
8. Offender profiling
9. They were destroyed during the London Blitz in the 1940s
10. Walter Sickert

FOOD

1. *The Forme of Cury* (possibly the work of King Richard II's master cook)
2. The Columbian Exchange
3. George I
4. Yorkshire Pudding
5. Finnan haddie, which is cold-smoked
6. The Hindoostane Coffee House
7. Cawl
8. Chung Koon
9. Harry Ramsden
10. Fanny Craddock

DRINK

1. Catherine of Braganza
2. Shepherd Neame
3. William Hogarth
4. R. White's Lemonade
5. The League of the Cross
6. Irn-Bru
7. The Government Wine Cellar (GWC)
8. Tizer
9. Ribena
10. Purple Ronnie

CECIL RHODES

1. Jersey
2. The Glen Grey Act
3. The Cape to Cairo Railway
4. Princess Catherine Radziwiłł
5. Kimberley
6. De Beers
7. Matabeleland, in what is now Zimbabwe
8. Muizenberg
9. The University of Oxford
10. Rhodesia

ROBERT GASCOYNE-CECIL

1. Hatfield House
2. Marquess of Salisbury
3. He said that they wouldn't elect a black man
4. Foreign secretary
5. Splendid isolation
6. Portugal
7. Venezuela
8. The Jameson Road
9. The Fashoda Incident
10. The House of Lords

SIR EDWARD ELGAR

1. The Wand of Youth
2. William Stockley
3. Jean Froissart
4. The Enigma Variations
5. St. John Henry Newman
6. *Othello*
7. Land of Hope and Glory
8. A.C. Benson

9. Master of the King's Music (or Master of the King's Musick)
10. *He Banged the Leather for Goal*

GILBERT AND SULLIVAN

1. The Bab Ballads
2. The Mendelssohn Scholarship
3. Thomas German Reed
4. *Thespis*
5. Savoy Opera
6. *The Sorceror*
7. *The Mikado*
8. The D'Oyly Carte Opera Company
9. The Carpet Quarrel
10. *The Grand Duke*

THE LONDON UNDERGROUND

1. The Metropolitan Railway, which originally ran from Paddington to Farringdon Street
2. Cut and cover
3. The Twopenny Tube
4. Charles Yerkes
5. Johnston (named after its creator, Edward Johnston)
6. Harry Beck
7. Bethnal Green
8. Transport for London (TfL)
9. Hampstead Station on the Northern Line, which is 58.5m beneath the surface
10. Charing Cross

EARLY BRITISH CINEMA

1. Roundhay Garden Scene
2. William Friese-Greene
3. *Incident at Clovelly Cottage*

4. Ealing Studios
5. Cecil Hepworth
6. Charles Urban
7. Quota quickies
8. Alexander Korda
9. The GPO Film Unit
10. Alfred Hitchcock

LEEDS

1. People of the fast-flowing river
2. John Harrison
3. Adam Baynes
4. Ralph Thoresby
5. Benjamin Henry Latrobe
6. Armley Mills (now the Leeds Industrial Museum)
7. Tetley's (aka Joshua Tetley & Son)
8. Almost 1kg of dripping. One person died in the Leeds Dripping Riot
9. The Barnbow Munitions Factory, which had been the most productive British shell factory
10. Montague Burton, the founder of Burton Menswear

THE BOER WAR

1. Farmer
2. Johannesburg
3. Lord Roberts
4. Paul Kruger
5. Ladysmith
6. A Christmas pudding and two flags
7. Pretoria
8. Lord Kitchener
9. Christiaan de Wet
10. Horses

BUCKINGHAM PALACE

1. The Manor of Ebury (or Eia)
2. William Winde
3. His wife, Queen Charlotte
4. John Nash
5. The new Houses of Parliament, after the Palace of Westminster was destroyed by fire. George IV's offer was declined
6. Queen Victoria
7. Lancelot 'Capability' Brown
8. Tsar Nicholas I of Russia
9. The palace chapel
10. The River Tyburn

EDWARD VII

1. Bertie
2. He saw him traverse Niagara Falls on a highwire
3. Nellie Clifden
4. Alexandra of Denmark
5. A Sunday lunch consisting of roast beef, Yorkshire pudding and potatoes
6. Baccarat
7. The Uncle of Europe
8. Kiss Hands (the term was more literal in Edward's time than it is now)
9. The People's Budget, which had been put forward by the Liberal government
10. Witch of the Air

ARTHUR BALFOUR

1. Bloody Balfour
2. First Lord of the Treasury
3. The Entente Cordiale

4. The Committee of Imperial Defence
5. The Fourth Party
6. The Souls
7. The Society for Psychical Research
8. The Balfour Mission, or the Balfour Visit
9. The International Lawn Tennis Club of Great Britain
10. Phlebitis (inflammation of a vein)

THE SUFFRAGETTES

1. New Zealand
2. John Stuart Mill
3. The Isle of Man
4. Emmeline Pankhurst
5. They were board games
6. Evaline Hilda Burkitt
7. Emily Davison
8. The Bodyguard
9. Constance Markievicz (as she'd stood for Sinn Féin, however, she declined to take her seat)
10. Nancy Astor

MARIE STOPES

1. Charlotte Carmichael Stopes
2. Pangaea (along with another supercontinent, Gondwana)
3. Robert Falcon Scott
4. *Married Love, or Love in Marriage*
5. Margaret Sanger
6. *The Authorised Life of Marie C. Stopes* (later republished as *Marie Stopes Her Work and Her Play*)
7. The Mothers' Clinic, Britain's first birth control clinic
8. Dr. Halliday Sutherland
9. *Our Ostriches*
10. MSI Reproductive Choices

HERBERT ASQUITH

1. East Fife
2. Winston Churchill
3. The minimum wage
4. The king agreed to create enough Liberal peers to get the Parliament Bill through the House of Lords, thereby packing the chamber
5. Ireland
6. The Agadir Crisis
7. The Shell Crisis
8. Lord Northcliffe, owner of (among other titles) the *Daily Mail* and the *Daily Mirror*
9. The graveyard at the Church of All Saints in Sutton Courtenay
10. The Liberals

VIRGINIA WOOLF

1. Julia Stephen
2. 22 Hyde Park Gate
3. The Hogarth Press
4. *The Voyage Out*
5. Clarissa
6. The Isle of Skye
7. Vita Sackville-West
8. Elizabeth Barrett Browning
9. Between the Acts
10. The River Ouse

THE BLOOMSBURY GROUP

1. Cambridge
2. G.E. Moore
3. Vanessa Bell (nee Woolf, wife of Clive Bell)
4. Charleston Farmhouse

5. *A Passage to India*
6. Roger Fry
7. Mary 'Molly' MacCarthy
8. The Dreadnought hoax
9. David Garnett
10. Wyndham Lewis

JOHN MAYNARD KEYNES

1. The India Office, in London
2. The Political Economy Club
3. The Heavenly Twins
4. The Economic Consequences of Peace
5. Probability theory
6. The General Theory of Employment, Interest and Money
7. The Bank of England
8. The Bretton Woods Conference
9. The bancor
10. Milton Friedman (the phrase was later popularised by President Richard Nixon)

DOCTOR CRIPPEN

1. Michigan
2. Cora Henrietta Turner
3. Holloway
4. Kate Williams, also known as Vulcana
5. Ethel 'Le Neve' Neave, who he'd initially hired as a typist
6. Belgium
7. The SS Montrose
8. Henry George Kendall
9. Lord Alverstone, the Lord Chief Justice
10. Pentonville Prison

GEORGE V

1. HMS Britannia
2. Albert Victor
3. Mary of Teck
4. The Festival of Empire
5. The House of Windsor
6. Rudyard Kipling
7. He delivered a Royal Christmas speech on the radio (the speeches are now televised)
8. Bognor, which gained the suffix Regis as a result and is now known as Bognor Regis
9. "Bugger Bognor!"
10. Trauermusik (Mourning Music)

ROBERT FALCON SCOTT & ERNEST SHACKLETON

1. Clements Markham
2. RRS Discovery
3. The Polar Plateau
4. Nimrod
5. Terra Nova, a whaling ship
6. Roald Amundsen
7. Captain Lawrence Oates
8. Observation Hill
9. The first land crossing of the continent, from sea to sea
10. Vivian Fuchs

THE OUTBREAK OF WORLD WAR ONE

1. The powder keg of Europe
2. Gavrilo Princip
3. The July Crisis
4. The Triple Entente
5. Wilhelm II
6. Belgium

7. The Schlieffen Plan
8. The British Expeditionary Force (BEF)
9. The First Battle of the Marne
10. The Race to the Sea

THE WESTERN FRONT

1. Chlorine gas
2. Tanks
3. He was the first person to open fire with a machine gun from a plane
4. The Battle of Verdun
5. Kitchener's Army
6. Live and Let Live
7. The Hindenburg Line
8. Passchendaele / Passendale
9. The Hundred Days Offensive
10. The Unknown Warrior

THE NAVAL WAR

1. The First Moroccan Crisis (aka the Tangier Crisis)
2. John Arbuthnot 'Jackie' Fisher
3. Winston Churchill
4. Hit by a self-propelled torpedo fired by a submarine
5. SMS Blücher
6. RMS Lusitania
7. Mustafa Kemal Atatürk
8. The Battle of Jutland
9. The North Sea Mine Barrage
10. Sopwith Camels

LORD KITCHENER & FIELD MARSHAL HAIG

1. Haig & Haig whisky
2. The Holy Land

3. The Mahdist War (which Britain joined on the side of Egypt)
4. The Rawalpindi Parade
5. Secretary of State for War
6. The famous Lord Kitchener recruitment poster
7. The Butcher of the Somme
8. HMS Hampshire
9. The Royal and Ancient Golf Club of St. Andrews
10. Alfred Frank Hardiman

BRITISH LIFE DURING WORLD WAR ONE

1. The Defence of the Realm Act (DORA)
2. William Willett
3. The pals battalions
4. The Richmond Sixteen, a set of conscientious objectors
5. *It's a Long Way to Tipperary*
6. The Canary Girls
7. The London Air Defence Area (LADA)
8. The Women's Peace Crusade
9. The Home Forces
10. Irish citizens

THE END OF WORLD WAR ONE

1. Wilfred Owen
2. First Sea Lord Admiral Rosslyn Wemyss
3. The Treaty of Versailles
4. *For the Fallen*
5. The Sykes-Picot Agreement
6. Woodrow Wilson
7. The League of Nations
8. The Imperial War Graves Commission, later the Commonwealth War Graves Commission
9. The Royal British Legion
10. Florence Green

DAVID LLOYD GEORGE

1. Welsh
2. Carnarvon Boroughs in the north of Wales
3. President of the Board of Trade
4. Marconi
5. Minister of Munitions
6. Robert Georges Nivelle
7. The Spanish flu pandemic
8. The Coupon election (after a coalition coupon given to candidates)
9. Communism
10. Sir Bertram Clough William-Ellis

THE IRISH WAR OF INDEPENDENCE

1. Arthur Griffith
2. The Ulster Volunteers, which became the Ulster Volunteer Force in 1913
3. Patrick Pearse
4. Dáil Éireann (Assembly of Ireland)
5. The Rescue at Knocklong
6. The United States Senate
7. Bloody Sunday
8. Black and Tans
9. Michael Collins
10. The Royal Ulster Constabulary

BRITISH COAL MINING

1. Coke
2. 1913 (with 287 million tonnes)
3. The National Union of Mineworkers
4. Woolley Colliery
5. Aberfan
6. The Three-Day Week

7. Orgreave Colliery, near Rotherham
8. The Miners' Wives Support Groups
9. They were part of the Kent Coalfield
10. Asfordby Colliery

NEWCASTLE

1. The Bridge of Aelius (Aelius was the family name of Emperor Hadrian)
2. Monkchester
3. Robert Curthose, son of William the Conqueror
4. The Hostmen
5. The Black Death
6. "To carry coals to Newcastle"
7. Richard Grainger
8. Stephenson's Rocket
9. The Maling pottery
10. Mott, Hay and Anderson

SUNDERLAND

1. Hastings Hill
2. The Venerable Bede
3. Freeborn rights
4. Glass manufacturing
5. Victoria Hall
6. Sir Henry Havelock
7. Henry Irving
8. The Mills bomb, a type of hand grenade that was used extensively by British soldiers in the First World War
9. Roker Park
10. James Herriot

THE BBC

1. Dame Nellie Melba
2. John Reith (aka Lord Reith)
3. George Newnes Ltd
4. *The Man With the Flower in His Mouth*
5. Marconi
6. The Radiophonic Workshop
7. The European Broadcasting Union (EBU)
8. Higgs and Hill
9. Kangaroos
10. Ceefax

MAIL

1. Master of the Posts
2. James I, in an attempt to retain control over Scottish affairs
3. Thomas Witherings
4. Bristol
5. He changed the system so that the sender, rather than the receiver, paid the cost of postage
6. The Penny Black
7. The name of the country of issue
8. William Mulready
9. The Post Office pillar box
10. Longsleddale

BONAR LAW

1. Outside the British Isles (he was born in New Brunswick, now part of Canada)
2. Robert Murray M'Cheyne (the subject of a biography by Andrew Bonar, hence Law's christian name)
3. William Jacks
4. The Khaki election
5. Parliamentary Secretary to the Board of Trade

6. Walter Long and Austin Chamberlain
7. Secretary of State for the Colonies
8. Throat cancer
9. George Canning (119 days, in 1827) and F.J. Robinson, Viscount Goderich (144 days, from 1827 to 1828)
10. *The Unknown Prime Minister*

STANLEY BALDWIN

1. Louisa MacDonald, one of the so-called MacDonald Sisters who were famous for having all married well-known men
2. The General Council of the Trades Union Congress (TUC)
3. The Organisation for the Maintenance of Supplies
4. Maternity health
5. The Hoare-Laval Pact
6. Guilty Men
7. The Café de Paris in Leicester Square
8. The iron gates
9. Astley Hall
10. Worcester Cathedral

RAMSAY MACDONALD

1. Trafalgar Square
2. Birbeck Literary and Scientific Institution (now Birbeck, University of London)
3. Thomas Lough
4. The working class
5. J.R. Campbell
6. The Zinoviev Letter
7. A National Government, which included Conservatives, Liberals and National Labour MPs
8. The Invergordon Mutiny
9. The British Empire Economic Conference, aka the Ottowa Conference
10. Lord President of the Council

GLASGOW

1. The Kingdom of Strathclyde
2. Saint Mungo
3. William Hunter (the museum is the Hunterian Museum)
4. Joseph Black
5. The Boys' Brigade (BB)
6. Red Clydeside
7. The Glasgow Razor Gangs
8. The Battle of George Square
9. Charles Rennie Mackintosh
10. The Bruce Report

THE JARROW MARCH

1. Palmer's Shipyard
2. The National Unemployed Workers' Movement (NUWM)
3. Walter 'Wal' Hannington
4. Ellen Wilkinson
5. Crusaders
6. The Peace Pledge Union
7. 11,000
8. *The Town That Was Murdered*
9. Alan Price
10. The March for Jobs

EDWARD VIII

1. HMS Hindustan
2. Prince John
3. Wallis Simpson
4. He was the first to fly in an aircraft
5. He chose to be depicted facing left, whereas tradition 6. dictated that he should have faced right (since each monarch was supposed to face the opposite way to their predecessor)
6. Jerome Bannigan, alias George Andrew McMahon

7. The Duke of Windsor
8. He gave a full Nazi salute
9. Governor of the Bahamas
10. Paris

GEORGE VI

1. Bertie
2. The Battle of Jutland
3. Lionel Logue, who helped him with his stammer
4. Bertrand Clark
5. Percy Metcalfe
6. Edward Wood, the 1st Earl of Halifax
7. They were invited onto the Buckingham Palace balcony, which is usually reserved for members of the royal family only
8. The United Nations
9. Emperor of India
10. London Airport, where he saw his daughter Elizabeth leaving for a tour of Kenya and Australia

ELIZABETH, THE QUEEN MOTHER

1. Glamis Castle
2. She laid it at the Tomb of the Unknown Warrior, in memory of a brother named Fergus who had died during the First World War
3. The Koh-i-Noor diamond
4. *The Queen's Book of the Red Cross*
5. The most dangerous woman in Europe
6. Empress of India
7. The Castle of Mey
8. Dick Francis
9. Camellias

10. It was placed on the Tomb of the Unknown Warrior, echoing something she'd done with her wedding bouquet almost eight decades earlier

ART

1. Creswell Crags
2. Nicholas Hilliard
3. The Royal Academy of Arts
4. Sugar (his company Henry Tate & Sons later merged with Abram Lyle & Sons to form Tate & Lyle)
5. L.S. Lowry
6. The BLK Art Group
7. Malcolm Morley
8. Gilbert & George
9. Young British Artists
10. Trafalgar Square's Fourth Plinth

BARBARA HEPWORTH & HENRY MOORE

1. Leeds School of Art (now Leeds Arts University)
2. West Wind
3. Unit One
4. St. Ives
5. Hoglands
6. Family Group
7. Abingdon Green, aka College Green, across the road from the Houses of Parliament
8. Winged Figure
9. Two Forms (Divided Circle)
10. Old Flo

OSWALD MOSLEY

1. Elizabeth Bowes-Lyon, the future wife of King George VI and mother of Elizabeth II
2. Fencing
3. Diana Guinness, née Mitford
4. Harrow
5. The Labour Party
6. The British Union of Fascists
7. The Blackshirts
8. The Battle of Cable Street
9. A single political entity covering all of Europe
10. *My Life*

NEVILLE CHAMBERLAIN

1. The Bahamas
2. Lord Mayor of Birmingham
3. Director of National Service
4. A word to the ladies
5. Oswald Mosley
6. A week off work with pay (leading to a growth in the number of holiday camps)
7. Plan Z
8. The Norway Debate
9. Lord President of the Council
10. Edward Wood, the Viscount Halifax

THE OUTBREAK OF WORLD WAR TWO

1. The Weimer Republic
2. The Treaty of Versailles
3. The Great Depression
4. The Enabling Act
5. The Sudetenland
6. The Munich Agreement

7. Danzig
8. The Molotov-Ribbentrop pact
9. Lebensraum
10. Poland

WINSTON CHURCHILL

1. Blenheim Palace, his family's ancestral home
2. General Kitchener
3. The Aliens Bill, which he saw as anti-Jewish
4. The gold standard
5. Blood, toil, tears and sweat
6. The Iron Curtain
7. The Nobel Prize in Literature
8. Duke of London
9. Honorary Citizen of the United States
10. Operation Hope Not

DUNKIRK

1. The Phoney War
2. The Manstein Plan
3. The Maginot Line
4. Operation Dynamo
5. Admiral Sir Bertram Ramsay
6. The tunnels in the cliffs beneath Dover Castle
7. Lille
8. The 'little ships'
9. "We shall fight on the beeches"
10. The Dunkirk Jack

DOVER

1. Portus Dubris
2. Maison Dieu
3. The River Dour

4. An earthquake, estimated at between 5.3 and 6 on the Richter scale
5. The Great Shaft
6. Captain of the English football team
7. Henry Hawley Smart, who wrote under the name Captain Hawley Smart
8. Hellfire Corner
9. The Golden Arrow
10. Vera Lynn

THE BATTLE OF BRITAIN & THE BLITZ

1. The Luftwaffe
2. Air Chief Marshal Hugh Dowding
3. Chain Home
4. Operation Sea Lion
5. The Hawker Hurricane
6. Eric Lock
7. The Few
8. Adlertag (Eagle Day)
9. Air Chief Marshal Keith Park
10. Sir Arthur 'Bomber' Harris

COVENTRY

1. St. Osburga (or Osburh)
2. Lady Godiva (or Godgifu in Old English)
3. Peeping Tom
4. Coventry blue (the cloth retained its colour well, leading to the phrase 'true blue')
5. The phrase is 'to send someone to Coventry', i.e to ostracise them
6. Samuel Watson
7. James Starley
8. The Daimler Motor Company
9. Father Forgive

10. Donald Gibson

THE AFRICAN CAMPAIGN

1. Operation Compass
2. Field Marshal Erwin Rommel
3. Malta
4. Operation Sonnenblume
5. The Desert Rats
6. Tobruk
7. The Second Battle of El Alamein
8. Operation Torch
9. Tunis
10. The Battle of the Mareth Line

THE ITALIAN CAMPAIGN

1. Operation Husky
2. His corpse was dressed as an officer of the Royal Marines and set adrift off the coast of Spain as part of Operation Mincemeat, which aimed to trick the Germans into expecting an invasion of Greece
3. Valletta, in Malta
4. Benito Mussolini
5. Cassibile
6. The Winter Line
7. Monte Cassino
8. The Gothic Line
9. Operation Grapeshot
10. The Surrender of Caserta

BRITISH LIFE DURING WORLD WAR TWO

1. Petrol
2. Minister of Food
3. Keep Calm and Carry On

4. Operation Pied Piper
5. The Home Guard
6. Eric Roberts
7. The George Cross
8. Abram Games
9. The Beveridge Report
10. Ivor Novello

ALAN TURING & BLETCHLEY PARK

1. A Turing machine
2. The Government Code and Cypher School (GC&CS)
3. The Enigma machine
4. The Golf, Cheese and Chess Society
5. Ultra (with the code Boniface also used on occasion)
6. The Cambridge Five
7. To exhibit intelligent behaviour that's equivalent to, or indistinguishable from, that of a real human
8. Cyanide
9. Laws that banned homosexual acts
10. Any historical legislation that banned homosexual acts

THE WAR IN THE PACIFIC

1. The Republic of China
2. Pearl Harbor
3. Thailand
4. The Chindits
5. Lieutenant-General William Slim
6. Operation Cartwheel
7. The Battle of Okinawa
8. Borneo
9. The Potsdam Declaration
10. He remained on Morotai island, and in 1974 he became the last 'Japanese holdout' to surrender

D-DAY

1. Operation Overlord
2. Operation Tiger, or Exercise Tiger
3. General Dwight D. Eisenhower
4. General Bernard Montgomery
5. Operation Fortitude
6. The Atlantic Wall
7. The River Orne and the Caen Canal
8. Gold Beach, Juno Beach, Omaha Beach, Sword Beach and Utah Beach
9. American journalist Martha Gellhorn
10. Hobart's Funnies

THE END OF WORLD WAR TWO

1. The Yalta (or Crimea) Conference
2. Karl Dönitz
3. *For He's a Jolly Good Fellow*
4. The Morgenthau Plan
5. The Percentages Agreement
6. The Eastern Bloc
7. The Universal Declaration of Human Rights
8. Operation Unthinkable
9. George Orwell
10. The Berlin War

CLEMENT ATTLEE

1. Beatrice Webb
2. Stepney
3. George Lansbury
4. Arthur Greenwood
5. The National Coal Board
6. The Marshall Plan
7. *Keep Left*

8. The Korean War
9. The Homosexual Law Reform Society
10. Ivor Roberts-Jones

ANEURIN BEVAN & THE NHS

1. He became a coal miner
2. Janet 'Jennie' Lee
3. Somerville Hastings
4. The Tredegar Medical Aid Society
5. *In Place of Fear*
6. Richard Crossman
7. *Emergency Ward 10*
8. Hounslow Hospital
9. Holby City
10. The George Cross

THE WINDRUSH GENERATION

1. MV Monte Rosa
2. Kingston
3. Clapham South
4. Lord Kitchener
5. Samuel Selvon
6. Claudia Jones
7. *To Sir, With Love*
8. The Notting Hill Carnival
9. Brixton
10. Paulette Wilson

THE COMMONWEALTH

1. Jan Smuts
2. The Statute of Westminster
3. Canada
4. Plan G

5. Marlborough House
6. Commonwealth Secretary-General
7. Scotland
8. Nigeria
9. Paul Carroll
10. Rwanda (which joined in 2009)

GAMES & TOYS

1. Noah's Ark
2. Jigsaw puzzles
3. Hollow-casting
4. The first British teddy bear
5. Meccano (which later went on to sell, among other things, Hornby Railway sets)
6. Airfix
7. Cluedo (or Clue in North America)
8. Scalex, which eventually became Scalextric
9. Palitoy
10. *Tomb Raider*

MOTOR RACING

1. Brooklands
2. The Indy 500
3. Mike Hawthorn
4. John Surtees
5. Nigel Mansell
6. Colin McRae
7. Woking
8. Lewis Hamilton (it was also his first race)
9. Jenson Button
10. Jaguar

ELIZABETH II

1. 17 Bruton Street in Mayfair, the house of her maternal grandfather
2. *The Little Princesses*
3. Canada
4. The Auxiliary Territorial Service
5. Sagana Lodge, in Kenya
6. Norman Hartnell
7. The United States Congress
8. Annus horribilis (horrible year)
9. The Republic of Ireland
10. Her Sapphire Jubilee (after 65 years on the throne)

PRINCE PHILIP

1. Mon Repos
2. HMS Calypso
3. The Royal Naval College, Dartmouth
4. Mountbatten
5. Broadlands, the home of Philip's uncle
6. Lieutenant Commander (in July 1950, a year before he left)
7. The Six Declines of Modern Youth
8. Dontopedalogy
9. Operation Forth Bridge
10. At least ninety years, i.e. until 2111 at the earliest

PRINCE CHARLES

1. Edward VII, his great-great-grandfather
2. Attend school (his predecessors had private tutors)
3. The Timbertop campus of Geelong Grammar School, in Victoria
4. *The Old Man of Lochnagar*
5. The Prince's Trust
6. He was present at the birth

7. Poundbury
8. *Coronation Street*, which was celebrating its 40th anniversary
9. He hired an official harpist, with the aim of supporting young musical talent in Wales
10. She became the Duchess of Cornwall

BRITISH TELEVISION

1. John Logie Baird
2. The coronation of Queen Elizabeth II
3. *The Grove Family*
4. Associated-Rediffusion
5. Barbara Mandell
6. Grace Archer
7. The Pilkington Report
8. The Wimbledon Championships
9. Countdown
10. The 1966 World Cup Final between England and West Germany, which drew 32.3m viewers

ANTHONY EDEN

1. Charles Grey, the 2nd Earl Grey
2. Backbencher
3. The Glamour Boys
4. He oversaw the lost post-Second World War unemployment figures, which were around 1%
5. Lionel 'Buster' Crabb (he's assumed to have died)
6. Frangleterre
7. Herefordshire cattle (he's said to have named one of them Churchill)
8. 'Rab' Butler
9. The World at War
10. Winston Churchill's War Cabinet

THE SUEZ CRISIS

1. Ferdinand de Lesseps
2. Gamal Abdel Nasser
3. Israel
4. The Protocol of Sèvres
5. Guy Mollet
6. Admiral (Lord) Louis Mountbatten
7. Port Said
8. The Six-Day War, between Egypt and Israel
9. Lester B. Pearson
10. The Eisenhower Doctrine

HAROLD MACMILLAN

1. The Battle of Flers-Courcelette, part of the Battle of the Somme
2. Macmillan, which had been co-founded in 1843 by his grandfather Daniel MacMillan
3. Foreign Secretary
4. The Bank Rate Tribunal (which declared that the allegations were unjustified)
5. Kiritimati, or Christmas Island
6. The Campaign for Nuclear Disarmament
7. Supermac
8. The Night of the Long Knives
9. John Profumo
10. The Carlton Club

BRITISH ANIMALS

1. William Hogarth
2. Old Martin
3. The Craven Heifer
4. Caesar
5. The King of Rome

6. Guy
7. *Blue Peter*
8. Heather the Leather
9. The Official Monster Raving Loony Party
10. Chief Mouser to the Cabinet Office

KITCHEN SINK REALISM

1. Angry young men
2. *It Always Rains on Sunday*
3. John Bratby
4. The Theatre Workshop
5. John Osborne
6. *A Taste of Honey*
7. Alan Sillitoe
8. Ken Loach
9. Alfie
10. William Roache

MANCHESTER

1. The Brigantes, although a sub-tribe called the Setantii might have been in control
2. Oversley Farm
3. Mamucium (possibly a reference to a breast-like hill, or a mother
4. The Salford Hundred
5. The Angel Stone
6. The English Civil War
7. The Manchester Ship Canal
8. Cottonopolis
9. The Peterloo Massacre
10. *The Guardian* (originally *The Manchester Guardian*)

THE SWINGING SIXTIES

1. Granny Takes a Trip
2. Roger Miller
3. Twiggy
4. Sex (or SEX)
5. Twiggy
6. The Ad Lib Club
7. John Stephen
8. *The Avengers*
9. Michaelangelo Antonioni
10. Tonite Lets All Make Love in London (sic)

FASHION

1. Gabardine
2. Donkey jackets
3. Charles Frederick Worth
4. Tattooing
5. Savile Row, named after Lady Dorothy Savile
6. Vidal Sassoon
7. Harris Sumrie
8. Pamela Rooke
9. Mods and rockers
10. Alexander McQueen

MUSIC

1. William Byrd
2. The Roud Folk Song Index (compiled by Steve Roud)
3. *The Lincolnshire Poacher*
4. Ralph Vaughan Williams
5. Benjamin Britten
6. The Strand
7. The Wire
8. Factory Records

9. *Wannabe* by the Spice Girls
10. Steve Brookestein

THE BEATLES

1. The Blackjacks
2. Johnny Gentle
3. Brian Epstein
4. *P.S. I Love You*
5. Beatlemania
6. Richard Lester
7. That's My Life (My Love and My Home)
8. Maharishi Mahesh Yogi
9. Billy Preston
10. *The Beatles at the Hollywood Bowl*

LIVERPOOL

1. Liver meant 'muddy' and pol meant 'pool' or 'creek'
2. King John
3. Banastre Tarleton
4. The White Star Line (aka the Oceanic Steam Navigation Company)
5. The (Royal) Albert Dock
6. The final surrender of the American Civil War
7. John Houlding
8. Adolf Hitler (Dowling was married to Hitler's brother Alois, who lived in Liverpool from 1911 to 1914, but there appears to be no proof that Adolf spent time in the city)
9. The Liverpool Poets
10. Tear gas (which had only previously been used in the UK in Northern Ireland)

HAROLD WILSON

1. Winston Churchill (in 1908)
2. President of the Board of Trade
3. Gnomes of Zürich
4. Homosexual acts
5. Pipe Smoker of the Year (followed by Pipeman of the Decade in 1976)
6. The Move
7. Girobank, via the Post Office network
8. The Open University
9. Muammar Gaddafi (the existence of this offer only became publicly known in 2009)
10. The Lavender List

FOOTBALL

1. The Freemasons' Tavern
2. Scotland
3. Scotch Professors
4. The Football Association of Wales
5. William McGregor
6. FIFA
7. Walter Winterbottom
8. St. Blaize and Hope Brothers
9. The United States
10. 4-2

DERBY

1. Æthelflæd
2. John Cotton
3. Bonnie Prince Charlie
4. John Lombe
5. The Derby Rib machine
6. Joseph Wright, aka Joseph Wright of Derby

7. James Plimsoll (the measure was the Plimsoll line)
8. They were the first mainline diesel locomotives
9. Ted Moult
10. A charter scroll, to mark the granting of city status to Derby (it had previously been one of the few English towns to have a cathedral)

ENOCH POWELL

1. The Professor
2. Viceroy of India (the position was about to be abolished)
3. The Hola Massacre
4. Minister of Health
5. The Rivers of Blood speech
6. Wolverhampton (his constituency)
7. Shadow Defence Secretary
8. The Morecambe Budget
9. The Ulster Unionists
10. A life peerage

BIRMINGHAM

1. The Saltley Handaxe
2. Metchley Fort
3. Peter de Birmingham
4. The Lunar Society of Birmingham (who met on the full moon)
5. The Moor Street Theatre
6. Upper Priory Cotton Mill
7. The Priestley Riots (named after the controversial philosopher Joseph Priestley)
8. Celluloid, which means that he invented the first man-made plastic
9. Baskerville (based on the work of John Baskerville)
10. Bird's Custard

GOLF

1. The Royal and Ancient Golf Club of St. Andrews
2. Thomas Kincaid
3. A fellow golfer, Duncan Forbes of Culloden, successfully pleaded for his life
4. Thomas Mitchell Morris, aka Old Tom Morris
5. Prestwick Golf Club
6. John Ball
7. The Belfry
8. He sold packets of seed at one penny each
9. Royal St. George's
10. Laura Davies

EDWARD HEATH

1. The organ scholarship at Balliol College
2. Enoch Powell
3. Selsdon Man (following the emergence of a policy document from the Selsdon Park Hotel)
4. Grocer Heath
5. Decimal Day, which saw the decimilisation of the previous £sd currency
6. The Admiral's Cup international yachting regatta
7. Monty Python
8. Operation Demetrius
9. Who Governs Britain?
10. Father of the House (which refers to the longest-serving MP)

BRITAIN IN THE EU

1. The Hague Congress, aka the Congress of Europe
2. The Council of Europe
3. The European Coal and Steel Community (ECSC)
4. President Charles de Gaulle of France

5. Norway
6. The Shetland Isles and the Outer Hebrides
7. The European Monetary System (EMS)
8. Michael Foot
9. The Maastricht Treaty
10. Sir James Goldsmith

PORTSMOUTH

1. Jean de Gisors
2. The loss of Normandy
3. The Mary Rose, a warship of Henry VIII
4. Spice Island
5. Arthur Conan Doyle (under the pseudonym A.C. Smith)
6. Peter Sellers
7. Lively Lady
8. A.E. Cogswell
9. The Tricorn Centre
10. The Spinnaker Tower

JAMES CALLAGHAN

1. The Royal Navy (during the Second World War)
2. The Inland Revenue
3. The Social Contract
4. The Great Debate
5. David Steel
6. *Waiting at the Church*
7. Keeper of the Cloth Cap
8. Labour Isn't Working
9. Great Ormond Street Hospital
10. The Great Offices of State (Chancellor of the Exchequer, Home Secretary, Foreign Secretary and Prime Minister)

THE WINTER OF DISCONTENT

1. The Stepping Stones Report
2. Ford of Britain
3. 5%
4. Lorry drivers
5. Fester Square
6. Larry Lamb, editor of The Sun at the time
7. Gravediggers
8. Crisis? What Crisis?
9. Saatchi & Saatchi
10. Plaid Cymru, the Ulster Unionist Party and the Scottish Labour Party

THE CONSERVATIVE PARTY

1. The Tamworth Manifesto
2. The Conservative and Unionist Party
3. Chairman of the Conservative Party
4. The 1922 Committee
5. George Arliss
6. The Industrial Charter
7. The International Democrat Union
8. The European Research Group
9. The Cornerstone Group
10. William Hague

MARGARET THATCHER

1. Mayor of Grantham
2. Chemistry
3. Finchley
4. Education Secretary
5. Britain Awake
6. The Iron Lady
7. Michael Heseltine

8. Augusto Pinochet
9. A statue
10. The Ritz, in Piccadilly

THE FALKLANDS WAR

1. France
2. Port Egmont
3. The Hope Bay Incident
4. Operation Rosario
5. General Leopoldo Galtieri
6. Rex Hunt
7. ARA General Belgrano
8. HMS Sheffield
9. The Battle of San Carlos
10. Stanley

PRINCESS DIANA

1. Barbara Cartland
2. She was a nursery school assistant
3. David and Elizabeth Emanuel
4. Queen Mary's Lover's Knot Tiara, which had originally been owned by the wife of George V
5. John Travolta
6. Peter Settelen
7. Martin Bashir
8. Landmines
9. Centrepoint
10. Althorp House

PRINCE WILLIAM

1. Wombat
2. A golf club
3. The University of St. Andrews

4. Counsellor of State
5. The Football Association
6. He slept rough for a night, near Blackfriars Bridge in London
7. Live in Wales
8. The East Anglian Air Ambulance
9. The Royal Foundation
10. Lupo

PRINCE HARRY

1. St. Mary's, in Paddington
2. The Blues and Royals
3. Forward Air Controller
4. Co-pilot and gunner for an Apache helicopter
5. The Invictus Games
6. The Australian Defence Force
7. The Royal Marines
8. Megxit
9. Silverstone Circuit
10. *The Me You Can't See*

NORWICH

1. Marketplace of the Iceni
2. William of Norwich
3. A staple port (as set out by the 1353 Statute of the Staple)
4. Robert Kett, who was executed at the end of Kett's Rebellion
5. The Strangers, or Elizabethan Strangers
6. The Norwich canary
7. The Norwich Post
8. Norwich Union
9. Colman's (known mainly for mustard and other sauces)
10. Billy Bluelight

JOHN MAJOR

1. Tom Major-Ball
2. Three O-levels (in History, English Language and English Literature)
3. The Guy Fawkes Club
4. One that was broadcast live on television
5. The Citizen's Charter
6. Black Wednesday
7. British Rail
8. The Maastricht Treaty
9. John Redwood
10. Cricket

CRICKET

1. Surrey
2. Marylebone Cricket Club
3. Hambledon Club
4. Gentlemen v Players
5. The White Conduit Club
6. William Lambert
7. John Nyren (in collaboration with Charles Cowden Clarke)
8. Edgar 'Ned' Willsher
9. Fred Lillywhite
10. W.G. Grace

BOLTON

1. Agricola
2. Roger de Poitou
3. Hall i' th' Wood
4. George Marsh
5. Prince Rupert
6. Samuel Taylor Chadwick

7. B. Hick and Sons
8. William Lever, Lord Leverhulme, who established Lever Brothers
9. Burnden Park
10. Fred Dibnah

TONY BLAIR

1. Ugly Rumours
2. Clause IV, which originally referred to the party's commitment to common ownership of the means of production
3. Alistair Campbell
4. The Bank of England
5. The Good Friday Agreement
6. The Freedom of Information Act
7. Sierra Leone
8. A Congressional Gold Medal
9. The United Nations, the United Station, the European Union and Russia
10. The Chilcot Inquiry

EDINBURGH

1. The Gododdin
2. Kenneth II
3. Holyrood Palace
4. St. Giles Street
5. James Craig
6. David Hume
7. The Honours of Scotland, including the Crown of Scotland
8. The Great Fire of Edinburgh
9. Cowgate
10. A military tattoo, with the first official Edinburgh Military Tattoo followed a year later

THE LABOUR PARTY

1. The Fabian Society
2. The Labour Representation Committee (LRC)
3. Keir Hardie
4. The Liberal Party
5. The Housing (Financial Provisions) Act
6. Hugh Gaitskell
7. Ken Livingstone
8. Millbank Tower
9. Dennis Skinner
10. Momentum

GORDON BROWN

1. History
2. Dunfermline East
3. James Maxton
4. The Consumer Price Index
5. The Financial Services Authority
6. Not Flash, Just Gordon
7. The Lancashire Plot
8. Eco-towns
9. The Climate Change Act
10. Bigotgate

RUGBY

1. Tripontium
2. Lawrence Sheriff
3. The Gunpowder Plot (they were staying at an inn in Dunchurch, a couple of miles outside the town)
4. Thomas Hughes
5. William Webb Ellis (although the story is believed by many to be a myth)
6. The modern-day rugby ball

7. Thomas Arnold
8. The Schism
9. Batley
10. The jet engine

DAVID CAMERON

1. The Smith Square Set (or the Notting Hill Set)
2. Nick Clegg, the Liberal Democrat leader
3. Andy Coulson
4. Austerity
5. Operation Ellamy
6. The Jewish National Fund
7. Tottenham Hale
8. Better Together
9. Greensill Capital
10. Alzheimer's Research UK

BREXIT

1. The Bloomberg Speech
2. The Anti-Federalist League
3. Gisela Stuart
4. The West Midlands
5. Diane James (Farage subsequently returned for a short period)
6. Article 50 of the Treaty on European Union
7. Michel Barnier
8. Operation Yellowhammer
9. 47
10. The Northern Ireland Protocol

THERESA MAY

1. The Bank of England
2. The Nasty Party

3. Home Secretary and Minister for Women and Equalities
4. Women2Win
5. The Hostile Environment Policy
6. The Snoopers' Charter
7. Confidence and supply
8. The contaminated blood scandal
9. Fields of wheat
10. In contempt of Parliament (this was in relation to legal advice about Brexit)

THE ENGLISH CHANNEL & THE NORTH SEA

1. Île Vierge
2. The Strait of Dover (or the Dover Narrows)
3. Lomea (which is now generally considered to have never existed)
4. The Devil's Hole
5. A tunnel running under the English Channel, connecting Britain and France
6. Piper Alpha
7. Russia (the British ships had been mistake for Japanese vessels, during the Russo-Japanese War)
8. Sealand
9. Matthew Webb
10. Louis Blériot

BOXING

1. His butcher and his butler (the butcher won)
2. He was the first English bare-knuckle boxing champion
3. John 'Jack' Broughton
4. He was the 9th Marquess of Queensberry, and he publicly endorsed a set of rules that became known as the Queensbury Rules
5. The Little Bridge Grounds
6. The Sweet Science of Bruising

7. William James 'Jimmy' Wilde
8. ANSWER
9. Joe Calzaghe
10. Nicola Adams

KINGSTON UPON HULL

1. William de la Pole
2. The Hanseatic League
3. Hull Dock Company was the first statutory dock company in Britain
4. William Wilberforce
5. Sir John Ellerman
6. Joseph Hirst
7. Trekking
8. Philip Larkin
9. The Cod Wars
10. UK City of Culture

BORIS JOHNSON

1. Bavaria
2. The Bullingdon Club
3. The Times
4. Allegra Mostyn-Owen
5. *Have I Got News For You?*
6. The Spectator
7. Henley
8. Drinking alcohol
9. *Seventy-Two Virgins*
10. Dominic Cummings

TENNIS

1. Leamington Spa
2. Walter Clopton Wingfield

3. Spencer Gore
4. William Renshaw
5. Dwight F. Davis
6. Slazenger (for tennis balls)
7. Table Tennis
8. Angela Mortimer
9. Henman Hill
10. Virginia Wade, who won Wimbledon in 1977

COVID-19

1. Severe acute respiratory syndrome coronavirus-2
2. Medway Maritime Hospital, in Chatham
3. York
4. Operation Rescript
5. Patrick Vallance
6. Scientific Advisory Group for Emergencies
7. Dominic Raab
8. Eat Out to Help Out
9. She became the first person to receive a COVID-19 jab
10. Jenny Harries

THE FUTURE...

1. Airstrip One
2. Spaceports
3. Dan Dare
4. Birmingham
5. J.G. Ballard
6. The Vogons
7. P.D. James
8. The Daleks
9. The Eloi
10. Along with the rest of the world, it will be absorbed by the Sun, which will enter its Red Giant phase and expand beyond Earth's current orbit

Which classic novel features the Meryton Ball? What's Little Dorrit's first name? A cat named Behemoth features in the work of which author?

Trotsky's Book of Literary Quiz Questions contains 3,160 questions on literature from around the world. Categories include General Knowledge, Thrillers, Romance, Horror, Science Fiction and Poetry and many more, as well as rounds on more than thirty authors.

Trotsky was a Jack Russell terrier who sat through many pub literary quizzes. This book was written in his memory, and any profits will go to local charities / good causes.